Preoccupations
in Australian Poetry

P9-CTB-055

Preoccupations
in Australian Poetry

JUDITH WRIGHT

ILLINOIS CENTRAL COLLEGE
LEARNING RESOURCE CENTER

MELBOURNE
OXFORD UNIVERSITY PRESS
LONDON WELLINGTON NEW YORK

35978

PR
9461
.W7
1966
c.2

*Oxford University Press, Ely House, London, W.*1

GLASGOW NEW YORK TORONTO MELBOURNE WELLINGTON
CAPE TOWN SALISBURY IBADAN NAIROBI LUSAKA ADDIS ABABA
BOMBAY CALCUTTA MADRAS KARACHI LAHORE DACCA
KUALA LUMPUR HONG KONG

Oxford University Press, 7 Bowen Crescent, Melbourne

First published 1965
First paperback edition 1966

Registered in Australia for transmission by post as a book
PRINTED IN AUSTRALIA BY BROWN, PRIOR, ANDERSON PTY. LTD.

Contents

CONTENTS

Author's Note

This book makes no pretension to being either historically or critically exhaustive in the field of Australian poetry. There are numerous writers, particularly of the present day, for whose work I have much admiration, but with whom I have not attempted to deal. This is because I have tried here to concern myself less with textual or critical judgements than with certain attitudes and aspects in Australian writing.

My choice of poets is therefore not to be taken as indicating my own literary canon. I have written of them, and of their works, rather because they have seemed to me key figures in the movement of Australian poetic consciousness, or because in one way or another certain of their poems seem to me to illustrate these attitudes and aspects.

Acknowledgements

I thank the following authors and publishers for permission to quote from work still in copyright:

Angus & Robertson Ltd for permission to quote from the works of Christopher Brennan, Henry Lawson, Hugh McCrae, Shaw Neilson and Bernard O'Dowd, and for the quotations from *Australian Bush Ballads* and *Old Bush Songs* edited by Stewart and Keesing; John Blight for permission to quote from *The Old Pianist* (Dymock's Ltd, 1945), *The Two Suns Met* (Angus & Robertson, 1954) and *A Beachcomber's Diary* (Angus & Robertson, 1963); David Campbell for the quotation from *Speak With the Sun* (Chatto & Windus, 1949); R. D. FitzGerald for quotations from *To Meet the Sun* (Angus & Robertson, 1929), *Moonlight Acre* (Melbourne University Press, 1938), *Heemskerck Shoals* (Mountain Side Press, 1949), *This Night's Orbit* (Angus & Robertson, 1953), *Between Two Tides* (Angus & Robertson, 1952), *Southmost Twelve* (Angus & Robertson, 1952); A. D. Hope for quotations from *The Wandering Islands* (Edwards & Shaw, 1955) and *Poems* (Hamish Hamilton, 1960), and from 'Conversation with Calliope' *(Texas Quarterly);* Jack Lindsay for quotations from *Life Rarely Tells* and *The Roaring Twenties* (Bodley Head); James McAuley for quotations from *Under Aldebaran* (Melbourne University Press, 1946), and *A Vision of Ceremony* (Angus & Robertson, 1956); Oxford University Press for the quotation from F. M. Robb's Introduction to the *Poems of Adam Lindsay Gordon* (1912); George Allen & Unwin Ltd and the author for the quotation from Bertrand Russell's *Mysticism and Logic; Southerly* and the executors of the late C. W. Salier for the quotation from his article on Charles Harpur; Kenneth Slessor for the quotations from *One Hundred Poems* (Angus & Robertson, 1944); Miss Christina Stead for the quotation from *Seven Poor Men of Sydney* (Peter Davies, 1934); and Francis Webb for the quotations from *A Drum for Ben Boyd* (Angus & Robertson, 1948), *Leichhardt in Theatre* (Angus & Robertson, 1952), *Birthday* (privately printed, 1953), and *Socrates* (Angus & Robertson, 1964).

INTRODUCTION

Australia's Double Aspect

∽

IT IS only necessary to look at Australia's literature, in order to see that for very many of her writers she has presented herself as the most difficult of technical problems. Before one's country can become an accepted background against which the poet's and novelist's imagination can move unhindered, it must first be observed, understood, described, and as it were absorbed. The writer must be at peace with his landscape before he can turn confidently to its human figures.

But in Australian writing the landscape has, it almost seems, its own life, hostile to its human inhabitants; it forces its way into the foreground, it takes up an immense amount of room, or sometimes it is so firmly pushed away that its obvious absence haunts us as much as its presence could do. Thus it haunts us in the novels of Henry Handel Richardson (where it is the ever-present, inexorably shabby and ugly background for the downfall of a man who is alien to it until his death) as it does in the passionate and over-coloured descriptions of Eve Langley in *The Pea Pickers*; and its influence is present by implication as much in Brennan's poetry, where landscape is deliberately universalized, as in the most aboriginal of Jindy jingle.

This is because Australia has from the beginning of its short history meant something more to its new inhabitants than mere environment and mere land to be occupied, ploughed and brought into subjection. It has been the outer equivalent of an inner reality; first, and persistently, the reality of exile; second, though perhaps we now tend to forget this, the reality of newness and freedom.

Since Harpur, the free-born descendant of transported convicts, chose to be the first poet of his country—

> 'Lo! 'tis the land of the grave of thy father!
> 'Tis the cradle of Liberty . . .'

and dedicated himself to dreams of a time when

'all men shall stand
proudly beneath the fair wide roof of heaven
as God-created equals . . .'

the two strains of feeling (for the conservative, the sense of exile,
and for the radical, the sense of liberty, of a new chance) have,
at least until very recently, been recognizable in all that was
written here.

This double aspect of the inner Australia, as we might call it,
has been matched and reinforced by the outer physical reality
of the country itself. As a land of exile, it could scarcely have
been more alien to all European ideas either of natural beauty
or of physical amenity; its unknown plants and animals, its odd
reversals of all that British invaders knew and understood of
their own country (in the habits of the eucalypts, almost incredu-
lously noted by early botanists, of shedding their bark seasonally
and retaining their leaves; the alternations of drought and flood;
the difficulties of soil and climate that made nonsense of the early
efforts of farmers unaccustomed to any but English conditions; the
transposition of the seasons, the unfamiliarity of the night sky.)
But from the beginning of settlement there were rebels who hoped
to make here a country that would lead the world towards new
concepts of human freedom—men like Harpur and like many
others articulate or inarticulate, who saw Australia as a great
opportunity to establish Utopia, 'meet cradle for the birth sublime
of just Equality', as Harpur put it—and to such men these differences scarcely counted. What did matter was the size and the
silence of this country, in which the law and civilization were
soon outdistanced by any traveller beyond the coastal settlements.

So from the first Australia, as a condition of life, loomed large
in the consciousness of her white invaders. She seemed either a
prison, a land to be escaped from as soon as possible or to be
endured till death, or to the few who saw Utopia in her, a new
country, a country of hope and faith. At first, at any rate, there
was little notion of her as a possible source of wealth and easy
living. The disciplines she imposed were too hard; the conditions
she made were too grinding; she had too little immediate wealth
to offer. There were in Australia no sources of easy money, until
the gold-rushes began; America's obvious abundance in furs,
forests, pastures and minerals had made her early settlers predict
and boast of her future as a great nation, but in Australia little
or none of such faith was possible. A distant dependency of

England, she had little to offer except hard work, loneliness and
dreadful isolation; and probably this loneliness caused her early
inhabitants to exaggerate her strangeness—the lost and ancient
quality that Lawrence later felt.

So Marcus Clarke wrote in all seriousness:

> What is the dominant note of Australian scenery? That which
> is the dominant note of Poe's poetry—Weird Melancholy
> . . . The Australian mountain forests are funereal, secret,
> stern. Their solitude is desolation. They seem to stifle in
> their black gorges a story of sullen despair. No tender senti-
> ment is nourished in their shade. In other lands the dying
> year is mourned, the falling leaves drop lightly on the bier.
> In the Australian forests no leaves fall . . . The very animal
> life of these frowning hills is either grotesque or ghostly.
> Great grey kangaroos hop noiselessly over the coarse grass.
> Flights of white cockatoos stream out shrieking like evil
> souls. The sun suddenly sinks, the mopokes burst out into
> horrible peals of semi-human laughter. The natives aver
> that, when night comes, from out the bottomless depths of
> some lagoon the Bunyip rises, and, in form like a monstrous
> sea-calf, drags his loathsome length from out the ooze. From
> a corner of the silent forest rises a dismal chant, and around
> a fire dance natives painted like skeletons. All is fear-inspir-
> ing and gloomy . . . Hopeless explorers have named (the
> mountains) out of their suffering—Mount Misery, Mount
> Dreadful, Mount Despair . . . The soul, placed before the
> frightful grandeur of these barren hills, drinks in their senti-
> ment of defiant ferocity, and is steeped in bitterness.[1]

So much for Australia's mountains. Her plains Clarke called
'shelterless and silent', her trees and flowers, in which Banks had
delighted, Clarke called 'grotesque and weird', 'the strange
scribblings of Nature learning how to write'. So far Clarke speaks
as an alien—as one of those for whom Australia was a land of
exile and terror. But he saw, too, the other side of the picture;
the side seen by Australia's first lovers, the rebels against civilization; for he goes on:

> Some see no beauty in our trees without shade, our flowers
> without perfume, our birds who cannot fly, and our beasts
> who have not yet learned to walk on all fours. But the
> dweller in the wilderness . . . becomes familiar with the

[1] Preface to *Poems of the Late Adam Lindsay Gordon* (Massina, Melbourne,
1880)

> beauty of loneliness . . . learns the language of the barren
> and uncouth, and can read the hieroglyphs of haggard gum-
> trees, blown into odd shapes, distorted with fierce hot winds,
> or cramped with cold nights, when the Southern Cross
> freezes in a cloudless sky of icy blue . . . and the Poet of our
> desolation begins to comprehend why free Esau loved his
> heritage of desert sand, better than all the bountiful rich-
> ness of Egypt.

The violent reaction of the European consciousness against
what it saw in this new country, and the conditions that had to
be endured here, has persisted until our own day. Its modern
reflection can be found in the novels of Martin Boyd, for instance, with their uneasy movement from Australia to England
and back to Australia again. In them, not only the characters
but the writing itself seems never at home in either country—
nostalgic for both, yet settled in neither. Boyd is no 'free Esau'—
for him the country stations that supported his families' fortunes
were 'all in remote burning plains, blasted by the January
sun . . . they were all built of corrugated iron and they all smelt
of sheep'. Civilization, for the people of Boyd's novels, in so far
as it exists here at all, is embodied precariously in a certain group
of people in Melbourne. Only the very youngest of his characters,
in a family Australian-born for generations, begins to come to
terms with the country through the medium of art. And though
this strain in our writing may seem to us now outdated, out-
grown, we should be honest enough to recognize that it was
and remains real enough to influence our feeling still in many
ways.

This contradiction, this inner argument between the transplanted European and his new country, takes many forms, but in
one way or another it is to be seen in almost every Australian
writer. In Christina Stead's *Seven Poor Men of Sydney*:

> Blount stirred himself and said: 'Why are we here? Nothing
> floats down here, this far south, but is worn out with wind,
> tempest and weather; all is flotsam and jetsam. They leave
> their rags and tatters here; why do we have to be dressed?
> The sun is hot enough, why can't we run naked in our own
> country, in our own land, to work out our own destiny? . . .
> This land was last discovered: Why? A ghost land, a con-
> tinent of mystery; the very pole disconcerted the magnetic
> needle so that ships went astray, ice and fog and storm bound

the seas, a horrid destiny in the Abrolhos, in the Philippines, in the Tasman seas, in the Southern Ocean, all protected the malign and bitter genius of this waste land. Its heart is made of salt: it suddenly oozes from its burning pores, gold which will destroy men in greed, but not water to give them drink. Jealous land! Ravishers over-bold! And lost legion! Our land should never have been won.'

That is, essentially, the cry of the exiled European; and it is in Henry Handel Richardson's great trilogy of novels that the story of the exiled European is most clearly set out. That is the story of Richard Mahony, for whom Australia was precisely the Antipodes; who, when he made money, promptly returned to England to spend it. Yet, like the families in Boyd's novels, he was no longer able to merge with his English background, and returned at last to Australia, to die there broken and deranged. Richardson is sparing with her descriptions of the Australian landscape; it is for most of the immensely long novel sketched in only as a background to Mahony's gradual and inevitable downfall. But the last book ends, not on a human note, but a natural:

Amid these wavy downs Mahony was laid to rest . . . A quarter of a mile off, behind a ridge of dunes, the surf driving in from the Bight, breaks and booms eternally on the barren shore. Thence, too, come the fierce winds which, in stormy weather, hurl themselves over the land, where not a tree, not a bush, nor even a fence stands to break their force.—Or to limit the outlook. On all sides the eye can range, unhindered, to where the vast earth meets the infinitely vaster sky. And, under blazing summer suns, or when a full moon floods the night, no shadow falls on the sun-baked or moon-blanched plains, but those cast by the few little stones set up in human remembrance.
. . . But, those who had known and loved him passing, scattering, forgetting, rude weeds choked the flowers, the cross toppled over, fell to pieces and was removed, the ivy that entwined it uprooted. And, thereafter, his resting-place was indistinguishable from the common ground. The rich and kindly earth of his adopted country absorbed his perishable body, as the country itself had never contrived to make its own, his wayward, vagrant spirit.

From one viewpoint one might look at Richardson's novel-sequence as a kind of attempt, on the part of the exile-consciousness, to understand and reconcile itself with the alien country that is gradually overcoming and changing it and with which in the end it must be merged. The novels make a kind of bridge between Europeanism and the unknown thing that is to be made of Europeans by Australia, and in them, perhaps, Richardson, herself doubly an exile, reconciled herself not only with her own hard childhood and the loss of her sensitive rebellious father, but with the Australia from which, though she was born there, she had herself turned away. That final image of the body of Mahony absorbed and annihilated by the country in which he had suffered as a stranger, is transformed from bitterness into peace by those two significant words—'rich' and 'kindly'. In them, it seems, Richardson forgives all the barren grimness, rawness and cruelty of the little town on the plains where Richard had suffered the last stages of his martyrdom—of the country that had seemed to Mary, as she travelled through it, 'the flattest, barest, ugliest country she had ever had the misfortune to see . . . the last word in loneliness and desolation'.

The unifying image—the image that brings peace for the first time since Mahony's bitter story began—is Mahony's grave. Just so, Harpur, taking on himself the task of becoming Australia's first poet, had cried—

'See, 'tis the land of the grave of thy father . . .'

It is curious—or perhaps not so curious—that this theme, of the European mind in contact with a raw, bleak and alien life and landscape, struggling with it in a suffering whose only consummation and reconciliation is found in death, is taken up again in Patrick White's *Voss*. 'You see', says Judd, the deserter and murderer, at the end of the book, 'if you live and suffer long enough in a place, you do not leave it altogether. Your spirit is still there'. And so, as Laura sums up the story, Voss through his death 'is still there in the country and always will be. His legend will be written down, eventually, by those who have been troubled by it.'

This, then, both Richardson and White, our two greatest novelists, have told us, is one way of reconciliation: where man has suffered, whether he is suffering, like Mahony, as an unwilling exile, or like Voss, as a dedicated seeker, the conflict of spirit and country ends in some kind of unity. By virtue of such suffering and struggle, the country becomes less alien to us: the vicarious sacrifice of Voss means to Laura, and to little Topp, the disappointed music-master, and to others, the possibility of understanding, loving and interpreting the 'sour colonial soil' on which they find themselves. 'Knowledge', says Laura, 'was never a matter of geography. Quite the reverse, it overflows all maps that exist. Perhaps true knowledge only comes of death by torture in the country of the mind.'

'Death by torture in the country of the mind'—it is perhaps too melodramatic a way of putting it, for any lesser man than White's particular explorer-Christ. Nevertheless, there is certainly a sense in which Laura's words are true for all white Australians; a certain kind of death is indeed what Australia has demanded of us, a death of some things in us, to make room, perhaps, for others. Change itself is a kind of death, and Australia has changed us.

Lawrence, whose insight both into people and places was often so sharply illuminating, saw in us the sign of this death; a kind of apathy, and emptiness, a void. He saw that something had gone out of the European consciousness, in this country, and that as yet nothing had taken its place. And he related this emptiness to the country itself, that country of 'the previous world—the world of the coal age! The lonely, lonely world that had waited, it seemed, since the coal age . . . What was the good of trying to be an alert, conscious man here? You couldn't.'

Those words strike farther home into the central relationship of the white Australian and his country, perhaps, than any written by the native-born. Lawrence saw what lies deeper in us than we know—the scar left by the struggle to conquer and waken, for our own purposes, a landscape that had survived on its own terms until the world's late days. Its only human inhabitants had been the aborigines whom we dispossessed—who were bound to the land we took from them, by the indissoluble link of religion and totemic kinship, so that our intrusion on the land itself became a kind of bloodless murder, even where no actual murder took place.

Our conflict both with land and people went deeper, perhaps, because there was in it so little of the heroic, so that we could not bolster up our self-esteem by boasting of our conquests; and because there was in it, too, so much of compromise. The country allowed us in easily enough; no battles were fought for it. The real battle was of a different order, not so much for conquest as for survival, and in surviving we found ourselves, for many years, living on Australia's terms rather than our own.

The weapons of the country were its emptiness, its sameness, its distances, its extremes of climate; the weapons of its settlers were endurance, persistence, a home-made ingenuity, and a sardonic attitude to the failures and reverses that they soon learned to expect. The struggle that developed these qualities necessarily took away, at the same time, the more specifically European virtue that Lawrence calls 'alert consciousness', and much else went with it also. So, in recent years, James McAuley writes of his countrymen—

'The people are hard-eyed, kindly, with nothing inside them;
The men are independent, but you could not call them free.'

The alteration that Lawrence sensed in us was not something superficial; it was not simply that the external customs and habits of life in civilized Europe had rubbed off in the struggle. Something had left us, had 'died by torture in the country of the mind'. White tells us that this is one way, at least, to true knowledge—to die is also to be reborn. But both Lawrence and McAuley would have it that, as yet, the emptiness remains. We have not yet, perhaps, reached that point of equilibrium at which we can feel that this country is truly ours by right of understanding and acceptance, and from which we can begin to grow again.

Perhaps this is why we tend still—in fact, increasingly—to crowd into cities in order to keep ourselves warm. We have not yet a culture in which both city and country have their proper place, each complementing the other; we have not assimilated the two ways of living to each other. The European never lived by bread alone; he had something else to sustain him, the sense of belonging to a tradition, of sharing in a long inheritance of achievement both of mind and heart which is symbolized in the names of countries—England, France, Italy, Greece—and which formed for him a kind of interpretation and framework for his own life and himself, his landscape and his cities. He shared, however vicariously and unconsciously, in an art, a literature and a culture that stretched far into the past.

But when he came to Australia—as Europeans are still coming—the older culture which had given his life a meaning beyond the personal, by linking him with the past, began to lose its power over him. It had authority still, but his real share in it dribbled away; for the true function of an art and a culture is to interpret us to ourselves, and to relate us to the country and the society in which we live.

So the new Australian (and all of us, to some extent, are new Australians) has in truth died a little. This is what our 'literature of exile' recognizes in us, and here it has the real importance of true literature. For if we reject outright the literature of nostalgia, we fail to understand something important about ourselves, and will not be able to set about making Australia into our real spiritual home. In the same way, if we accept it too whole-heartedly, and take too seriously the notion that ours is a transplanted community, we deny the second aspect of our situation as Australians—the opportunity that is given us to make our loss into a gain, to turn Australia into a reality, to become something new in the world; to be not, as Hope puts it, 'second-hand Europeans' timidly pullulating on alien shores, but a people who have seized the chance to make a new kind of consciousness out of our new conditions.

The 'literature of exile' points to something in us of lingering dependence and uncertainty, to a habit of mind (which shows itself particularly in conservative politicians today) that distrusts its own judgement and prefers 'second-hand Europeanism' to insecurely based Australianism. We have made much of our so-called newly emerging national consciousness, of our 'Australian legend'. But just what does the Australian legend, so far, consist in? We ought to look as closely as we can, for the past holds the clue to the present, and we ourselves are the present. So far as Australia is not yet wholly our country of the mind, it is because we have not yet understood and interpreted our relation to her.

The easy way of making a national legend was not for us. Australia presented a blank and negative front to our efforts at self-aggrandizement, either through easy wealth or heroic conquest. It seems possible that this fact has had something to do with the persistence, even up to the present time, of that 'exile-consciousness' I have pointed to in the work of various of our writers.

But what was in its time, new, is the second strain of feeling for Australia running through our literature, of a wholly opposite kind—the strain of feeling that begins most clearly, from a literary point of view, in the work of Harpur. This is the attitude that has arisen from the sense that here something new could be made, some kind of new relationship between men was mistily becoming possible. This second side of our consciousness forms a current that has found expression in the work of such writers as

Tom Collins, Henry Lawson, O'Dowd, Eleanor Dark, and others; it is the attitude that Russel Ward has documented in his recent book, *The Australian Legend*; it is, of course, what we mean, or what we ought to mean, when we talk of the importance of the work of the balladists and the *'Bulletin* writers' of the 'nineties and after.

To begin with, of course, it is significant that the feeling of being Australian—of belonging to this country and no other—should have taken its rise so evidently in a radical and political approach, and in writers who have regarded human relations as the starting-point of literature, human relations of a purely social and general kind. These writers are concerned much less with landscape or with the European past, with the subtler questions of human motive, than with the future. What gave them their particular brand of optimistic reformism was just that fact against which the 'exile-consciousness', the European consciousness, rebelled—the fact that, faced with unpredictable and uncompromising new conditions, the European culture to which the upper strata of our society clung has had to change, and has made way in important respects for something new.

Price Warung's famous version of the Convict Oath, which, as Ward points out, may well have been authentic, ought I think to be taken as a starting-point when we think of the development of this attitude. It runs,

> Hand to hand
> On Earth, in Hell,
> Sick or well,
> On Sea, on Land,
> On the square, ever. . . .
>
> Stiff or in Breath,
> Lag or Free,
> You and Me,
> In Life, in Death,
> On the Cross, never.

And though similar oaths may well have been current in other and older countries, among convicts and men otherwise at cross-purposes with vested authority, this oath or the attitude it represents is for Australia the germ of the 'something new' that we now feel to be in some sense our own, and that passed into our literature in the work, especially, of Lawson and Furphy. It epitomizes the basic attitude between man and man that enabled the bush workers to survive as they travelled their hard tracks from job to job, and that helped the early settlers to face their hardships.

But more than that, it represents the bare bones of human relations; that which has made it possible for man himself to survive in the world and build his societies. It is, one might say, the basic oath of all men, in society; since no man can survive alone, but everyone is dependent on his neighbour in a mutual bargain of trust. The difference, in what was best in the Australian interpretation of it, is that mutual trust implies for us equality between man and man, equality of a kind that transcends the necessary difference of circumstances and work and intelligence and income. As Harpur put it, so at our best we think of ourselves, standing as 'God-created equals'.

Now this *is* a new thing, this sense in the best of us that we are equals; and Furphy and Lawson were supremely right in seizing on it as their deepest theme. The danger today is that, in our present reaction against the often over-sentimentalized emphasis on 'mateship' and the 'Australian legend', we may forget the truth that lies behind it and thereby lose the strength it gave us. For it did, in fact, form the basis of such real Australianity as we have.

Of course, it has been used both falsely and shallowly. Also, the radical writers who took the equality of man as their theme have shared a kind of optimism about the nature of man—Australian man, at any rate—that seems nowadays to leave out a good deal. This particular kind of optimism was always a necessary ingredient in the radical reformism that put its faith in the perfectibility of man, from Godwin and the Encyclopaedists onward; the notion of original sin was as old-fashioned, to such reformism, as the notion of human perfectibility begins to look to us today. But we ought not to dismiss that notion until we are sure we have understood just where its bearing lies. It is worthwhile trying to separate, in the work of these writers, what is sentimental and temporary from what is basic and true for us as well as for them: to free them, that is, from the limitations of their time and to see them in proper perspective.

In their work we find the chief difference between, say, the Australian and American dreams. Where the American dream made use of the competitive individualistic element in life, the freedom of any man to become richer and better than his fellows by hard work and emulation, the Australian dream emphasizes man's duty to his brother, and man's basic equality, the mutual trust which is the force that makes society cohere.

If it is universalized, it holds the key not only to our proper nationhood, but to the unifying of Australia's double aspect, firstly as a society of transplanted Europeans, and secondly as a new country with a separate contribution to make in the world.

Certainly we have lost something in our struggle in the country of the mind, but it is possible now to see that we have gained something too, even if we are not yet conscious of what it is. We are becoming identified with this country; we are beginning to know ourselves no longer exiles, but at home here in a proper sense of the term. We are beginning to write, no longer as transplanted Europeans, nor as rootless men who reject the past and put their hopes only in the future, but as men with a present to be lived in and a past to nourish us.

CHAPTER I

Charles Harpur

∽

POSSIBLY the strangest fact in the history of Australian poetry is the neglect and ignorance of the work of one of the best of its early poets. It is this fact that makes it difficult to write, as yet, what should be written; a dispassionate study of Harpur in relation to his time and ours. One has first to give an account of his work, since no reliable collection of it yet exists; one has to attempt, in fact, an evaluation of a poet who exists largely in manuscript, and whose manuscripts require much work of collation and comparing.

But there is one thing that does emerge from a reading even of the biased and incomplete collected volume posthumously published and never reprinted—that Harpur's claim to be regarded as the first poet of his country is better founded than has yet been allowed, and that he is also a better poet than many of those who followed him.

He is the first of our poets, too, in whom we can study the beginning of the split-consciousness that affects Australian writing even to our day—the contrary trends that reached their clearest expression in those very different writers, Brennan and Lawson. We are, and have always been, two people in one—a race of Europeans exiled from their own mainstream of development, yet carrying on that stream within themselves, and a race different in themselves because their environment and their influences are different. In this book I try to discover the implications of this double aspect of Australian consciousness; to study Harpur's work is to see it in operation, for the first time, and to mark its effect on a poet who consciously accepted his own difficulties and tried to reconcile them into poetry.

We have never given Harpur his full importance in our literary history, and we have carried our neglect of him to the point of leaving his works almost unread and almost unexamined. There were no doubt reasons for this neglect, in his own time. Harpur was born of convict parents; he was native-born at a time when nothing good was expected of Australians; and he professed a political point of view which many nineteenth-century Australian literati with their parochial conservatism, their admiration for Empire and their anxiety to forget Australia's convict origin, could only abhor. In addition, he was during his lifetime an unsuccessful man, and after his death his works were edited into innocuousness by a man who evidently understood little either of poetry as such or of Harpur in particular.

What is strange is that this misrepresentation was so long uncorrected. The only edition of Harpur's work available in public libraries (except for a fairly recent collection of his love-sonnets) remains the old and garbled edition of 1883. It is to be hoped that a new and scholarly edition will be published soon, but meanwhile it is almost impossible to arrive at a definitive estimate of his work.

All that can certainly be said, until more work is done on the manuscripts, is that at least fourteen of the major poems have been considerably abbreviated, without mention of this, in the so-called *Collected Poems,* and in several cases they have been abbreviated in such a manner that the point of the poem has been lost; and that of the minor poems a number have not been printed at all, and these not necessarily among the least important.

C. W. Salier and Harpur's biographer, J. Normington-Rawling, are among the extremely few critics who have made any thorough study of the original Harpur manuscripts. In an essay in *Southerly* Salier writes:

> I strongly incline to the view that rational criticism will come to see Charles Harpur as a unique and remarkable figure . . . a deeper-thoughted, wider-interested, more varied and versatile, and more masculine poet than has hitherto been conceived, who not only thought himself but really was, in a much higher degree than some critics have recognized, truly Australian.

And he says also,

> Until much further work is done on the Harpur MSS—all of it—and the various and in many instances numerous versions of the individual poems have been compared, the 1883 text must lie under grave suspicion of containing an unduly high proportion of matter that is not genuine

Harpur . . . This necessarily severely discounts much criticism of Harpur as a poet—such criticisms having for 60 years been based for the most part on the 1883 Poems . . .'[1]

This extraordinary indifference to the poet whom every critic allows—whatever may be his judgement on Harpur's poetry as far as it is known—to be our first important poet and among the few outstanding literary figures of the nineteenth century, reflects very greatly on the state of Australian literary criticism and research, but it seems, the more one reads of the Harpur manuscripts, to be only a logical extension of Harpur's misfortunes and misrepresentations during his life. The record left in his notes and essays, and in his poetry itself, is that of a man of incorruptible sincerity, earnestness and personal pride, pursued by many misfortunes, some of his own making but most arising out of his circumstances. To be born of convict parents (though he speaks of them with affection and seems never to have been embarrassed by remembering them) was in itself enough to bar him from a certain kind of society where he might have hoped for an audience for his poetry. And though he had friends, including Henry Parkes, who were willing to extend a helping hand, and though after long suspense and doubt Mary Doyle (his 'Rosa') did consent to marry him, Harpur was not born, it seems, to be happy or successful.

Of his personality, Kendall wrote in later years

But when the fiery power of youth
Had passed away and left him nameless,
Serene as light and strong as truth
He lived his life, untired and tameless . . .

No soul was he to sit on heights
And live with rocks apart and scornful.
Delights of men were his delights,
And common troubles made him mournful.

The pathos worn by wayside things,
The passion found in simple faces,
Struck deeper than the life of springs
Or strength of storms and sea-swept places.

External circumstances were an almost overwhelmingly important factor in Harpur's career. He was born into a society which, in the nature of its being and its preoccupations, had little

---

[1] C. W. Salier, *Southerly No. 1/1951*

use for poetry or literature. Its concern was to subdue an un-touched country, and its standards were set by physical hard work and by material values. It was a society in which what counted was not thought, but action; there were no rewards for learning or for art, except the scorn of the successful man who had got along well enough without either. So Harpur had practically no audience in his own land, and except for a few perceptive and intelligent men such as Parkes, he had no friends either.

Nor could he hope—though in fact he did hope—for recognition in England. His parentage, his lack of formal education and his birthplace were all against this. Who could imagine such a phenomenon as an Australian poet—in days when the notion of even an American poet was merely laughable? So Harpur's manuscripts, notes and verses which begin in his early years with so naïve an enthusiasm, so boyish a hope, are heartbreaking to read as his years increase and bring him more and bitterer dis-appointments and neglect.

Yet he continued to write, until his last days, though his powers began to flag and his first freshness left him. In a sonnet written for Parkes, he once lamented with bitter irony:

> While others dip their fleecy flocks, and store
> Bright gold, I've only so much *verse* the more
> . . . A vagrant, and the cause still, all along,
> This damned unconquerable love of Song.

And in fact he left a body of verse and criticism much larger and more ambitious in scope than his published volume even hints at.

Though, as the son of convict parents, Harpur had good reason for rebellion against what was harsh in English law and the English class-system, and though he lost no opportunity to urge that nothing of the same kind be allowed to establish itself in Australia, he is not basically a 'political' poet. Certainly he pub-lished a number of political and satirical verses (there was a market for these, and but little market for poetry as such); but they tend to sound rather ponderously idealistic, set beside the more scurrilously personal journalism of the day. However, he could point his scorn acutely enough, as in the sonnet in which he attacked Wentworth's proposal to introduce an aristocratic order—immediately nicknamed the Bunyip Aristocracy by the irreverent:

In Sheepshanks we behold a destined peer,
And Oxtail's stockmen shall 'my-lord' his son!

And he could speak plainly in his indignation too, as in 'Another Sonnet on the Proposed Recurrence to Transportation', which begins

The shame of Bondage is upon the land
Even yet, and a wild cry of Blood complains
To heaven like Abel's . . .

But increasingly his bitterest complaints are of the 'cloddishness' of the society he lived in, and of his friendlessness and disillusion; his early poems are here and there footnoted bitterly in a later hand, as in the manuscript of his 'To the Spirit of Poesy':

Yet do not thou forsake me now
Poesy, with Hope together.

. . . Ah misery, what were then my lot,
     Amongst a race of unbelievers:
Sordid men who all declare
That earthly gain alone is fair
And they who pore on bardic lore
     Deceived deceivers,

That to believe Mind yet shall weave,
Even though with armed Oppression coping,
A prophet-banner, which unfurled
Shall herald Freedom through the world,
And tell to man his perfect plan
     Is Folly hoping?

Half at rest upon thy breast
     How often have I laid me, musing
That in the golden eventide
All the dead to Thought allied
Around me dwelt, unseen yet *felt,*
     Great hopes infusing . . . .

To this poem in its early form, two notes are appended. The first reads in part ' . . . How much all that is immortal in me has been wronged by the society I have been compelled to herd with during the best years of my life'. The second, in an older and feebler hand: 'During my whole manhood I have had to mingle daily amongst men . . . who have faith for nothing in God's glorious universe that is not, in their own vile phrase, "money's worth".'

Such notes and poems are sad reading; but they are not, however much we may have to take them into account, the important fact about Harpur's work, nor would he himself have wished them overemphasized. Harpur believed himself to be a poet, and in the best of his work he had a well-justified faith. In his comparatively early poem, 'The Dream by the Fountain', he set himself the task of becoming the first authentic voice of a new nation in whose future, even at his depths of disappointment and despair, he never quite lost faith.

> Be then the bard of thy country! O rather
> Should such be thy choice than a monarchy wide!
> Lo! 'tis the land of the grave of thy father;
> 'Tis the cradle of liberty! Think, and decide.'

So spoke his muse, the 'muse of the evergreen forest', Australian Nature; and he never quite lost his conviction that his work would be a lasting landmark in his own country, though he died almost unrecognized.

Harpur, then, was that rarity, a conscious poet with a set task and a knowledge of the part he was playing. His choice of his lifework was deliberate, and he set about studying English poetry, not in order to imitate the fashions of his time, but to learn his art and to adapt English technique to his own purpose. He left a series of Rhymed Criticisms to mark his studies in English poetry, and many of his judgements are fresh and vigorous even today. He had a splendid ear, a clear mind and a true appreciation of language. Take his comment on Chaucer's 'Poor Scholar':

> What a noble draft is that! And with what a fine couplet does it conclude! It is the true English heroic couplet, not composed, like Pope's, of two lines having each a caesural balance, but flowing freely forth, and yet at the same time open to every variety of modulation. And notwithstanding all that has been dinned abroad to the contrary, I cannot help thinking the true English heroic verse the best of all kinds of verse—entire, compact, continuous and yet admitting of all the heroic pauses being located anywhere in it, from the first syllable to the last.[2]

And his Rhymed Criticism of Dryden is a good example of his

[2] MS. book 1847-1848, in the Mitchell Library, Sydney

capacity for absorbing a style without losing his own strength
and judgement:

Not much I love him, yet perforce admire
The vigorous rage of his material fire!
Though prodigal of verse, and coarse of phrase,
Built durably are all his better Lays.
His lines, like pleasant brooks, now warbling go,
And now, like mountain floods, they thunder as they flow.[3]

It was natural that his chief mentors in poetry should have
been Shelley and Wordsworth: Shelley whose fiery rational
libertarianism lighted in him an equal flame, and set him to
dream of his new country as 'a meet cradle for the birth sublime
/Of just Equality . . .' and Wordsworth, whose doctrine of the
integral relationship of man and nature found an immediate response in Harpur's own love of the mountains and valleys of his
Hawkesbury country.

But it is Wordsworth and not Shelley whose voice we hear
translated when Harpur speaks; Shelley's light-diffused lyricism
has little in common with Harpur's plain and sometimes grating
speech, but with Wordsworth he shares a quality of rocky endurance, of singleness and, at his best, of embracing vision. It is
a likeness, not an imitation—the grain of Harpur's mind runs as
does that of Wordsworth, and though Harpur spoke of Coleridge's poetry very highly ('I think I have, or have had, a greater
admiration for the poetry of Coleridge than for that of any of
his contemporaries') he makes clear the importance of Wordsworth in his life as a poet, in a sonnet worth quoting:

How much, O Wordsworth! in this world how much
Has thy surpassing love made rich for me
Of what was once unprized! A nameless tree,
A wilding flower—the merest hues that touch
The common clouds—lit summits—verdant leas,
With every woodland murmur, every song
Of bird or brook, as heard to gush along
In each fresh on-scape of some bough-caught breeze,
Have thence a charm to fill my bosom's core
And gift me with a vast capacity
For innocent joy: such as was mine before
Not even in boyhood, and that comes thus free
From things on all hands *now*, because they store
Some inspiration of thy poetry!

[3] Rhymed Criticisms with Prose Notes, MS. book C376, Mitchell Library

These two influences, the Shelleyan and the Wordsworthian, were most fortunate for Harpur as a poet. Probably no other influences could have given him what he needed most—firstly, an attitude to his own landscape that had within it the seeds of a true understanding and appreciation of its quality, and secondly, a fearless independence of self-dedication that sustained him in his long battle with the ignorance and prejudice of his countrymen. The first—the Wordsworthian attitude to nature—enabled him to universalize his perceptions and images, so that the Australian countryside which others still found so monotonous, hostile and distasteful became for him a vision of beauty no less real for being his alone. The second, his conviction of the importance of his task, enabled him to lay a firm basis for Australian literature (how firm I shall try to show) by combining the best in contemporary English poetry with the best that he could forge of what already lay to his hand. In his work, Australian poetry was to become the voice of a new country certainly—

> Lyre of my Country, first falls it to me
> From the charm-muttering Savage's rude-beating hand
> To snatch thee, that so thy wild numbers may be
> No longer but writ on the winds of thy land.

('To the Lyre of Australia')

but that voice was to speak against the background and with the support of already-existing tradition.

Harpur understood that this must be so, if Australian literature was to speak with a true voice. It was with good cause that he hated the traditions and institutions that had rejected his parents and sent them to die in a strange land; but he was prudent and honest enough to recognize that an Englishman in process of becoming an Australian must speak with an English voice before finding his true accent. And his love of English poetry was ardent and discriminatory enough to make it certain that his choice of style and language suited the task he was to carry out. He was not seduced by Tennyson from the plainer paths of his Wordsworth; and the reasons he gives for his dislike of much of Tennyson are illuminating and entertaining:

> My dislike . . . is founded not so much on special grounds of judgment, as on general dissimilarities of mental habit. He is an old-world 'towney'—a dresser of parterres, and a peeper into parks. I am a man of the woods and mountains—

a wielder of the axe, and mainly conversant with aboriginal nature; a man made stern and self-reliant, and thence plain and even fierce, by nearness (if I may so speak) to the *in-cunabula mundi.* Hence poetry, with him, should be nice and dainty, rather than wise and hearty: while to affect my admiration, it must be free, bold and open, even at the risk of being rude.[4]

If Kendall had been able to exercise such stern and proper judgement of the suitability of Swinburne and Tennyson to the Australian scene, he would certainly have been a stronger, and probably a better, poet. But for Harpur's task, especially, he could have found no better master than Wordsworth, with his doctrines of plain speech, plain living, and communion with nature; the latter two of these were forced upon Harpur in a manner that Wordsworth never experienced, and to forge a poetry from them Harpur needed a doctrine such as the first. Wordsworth gave him not only an aim, but a method, in his task of discovery.

For us, Australia exists as a known whole with certain qualities: it is a country mapped and interpreted not only physically but in literature. For Harpur, it was an isolated convict-colony, despised by its inhabitants for the most part, still largely unexplored, without literature or pride or nationhood, with little to its credit, and seen through European eyes as ugly, barbarous and monotonous. It was for Harpur to become its first poet and interpreter, and this he had to do without audience or encouragement. Moreover, he recognized that it was also for him to establish a basis from which Australian poetry might begin, and by combining the English poetic tradition with the best that its lowly colony had to offer, to speak in the voice of a new country without rejecting what English tradition could give.

One reason for the neglect of Harpur's work, among many, was probably that when he wrote his mentor, Wordsworth, was falling out of fashion and the impulse of the early Romantics was already almost spent. The poetic influence of the 'forties and 'fifties was Alfred Tennyson—and Harpur's opinion of Tennyson I have already quoted. The plainer virtues of Wordsworth, which Harpur largely shared, were now unpopular; the mid-Victorian showiness and conventionalism of thought that were so bad an

4 MS. book A90, Mitchell Library

influence on Kendall were much more to the taste of colonial society. So as Harpur grew old the chance of the recognition he hoped for receded farther and farther. His poetry was considered not only rough and uncouth, but imitative. In fact, Kendall's verse was a great deal more imitative than Harpur's; Harpur is rather a follower of Wordsworth than an imitator, but Kendall at his worst is indeed Swinburne-and-water.

Undoubtedly Harpur's poetic tools were borrowed; but they were not borrowed unthinkingly, as his Critical Notes amply demonstrate. His diction and metres are frequently Wordsworthian; but as I have tried to show, his mind and thought are Wordsworthian also, yet independently so. He used the tenets and the prosody of his masters as they should be used, not as an imitator, but as a man uses borrowed tools to make something of his own. He had the pride and the humility of a poet; pride in his vocation and humility before Poetry itself as something more than the individual poet. His prayer to his muse is illuminating:

> . . . Still let thy grace my being leaven—
> Thy mystic grace—that face to face
> Full converse I may hold with nature,
> Seeing published everywhere
> In forms, the soul that makes her fair,
> And grow the while to her large style
> In mental stature.

('To the Spirit of Poesy')

Harpur's adaptation of the idioms of early Romanticism relieved him of the main part of his burden, the burden of finding a technique and a means of expression, and allowed him to concentrate upon his larger task of imagining his country—an Australia that did not yet exist. The remarkable thing is that he succeeded so far in doing this—how far, one cannot realize without an attentive reading of his work as a whole.

It would, of course, have been impossible for him at this time to have had the kind of appreciation of the Australian landscape that is possible nowadays. It is important for us to realize this, for it is the key to understanding all early Australian writing. Australian writers began under a handicap that no other new-world literature has had to face in the same measure. The visual, the tactile and the physical qualities of Australia are unique, and the European background of her new inhabitants singularly unfitted them to appreciate this country.

Moreover, Australia was settled late, and settled in circumstances that did not predispose her immigrants to love her. It was not only fashionable, it was inevitable, to disparage everything about the country; the question of beauty never arose, in the early days of the colony when the struggle was merely to prove the country's ability to support life. It was scarcely surprising that Harpur's vow of devotion to his country and its 'yet-to-be-famed' beauties gave rise to little but derision. Poetry and Australia seemed an impossible juxtaposition.

Harpur began, however, with a certain advantage; he was born and lived his early years in the Hawkesbury country, where the foothills of the Blue Mountains rise to westward and where the Hawkesbury River runs through their folds. This was eminently the country for a naturally Wordsworthian bent to find its fulfilment, and Harpur uses his early environment to the full in his later poetry.

Some of his best and most visual passages centre round these mountains that haunted his boyhood:

> But when the sun had wholly disappeared
> Behind those mountains—O what words, what hues
> Might paint the wild magnificence of view
> That opened westward! Out extending, lo!
> The heights rose crowding with their summits all
> Dissolving as it seemed, and partly lost
> In the exceeding radiancy aloft;
> And thus transfigured for awhile they stood
> Like a great company of archaeons, crowned
> With burning diadems, and tented o'er
> With canopies of purple and of gold.

> ('The Creek of the Four Graves')

And later in the same poem he describes them after sunset:

> Against the twilight heaven—a cloudless depth
> Yet luminous with sunset's fading glow;
> And thus awhile in the lit dusk they seemed
> To hang like mighty pictures of themselves
> In the still chambers of some vaster world.

This is almost a painter's rendering, in its glowing solidity, its relation of sky to earth. Light, distance and depth move Harpur to his best poetry, as in his vision of the mountain forests answering to breeze and sunlight:

B

> . . . in the breeze that o'er
> Their rough enormous backs deep-fleeced with wood
> Came whispering down, the wide upslanting sea
> Of fanning leaves in the descending rays
> Danced interdazzlingly, as if the trees
> That bore them, were all thrilling—tingling all
> Even to the roots, for very happiness:
> So prompted from within, so sentient, seemed
> The bright quick motion . . . .

The long poem 'A Storm in the Mountains' contains some of his best descriptive passages. And here, as in the passages quoted, the success he achieves is in the terms of his relationship of earth and light, of landscape and weather:

> The fierce refracted heat flares visible—
> Lambently radiant, like the lustrous hem
> Of an else-viewless veil held trembling over them . . . .
> . . . Cloud on cloud dark-rolling into one
> Tremendous mass of latent thunder, there
> Vastly incumbent on the darkening air.

Harpur's poetry, with its faults and virtues, is well exemplified here. It depends for its effect, at its best, upon its structure and movement, not on versification; but the structure is solid and can be tested, and the movement is varied and supple. It is an accent and a structure wholly different from that of Kendall, whose gentle and wistful cadences betray his weaknesses as a structure-maker.

There is a curious resemblance, pointed out earlier by another critic, between Harpur's early landscape poetry and the paintings of such men as Conrad Martens and Louis Buvelot, early interpreters of the Australian scene. The emphasis of these paintings falls, not upon the differences of Australian landscapes from English, but upon their broad likenesses. Gum trees, seen close up, are not in the least like oaks and beeches; but from a distance all forests are much alike, a dark clothing for landscape, for contours which differ little from country to country. This contour, this clothing, the early painters chose to paint, and the light in which they chose to paint them is a little darkened, twilight rather than high noon, so that the violence of Australian light itself is dimmed and the landscape left a little indistinct. It is a generalization, not a particularization, of landscape; as though, in a process of aesthetic digestion, the easier and more familiar aspects of the country were chosen first. It was not until the 'nineties that Streeton, the first truly indigenous painter of importance, showed Australians the quality of their own light and the brightness of their sky and water.

In the same way, Harpur's treatment of the forests and hills of the Hawkesbury country is blurred and generalized by distance; there are no images that would be startling or unfamiliar to an English reader. Yet the chief impression that remains of it is a true picture; the landscape is dark, perhaps, but it reflects the sunlight descending, it seems, from great heights; it glows with radiance, it glitters with leaves. Colour is practically nonexistent (in Harpur there are almost no colour-words; his sunsets are a glowing depth, not a coloured arrangement of clouds); the landscape is massed, not detailed; but the description is, for anyone who has looked westward over the hills of the Hawkesbury country, both exact and illuminating.

Harpur's voice, unhappily, changes as he grows older and more disappointed; it loses its conviction, it becomes wistful, sometimes shrill, sometimes vituperative and self-pitying; but he retains to the last his command of the sentence, his capacity to weave it into the formal pattern of a poem, and his capacity to make his sentence follow and express the line of his thought.

> . . . 'Tis gone too—the frank trust is gone forever
> Wherewith I afterwards essayed the world,
>   And first the flag unfurled
> Of my own individual endeavour!
> Youth's unworn bravery I strive in vain
>   To gather back again . . . .
>
> My weary soul methinks derives some gain
> Of strength even from the pain
> Attendant upon Memory: transfusion
> Over a life so lossful—strength to know
>   The personal end of woe:
>
> And thence to feel, the future can bring little
> That was not typed in what time brought before—
>   And to expect no more.
>
> ('The Losses of the Past')

As a poet, Harpur is more consistent, more firmly himself, than Kendall later was, but still his work is uneven and often uncertain. It was natural that it should be so; he was working

virtually alone, cut off from encouragement and appreciation.
Yet at his best his accent is unmistakable, his voice cuts through
the clutter of early-Victorian style and mannerism:

> . . . the flaming steps
> Of thy unspeakable speed, which of itself
> Blows back the long strands of thy burning hair
> Through half the arch of Night . . .
>
> ('The Comet')

> . . . Or down the flickering glades
> Ghastfully glaring, huge dry-mouldered gums
> Stood 'mid their living kin as banked throughout
> With eating fire, expelling arrowy jets
> Of blue-tipped, intermitting, gaseous flame,
> Boles, branches—all! like vivid ghosts of trees.
>
> ('The Bushfire')

> The stars in their bright order still
> Cluster by cluster glowingly revealed
> As the slow cloud moved on—high over all—
> Looked wakeful—yea, looked thoughtful in their peace.
>
> ('The Creek of the Four Graves')

> But the Dead
> Have this immunity at least—a lot
> Final and fixed, as evermore within
> The gates of the Eternal. For the past
> Is wholly God's and therefore, like himself,
> Knows no reverse, no change—but lies forever
> Stretched in the sabbath of its vast repose.
>
> ('Obituary Lines for his Father')

> As when to crown some sage's theory
> Amid heaven's sisterhoods into shining view
> Comes the conjectured star—his lucky name
> To halo thenceforth with its virgin flame.
>
> ('To ————')

Such lines and images as these, though they are not as frequent
as they should be, can be set against plenty of poetic dross. But
even at his worst Harpur retains one great and decisive advantage over Kendall and Gordon—that he thinks, and that he
can think with power and poetry. His frequent pedestrianism,
his bathos and badness are not the faults of weakness and irre-

solution, but of failure in the endeavour to express some too in-choate idea. Harpur can write extremely poorly, but his badness is idiosyncratic, part of himself; it is not the badness that comes from lack of anything to say, but from a losing struggle with time and argument, or with the attempt to acclimatize English poetry.

For he did attempt that difficult feat, in such poems as 'The Creek of the Four Graves' (which in its form as published in the 1883 edition, though it is seriously incomplete, is not only the first narrative poem set in Australia, but remained the best for many years); in 'The Bushfire', 'Dawn and Sunset on the Snowy Mountains', the long and unsuccessful narrative-descriptive 'The Kangaroo-Hunt' and many others. 'The Kangaroo-Hunt', curiously though it mingles allegorical abstractions and descrip-tion of Australian birds and beasts, might now be published if only for its notes on early Australian customs and on the various fauna and flora that are mentioned; and the same may be said of 'Lost in the Bush', with its Crabbean couplets and its sharp description of the bush-labourers among whom it is set.

What, on the whole, one is left with, when one considers Harpur's work both in the manuscripts and in the suspect 1883 edition, is a poet to whom less than justice has been done. This being so, it is difficult not to fall into the opposite error, of claiming too much for him; he is, after all, a prouder and a more incorruptible figure than Kendall, and in some senses a more original and better poet.

How good a poet, in fact, was Harpur? To remember all his difficulties and troubles is dangerous, just as it is when we think of Kendall; Kendall is excused many weaknesses because of his unhappiness. This is not good criticism, but apologia. Harpur, bitterly as he felt the neglect of his work and the poverty that overtook him, would have preferred to be judged as poet only; he had that strength. Let us ignore his handicaps and look at his achievements.

Two of his most ambitious poems—'The Creek of the Four Graves' and 'A Storm in the Mountains'—are at least successful in their genre, which is, and is intended to be, descriptive and narrative only. They are essays in the use of pentameter, always Harpur's favourite measure and the one that most suited his staunch and rather prosy attack. The much anthologized 'Mid-summer Noon in the Australian Forest' is, in spite of hackneying, a detailed and true observation as far as it goes, pleasant in versification, unassuming yet strongly structured. Moreover, it is proof of Harpur's feeling for language. If a poem is musical, it is likely to be not only a pleasing poem but a good one; this poem has, for Harpur, a remarkable musicality.

> Only there's a drowsy humming
> From yon warm lagoon slow coming:
> 'Tis the dragon-hornet—see!
> All bedaubed resplendently,
> Yellow on a tawny ground—
> Each rich spot nor square nor round,
> Rudely heart-shaped, as it were
> The blurred and hasty impress there
> Of a vermeil-crusted seal
> Dusted o'er with golden meal.

The poet who wrote that verse, with its sleepy buzzing drone, and its curious and exact observation, was a master of language, even if haste and crudity and poeticisms mar his work in other places. We cannot deny Harpur his due as poet proper.

But, though description is one of his strengths, I have called him above all a poetic thinker (no frequent distinction in Australian poetry). His most considerable attempt is not published at all in the 1883 edition; and it may be that no version in the manuscripts is final. But it remains a surprising and moving piece of work to come from any poet in the first half of the nineteenth century—since we have agreed to leave out of consideration Harpur's isolation and poverty.

The poem, 'The World and the Soul'[5], in blank verse, is an attempt to account for the relationship of world and soul—no less; and the viewpoint which Harpur chooses is a kind of mystical evolutionism. But evolution is something which Harpur sees as in terms of a preparation for consciousness; not only for the consciousness of man, though he is the world's 'present king', but for later and higher forms of consciousness, 'new successions in the scheme of life', 'progressive changes in the sum/And increment of that divine idea/Whereof the earth's so solid-seeming bulk/Is, with its fleshly populations whole, the vesture.' The world is, for Harpur, one among many other possible worlds, 'that strew/The neighbouring heavens with seats of being'; but all worlds alike 'exist in Him';

5 MS. book A89, Mitchell Library

As being but the million-featured modes
Of his star-seeing Thoughts:—each several thought
A shining link in one eternal chain
Of progress—to Perfection.

And the Soul is 'beyond the swoop of chance, and lifted high
/Out of the crash of matter'; not because she is separate from the
World, but because she is rather its final expression; indestruc-
tible, she may be reborn by transmigration in any of those other
worlds. For she is

An ultimate idea of all that went before,
A Spirit of Thought, and thence a child of that
In which the world began and hath its end.
. . . Thus, ancestrally a spark
From God's internal brightness, goes she forth
To die not, but to clothe for evermore
Her mighty life and wondrous faculties
In robes of beauty and of use, and all
The comforting integuments that sense
Weaves for her wearing, in the loom of Time,
Out of the hoards and harvests of the Earth.

It is, perhaps, by this poem that Harpur should be judged
as a thinker. It is no longer possible for his own time to judge
him—and in this as in other things contemporary judgement
would have had its value, for though the poem is sternly
original, the ideas it expresses have not the same atmosphere for
us now that they would have had to a reader in the early 'fifties,
when the poem appears to have been written.

To begin with, the very subject of the poem is clearly highly
controversial and suspect, to the kind of audience that Harpur
could command. It is scarcely to be wondered at, not only that it
remained unpublished during his lifetime, but that it was even
omitted from the posthumous volume. The notion of physical
evolution, which forms the background of the evolution of consciousness in the poem, was then and for many years after the
poem was written, scarcely likely to find favour with Harpur's
readers; nor was his version of the nature and mission of the soul
apt to meet with approval. But the poem is certainly his credo as
a philosophical poem, and it is more important in its implications
than either of his other long poems with non-Australian themes
—'The Tower of the Dream,' and 'The Witch of Hebron' (the
latter of which is greatly truncated in the *Collected Poems*).

These two poems are in the nature of set-pieces, perhaps intended to attract attention to the poet and his work, for neither of them sounds wholly convincing when set against the rest of Harpur's poetry, and though 'The Tower of the Dream' contains much interesting imagery, the subject, like that of 'The Witch of Hebron', is not a good vehicle for Harpur's earthy and discursive style. But 'The World and the Soul', laborious as it occasionally becomes, is a genuine piece of metaphysical poetic thinking, an attempt to describe an original and interesting view of the universe, which Harpur seems to have arrived at for himself.

Certainly, the world-view which he professes here may no longer sound very unusual to anyone who is familiar with the thought of Nietzsche, Darwin, Bergson and the Indian mystics; but given Harpur's circumstances and the time in which he lived, it is clear that we must credit him with a great deal more capacity as a thinker than we have done heretofore. The view of man in relationship to God and nature expressed in the poems is clearly and logically stated, it is fearlessly comprehensive, and it is positive enough to give us a clue to the doggedness of dedication with which Harpur clung to his chosen profession—the profession of bard and mentor to an as-yet scarcely existent nation—in the face of all contempt and disregard.

Harpur's independence of mind is shown in his Critical Notes on contemporary poets; his admiration for Coleridge's poetry was tempered by rejection, on grounds he thought sufficient, of Coleridge's Kantianism. The notion that things-in-themselves are unknowable could clearly form no part of Harpur's thinking, since to him consciousness is not merely the end to which evolution works, but the means by which the soul comes to know the world and itself as existing in God—as 'the million-featured modes Of His star-seeing Thoughts'. For Harpur, in effect, consciousness is creative of farther and higher consciousness; and consciousness is not separate from the world but is 'a child of that/ In which the world began and hath its end'; it is continuous with the pre-conscious, and leads to farther and more developed forms of itself, and at last to perfection in God. That is why, though he occasionally wrote political verse, Harpur is not a political poet; for him man is not a political animal, but a spark of godhead, creating through sense 'out of the hoards and harvests of the earth' a robe 'of beauty and of use' for the soul's wear.

Basically, Harpur is a far more religious poet in the proper sense of the word than was Kendall, who wrote conventional religious poetry without any deep feeling or thought. Harpur's poetic sense is far deeper; his grasp of the issues of his time far wider. That he achieved so little recognition, that the most important part of his work remained unpublished in his own time and remains unknown today, has been a tragic loss to the development of Australian poetry.

It was, in fact, the philosophical standpoint Harpur took up, under Wordsworthian influence, that made him the first poet able to accept and delight in the strange new landscape of Australia. If Nature is accepted as Harpur accepted it, as part of man and of his consciousness, the strange and the unusual lose their repugnance and become part of the variety and beauty of life, to be loved and understood for their own sake. Harpur accepted Australia thus; his muse became the Muse of the Evergreen Forest, of Australian nature in particular; the forms of nature around him ceased for him to be alien and were part of his life and consciousness.

CHAPTER II

Henry Kendall

∽

WHEN HARPUR died in 1868, the social climate of Australia had changed a great deal since his birth. With the colony now no longer a rubbish-tip for England, but a promising young producer of wealth, with increased population and increasing self-confidence as her isolation lessened, Australia seemed well on the way to becoming what Harpur had hoped she would be, a nation in her own right.

But it did not look as though the kind of nation he had worked for was at all likely to emerge from these colonies. The 'tree of liberty' that he had once called on Australians to plant and tend was not putting out the shoots that he had dreamed it might. Men certainly did not seem to be turning from the pursuit of wealth to the pursuit of more fundamental values; the libertarian society might be in course of growth, but it was founded rather on the opportunism of the gold-rushes than on the exercise of reason and compassion in man.

Above all, there did not seem to be, with the increase in wealth, any more time or inclination for the cultivation of Australian poetry or the recognition of such poets as Australia already had. Overseas, England was busy aggrandizing her Empire and her possessions, and her young Australian colonies seemed content to trail in her wake, picking up such gold and silver as dropped from her pockets, and occupied much more with the market prices of wool and cattle, the getting of gold and the terms of trade than with the things of the mind.

It was little wonder that poor Harpur felt more and more bitterly as he aged that the lot of the self-appointed poet and prophet was a hard one. It seemed that his always detested enemy, 'money's-worth', was to be the victor.

But he had, in his last years, at least one disciple. The young Henry Kendall, poor and not well educated but an aspiring poet, discovered Harpur's verse and adopted him as master; and after a seven-year correspondence, when Kendall was still in his twenties and Harpur in his last years, the two met. How consoling

and restorative Harpur found their brief friendship, his sonnet to
Kendall bears witness:

> Said Chaucer in his old days, when the sun
> Of his poetic life was wearing low.
> 'To me now from afar come tidings none
> From spirits that once, with a congenial glow,
> Did glory in my glory long ago—
> Nay, even my neighbours, as in scorn 'twere done,
> Ignore me'—*and* to a like tune might run
> My story ever as I older grow.
> 'Tis much then, in this dearth on every hand
> Of sympathy, and in my loneness here,
> To have, through votive lines so sweetly bland
> (Yet bravely worshipful) as thine, such clear
> Assurance of how well my Native Land
> Shall yet atone for all—holding my memory dear.

The 'lines' Harpur spoke of were probably the enthusiastic
anapaests addressed to 'C.H.', in which Kendall exclaimed:

> I would sit at your feet for long days
> To hear the sweet Muse of the Wild
> Speak out through the sad and the passionate lays
> Of her first and her favourite child . . .
>
> I would sit at your feet, for I know
> Though the World in the Present be blind,
> That the blossoms of Promise will blow
> When the ages have left you behind.
>
> I would sit at your feet, for I feel
> I am one of a glorious band
> That ever will own you and hold you their Chief
> And a Monarch of Song in the land!

Kendall's devotion to Harpur's poetry may have waned later,
but his elegy for Harpur, written on the elder poet's death, is
sincere and tender, though perhaps it does not show much
understanding of Harpur's work and character. Nevertheless,
Kendall saw that Harpur had been the first to experience and
appreciate the problems of Australian poetry, and that his
strength and endurance had set him above his circumstances.

> So we that knew this singer dead
> Whose hands attuned the harp Australian,
> May set the face, and bow the head
> And mourn his fate and fortunes alien.

The burthen of a perished faith
Went sighing through his speech of sweetness,
With human hints of time and death
And subtle notes of incompleteness.

But when the fiery power of youth
Had passed away and left him nameless,
Serene as light and strong as truth
He lived his life, untired and tameless.

And far and free this man of men
With wintry hair and wasted feature
Had fellowship with gorge and glen
And learned the loves and runes of Nature . . .

We scarcely recognize Harpur's poetry, in the man who 'had fellowship with gorge and glen'—though it was in fact, the mountains that Harpur most loved—and 'who learned the loves and runes of Nature'; in fact this sounds more like an idealization of Kendall's own ambition as a poet, than of Harpur's actual achievement, which was directed far more to human than to natural phenomena. But Kendall recognizes this, in his final verses;

No soul was he to sit on heights
And live with rocks apart and scornful.
Delights of men were his delights
And common troubles made him mournful.

The pathos worn by wayside things,
The passion found in simple faces,
Struck deeper than the life of springs
Or strength of storms and sea-swept places.

Though the poem is not a particularly good characterization of Harpur's work, it has the virtue of generosity; and Kendall had cause to pay Harpur tribute, for many of Harpur's themes found their way, in one form or another, into Kendall's poetry.

So, in 'The Glen of Arrawatta', Kendall took up both the theme and the form of Harpur's 'The Creek of the Four Graves', though the poem is neither as dramatic nor as thoughtful as Harpur's original. In 'The Muse of Australia', Kendall addresses the same figure that Harpur had met in 'The Dream by the Fountain'; though Kendall laments that the Muse has not descended for him . . . he has only caught

a glimpse of her face, and her glittering hair,
And a hand with the Harp of Australia . . .

And so, too, he takes up the theme of Harpur's poem, 'The
Voice of the Swamp Oak'—first in his early poetic years, with
'The Wail in the Native Oak', then, twelve years later and with
bitter recollection, in 'The Voice in the Wild Oak'.

This identification with various of Harpur's indigenous themes
is interesting, and I think it can be shown to be significant. Kendall, who began as Harpur's acknowledged disciple, came to
think a good deal less of his verse than he had done as a young
man. Possibly he was influenced at least in part by the poor
opinion his other friend and mentor, James Lionel Michael, held
of Harpur's work. There is, in Sydney's Mitchell Library, a copy
of Harpur's book *A Poet's Home,* presented by Kendall to
Michael. It has been heavily marked—first by Kendall, approv-
ingly; then by Michael, with severe marginal comment. Yet it
seems that Kendall continued to feel Harpur's themes as a challenge to his own poetic powers; and his response, in 'The Voice
in the Wild Oak', was a summing-up of his own life in terms of
the poetic image that Harpur had first used.

So the link between the two poets needs to be examined carefully. Harpur's own poem (written, it would seem, fairly early)
was published in 1862 in *A Poet's Home,* and the Kendall-
Michael copy in the Mitchell Library has this poem heavily
marked by Kendall, apparently in approval. The poem is slight
enough, in comparison with some of Harpur's other work, but
Kendall may well have felt that in it an entirely indigenous subject was for the first time successfully handled and its special
quality conveyed.

THE VOICE OF THE SWAMP OAK

Who hath lain him underneath
A lone oak by a lonely stream;
He hath heard an utterance
Sadder than all else may seem.

Up in its dusk boughs out-tressing
Like the hair of a giant's head,
Mournful things beyond our guessing
—Day and night are uttered.

Even when the waveless air
May only stir the lightest leaf,
A lonely voice keeps moaning there
Wordless oracles of grief.

But when nightly blasts are roaming
Lowly is that voice no more;
From the streaming branches coming
Elfin shrieks are heard to pour.

While between the blast on-passing
And the blast that comes as oft,
'Mid those boughs dark intermassing
One long low wail pines aloft.

Till the listener surely deems
That some weird spirit of the air
Hath made those boughs the lute of themes
Wilder, darker than despair.

Darker than a woe whose morrow
Must be travelling to an end—
Wilder than the wildest sorrow
That in death hath still a friend.

Some lonely spirit that hath dwelt
For ages in one lonely tree—
Some weary spirit that hath felt
The burthen of eternity.

Kendall's particular interest in this poem was apparently less from the point of view of a connoisseur of verse than of a poet who intended to take up the task of translating and interpreting the new images around him. It is the subject, and Harpur's approach to it, that interest him; the technique he does not seem to have admired, to judge from his own attempt at the subject, which is much looser, more rhapsodic, and in an anapaestic metre (imitative of Tennyson's enormously popular 'Locksley Hall') that unfortunately does not help Kendall's own essential lack of prosodic control and economy. This metre requires a high degree of organization of the poetic sentence, and a pressure which shall keep it flowing strongly throughout; otherwise the long looping lines of anapaests begin to droop like faded garlands.

Kendall's poem, in fact, is not only sadly inflated, but it displays his own worst faults—the way in which his eye constantly strays from the object (that object on which, as Wordsworth remarked, the poet's eye must be fixed) to himself. One extract will be enough to display its loose sentimentalities:

. . .And I caught a glimpse of sunset fading from a far-off wild,
As I sat me down to fancy, like a thoughtful wistful child,
Sat me down to fancy what might mean these hollow hopeless tones
Sooming round the swooning silence, dying out in smothered moans,

What might mean that muffled sobbing? Did a lonely phantom wail
Pent among those tangled branches, barring out the moonlight pale?
Wept it for that gleam of glory wasting from the forest aisles,
For the fainting gleam of glory, sad with flickering sickly smiles?

This gives a convenient illustration of the way in which Kendall, though he may set out to write about something in the external world, keeps slipping back into subjectivity. The object —a landscape, an explorer's journey, a river—tends to become blurred and unrecognizable, swallowed up by the poetic sentiment. So in comparing Harpur's treatment of the Swamp Oak theme with Kendall's own first treatment of it, the difference in approach is obvious; in Harpur's poem the theme is presented as it is refracted through the poet's consciousness, but the poet himself does not appear; in Kendall's the 'mournful wistful child' who is the poet sits, as it were, in the middle of the poem and is its real subject.

Perhaps this contrast is due as much to certain facts of the time that Kendall lived in, as to his own character. To a modern taste, the unpretentious simplicity of form and treatment which Harpur inherited from Wordsworth is greatly preferable to the sentimental subjectivity into which other mid-Victorian poets, as well as Kendall, too easily slipped.

Moreover, the poem throws a strong light on the fact that the poetic mid-Victorianism of Tennyson and Swinburne was probably the most unsuitable influence for Australian poets that could be imagined. Harpur had had the right instinct when he had repudiated Tennyson, that 'dresser of parterres', in favour of a 'plain, even a rough' style. When Kendall abandoned Harpur's method in favour of the more fashionable styles, he determined his own poetic fate. A writer with real strength and stability might have fought beyond the influence of England and forged himself an expressive stylistic instrument. But Kendall, unlike Harpur, had not subjected himself to the stern poetic discipline of reading and judging for himself.

A simpler and stronger line, a practice of verbal economy, a study of poetic structure, might have given us a different poet. As it was, Kendall's besetting faults went uncorrected by better examples.

But as time went on, Kendall learned to simplify his ornament and, in his best poems, to speak plainly; and where he is impelled by true emotional pressure, he can manage his phrasing and sentences with real lyrical art. So, in 'The Voice in the Wild Oak', written twelve years later than 'The Wail in the Native Oak', much more control is shown. The poem is self-occupied still; but there is in it less mawkishness than genuine regret for the vanishing of his old dream—the dream of interpreting Australia.

> Twelve years ago, when I could face
> High heaven's dome with different eyes
> In days full-flowered and hours of grace,
> And nights not sad with sighs,
> I wrote a song in which I strove
> To shadow forth thy strain of woe,
> Dark widowed sister of the grove—
> Twelve wasted years ago.
>
> . . . But I who am that perished soul
> Have wasted so these powers of mine
> That I can never write that whole
> Pure perfect speech of thine . . .
> And still the life that lives in thee,
> The soul of thy majestic lay,
> Remains a mystery . . .

So the theme of the Swamp Oak, begun years before, comes to an end, and in the three poems in their sequence we can get a glimpse of what had happened to poetry in Australia, during the fifty years from 1833, when Harpur began his serious work, to Kendall's death. For there are practically no other candidates, worth serious consideration as poets, during that half-century; serious poetry, as opposed to folk-verse, found scarcely any other exponents.

It is relevant to wonder what had happened to the Lyre which Harpur had snatched 'from the charm-muttering Savage's rude-beating hand', at the command of his Muse. This Muse had also occupied a great deal of Kendall's thoughts; but as he confessed, this occupation was rather the search for her than the doing of her bidding.

> I never can reach you, to hear the sweet voice
> So full with the music of fountains!
> Oh when will you meet with the soul of your choice
> Who will lead you down here from the mountains?
>
> ('The Muse of Australia')

But though Kendall reproached himself for his failure to entice the Muse, the fault lay probably not so much in him as in what happened during those fifty years.

For Kendall's minor though real talent was not strong enough to stand up against the current of his times, or to turn them to poetic advantage. Like Harpur's, his fate and fortunes were 'alien', perhaps the more so in that his poetry was, on the whole, better received than that of Harpur. For what was expected of a poet in mid-Victorian Australia was very different from what Kendall had begun by expecting of himself; and the kind of pressure that was put on him resulted in a further weakening and sentimentalizing of his lyrical gifts. Harpur, unlucky as he thought himself, at least had never suffered that ultimate distress of having used his gift for ends that corrupted it. Anyone who reads a complete collection of Kendall's verse will realize that he was not so fortunate; or perhaps not so strong.

For the ascendancy of the devotees of 'money's-worth' meant that poets, to be successful, must accept the values of 'respectability'. The independent man, 'spherical and so far God-like', whom Harpur had dreamed of seeing in his time, did not grow out of the young Australia; the values that Harpur had upheld in his visionary younger days had gone no farther.

In Europe, the current of consciousness was leading more and more to a rejection of all such personal values. The increasing gap between intellect and feeling progressively weakened the work of English poets during the nineteenth century, after the death of the Early-Romantic movement.

No reconciling image took the place of the Wordsworthian nature-worship which was undermined by Coleridge's desperate clearsightedness:

> O Lady, we receive but what we give,
> And in our life alone does Nature live.

Out of that widening abyss rose the sad questionings of Arnold, for whom only poetry herself could now seem a reconciling force; the technical accomplishment and verbal grace of Tennyson; the embroidered metrical experiments of Swinburne and his empty celebration of the physical. Poetry had been deprived of anything to say; and rationalism and positivism flourished while religion was gradually relegated to the status of an unconvincing fairy tale.

All this had its natural repercussions in Australia. The 'worldly men' seemed abundantly justified in their common-sense occupation of carving out as much for themselves as possible. The fittest, it seemed, were to survive, and survival was the chief value; the fittest were obviously those who owned most and cared least for the survival of the rest. In the 'nineties, Barcroft Boake's embittered ballad, 'Where the Dead Men Lie', was to be the barbed comment on the effect of all this in the development of Australia.

So, probably, Kendall's projected affair with the Muse of Australia was doomed from the beginning. But, for the first time, poetry entered the lists in another guise. An Australian poet, if not Australian poetry, became almost a necessary adjunct to the national life.

Australia was becoming conscious of her growing importance. In 1877 a touring English cricket team was actually defeated by an Australian side. In 1879, an Australian newspaper, beating the drum for the coming Sydney International Exhibition, offered a prize of £100 for a poem on that subject, and Kendall won it. (The poem, *Cantata, written expressly for the Opening Ceremony of the Sydney International Exhibition* was published in 1879 and, naturally, was one of the worst he ever wrote.)

He attained celebrity; his next book, *Songs from the Mountains,* published in the following year, was for the first time a financial success. Australia had a national poet—her first, as everyone declared. Kendall—who had once hailed Harpur in the same glowing terms—does not seem to have protested.

Australia needed a poet (other nations had them); and Kendall seemed suited for the job. He made no exigent demands on her, as in his place Harpur would certainly have done. His lyrics, even those written in poverty and semi-starvation, reproached nobody but himself. They were rhetorical, they were sentimental, they were full of poetical words like 'swooning' and 'glen' and 'vale'; the best of them were praised by overseas critics and even the worst contained nothing unsuitable for a young lady's album.

Kendall had become, at last, a romantic figure. After a life of varied misery, he died in a state of comparative fame and comfort. No one need grudge him that, and much more. He had suffered a great deal, and in doing so he had learned far more about himself and his poetic limitations than his reviewers ever knew.

So there is a sense in which Kendall is not one poet, but two— the figure in Australian literature, and the private poet, filled with a desperate self-reproach and yearning, who is beginning to emerge more clearly in the perspective of years. For that he was indeed a poet, with real lyrical ability, is clear in the few poems whose emotional temperature is high enough to generate an inner pressure and sincerity of speech. There are not many of them. 'September' is too much a set-piece, though it has charms; the two Prefatory Sonnets, though they have a melancholy and disarming simplicity, and are perhaps the poems that attain most clarity, are in a sense public apologias; they do not arise out of an urgent poetic necessity to communicate. But in 'Orara', 'Mooni', 'The Bellbirds', 'After Many Years' and 'To a Mountain', we hear the voice, not of the poet Kendall had hoped he would be, but of the poet he was capable of being.

Later, I want to examine these poems; but at present it is necessary to look more closely at the effect on Kendall of the factors I have mentioned as frustrating and misleading his gifts. The most obvious of them, of course, is to be found in the occasional verses, those that he may have felt his position as Australia's only poet demanded of him.

But to read these is to get a distressing glimpse of the corruptions of popularity—of an acquiescence in the foolishnesses and hypocrisies of his time that amounts to betrayal of all that he had hoped for from his poetry. There are the two quite hysterical sets of verses written on the occasion of the visit of the young Duke of Edinburgh—a youth for whom, it seems, apart from his position not much could be, or ever was, said—and of his wounding by an insane and unfortunate young Irishman during his visit to Sydney. The incident, no doubt deplorable in itself,

roused the most violent passions, both against Ireland and for
Royalty; but Kendall outdid the most extravagant, and his 'Australia Vindex' and 'The Larrikin' can scarcely be read without a
tremor of distaste for their fawning vehemence.

Here is one verse from 'The Larrikin'—and not the most objectionable:

A blossom of blackness, indeed—of Satan a sinister fruit!
Far better the centipede's seed—the spawn of the adder or newt!
. . . The prison, the shackles and chain, are nothing to him
    and his type:
He sings in the shadow of pain, and laughs at the impotent
    stripe!

It was not in the 'weakness' deplored by the respectable, his
tendency to find comfort in the bottle, his shy solitary nature
and his difficulty in earning a sufficient living, that Kendall's real
failure lay; and we may even doubt that when he lamented his
'wasted years' it was of such matters that he was really thinking.
Rather it was his weakness in seeking popularity at the expense
of rigid poetic honesty. The kind of acclaim he gained from such
patriotic odes and sententious verses, and from his few attempts
at the bush narratives and racing ballads that had given Gordon
his celebrity, but which were somewhat outside Kendall's
experience and poetic ambit, was corrupting to his poetic gift:
for it meant that he was forced into sentimental falsities and
away from reality and his own imaginative potentiality. Sentimentalism is precisely this forcing of feeling where none exists;
and Kendall was often guilty of this.

Poems like 'Lilith', 'Galatea', and 'Merope'—those 'classical
subjects' admired by his time—poems like 'The Glen of Arrawatta', and 'A Death in the Bush', written largely because Harpur had written narrative poems of the bush; and the Biblical
subject-poems, colourless and unfelt; these make up the largest
part of Kendall's output, and in few of them can we find the ring
of genuine feeling, except where, reverting to his own unfortunate
condition, Kendall allows himself to enter the poem in person.
So in 'Euterpe' we suddenly hear a voice we can recognize:

Here and here my days are wasted, shorn of leaf and stript of
    fruit,
Vexed because of speech half-spoken, maiden with the mar-
    vellous lute . . . .

Much more authentic, because much less inflated, than these poems are his unadorned sketches of Jim the Splitter and Bill the Bullock-driver; Jim who was

> . . . bred in a bangalow-wood,
> And bangalow pith was the principal food
> His mother served out in her shanty—

and

> Poor bullocky Bill! In the circles select
> Of the scholars he hasn't a place,
> But he walks like a *man,* with his forehead erect,
> And he looks at God's day in the face.
> For rough as he seems, he would shudder to wrong
> A dog with the loss of a hair . . . .

But Kendall did not pin much faith on these sketches, or on his racing ballads or his attempts at bush narratives. He felt himself rather to be a nature-poet; for him the 'Harp of Australia' would be awarded by her Muse to the poet who made

> Not songs, like some, tormented and awry
> With passion, but a cunning harmony
> Of words and music caught from glen and height
> And lucid colours born of woodland light . . .

And 'the song that once he dreamed about' was to have been 'to the tune/Of woodland music set'.

On the strength of these ambitions of Kendall's and the few poems which seem to support his claims to be a poet of nature, it is an accepted commonplace that he is our first real depictor of Australian landscapes. A. G. Stephens was the main authority for this, but it has been repeated by critics ever since. In apology for the evident un-Australianness of most of his landscapes, the author of the article on Kendall in *Australian Literature* remarks 'it happens that the south-eastern portion of the continent, whence he drew inspiration, is less differentiated than the interior from European scenery.' And this author also tells us that Kendall's feeling for nature is 'intenser' than Harpur's.

But to anyone reading these few important poems of Kendall's with thorough attention, it becomes evident that they do not arise out of, or contain, the delight in or the detailed observation of outward scenes that is found—not to put too high a value into the other scale—in the work of John Thomson in England, or Barron Field in Australia—let alone of a true nature-

poet like Clare. There are no flowers here—except the wattle,
which had already been sung in bush ballads—yet Kendall must
have known the extraordinary flowering of the Hawkesbury
country with its variety and colour. The only trees mentioned—
apart from Harpur's own river-oak—are trees with vaguely
European names like 'cedar' and 'sycamore'; yet Kendall worked
with a timber firm and must have known the names of many
other trees and their habits. There are few birds, if we except a
mention of the lyrebird, and the bell-birds of the well-known
poem; and no animals.

Kendall's landscapes are, in fact, undifferentiated and without
life or inhabitants. Moreover, the landscapes themselves are
covered in a vague veil of generalization under which nothing
is really recognizable, nothing different from anything else. The
Orara, the Mooni, Narrara Creek—all are spoken of in just the
same terms; without the names, we would not know one from
another. All is disguised under indistinct adjectives and musical
poeticism:

> The ways of the frost have been filled of the flowers,
> While the forest discovers
> Wild wings, with the halo of hyaline hours
> And the music of lovers . . .
> O season of changes—of shadow and shine—
> September the splendid! . . .   ('September')

> Still to be by Mooni cool—
> Where the water-blossoms glister,
> And, by gleaming vale and vista,
> Sits the English April's sister
> Soft, and sweet, and wonderful.
>   ('Mooni')

> The singing silver life I hear,
> Whose home is in the green
> Far-folded woods of fountains clear,
> Where I have never been.
>   ('Orara')

Or—perhaps the best of these water-images:

> By channels of coolness the echoes are calling,
> And down the dim gorges I hear the creek falling;
> It lives in the mountain, where moss and the sedges
> Touch with their beauty the banks and the ledges;

Through breaks of the cedar and sycamore bowers
Struggles the light that is love to the flowers . . .

('The Bellbirds')

But these pictures are less descriptive than emotive—they are not the work of an enthusiastic observer of nature. Think of Clare's

There the gay river, laughing as it goes,
Plashes with easy wave its flaggy sides,
And to the calm of heart, in calmness shows
    What pleasure there abides,
To trace its sedgy banks, from trouble free . . .

('Summer Images')

or his

. . . little sinky foss,
Streaking the moors whence spa-red water spews
From pudges fringed with moss . . .

('To the Snipe')

Compared with these intimately seen pictures, Kendall's is subjective poetry, whose vague enthusiasms are expressed in equally vague pictures; the moss and the sedges 'touch with their beauty' the banks; the light is 'love to the flowers'. The features of the landscape are not described, but used as emotional notations; the reader accustomed to the Romantic connotation of such images is expected to respond to them with the proper reaction, but he is scarcely shown anything in its visual or audible reality. The whole scene, in fact, is like a nineteenth-century photographer's background, with waterfalls and mountains complete; the figure in the foreground is the important part of the picture, and this figure, wistful and frustrated, is the poet himself.

The stock character of Kendall's landscapes is obvious enough. He admitted it himself, in fact, in the second of his Prefatory Sonnets, where the 'stranger' treads 'the cedar dells', 'shot through with sunset', and 'hears the breezy ring of elfin bells/Far down by where the white-haired cataract booms'. This is exactly the kind of scenery of 'Orara' and 'Mooni'; yet it is not, in this sonnet, an Australian scene, but 'Syrian'.

However, these poems, even when we recognize their lack of differentiation and refuse their claim to be what Kendall thought they were, poems of Australian Nature, retain their interest and charm, and their power to make us feel that these rivers and valleys and glens and glades, however artificial they may look,

mean something. I want to suggest that what is compelling in
them is not any recognizable resemblance to actual landscape,
but the deep-rooted source of the images: that, in fact, the foreground figure is not only Kendall, but humanity.

> There is a river in the range
> I love to think about;
> Perhaps the searching feet of change
> Have never found it out.

So Kendall wrote in 'After Many Years', meditating on his
own loss of inspiration and his weariness. It is to rivers, creeks,
glens and valleys and 'secret hollows dear to noontide dew' that
Kendall's poetry constantly turns; and we may notice that the
feeling of this water imagery is always wistful, yearning and
frustrated, and that it is to the sources of the rivers, and to the
past, that the yearning is directed.

> Ah, brook above the upper bend,
> I often long to stand
> Where you in soft, cool shades descend
> From the untrodden land!
>
> ('Orara')

> Soul of mine from sin abhorrent
> Fain would hide by flashing current
> Like a sister of the torrent,
>   Far away by Mooni's springs.
>
> ('Mooni')

> With the years of the youth and the hairs of the hoary,
> I sit like a shadow outside of thy glory,
> Nor look with the morning-like feelings, O river,
> That illumined the boy in the days gone forever.
>
> ('Narrara Creek')

In fact, this scene that haunts Kendall's poetry, these rivers
that rouse in him so much melancholy and longing, are not so
much realities as symbols. They are more like recollections, visions
of the past to which the poet longs to return.

But the longing goes farther than mere return to their banks;
it is a longing for vanished youth, and even for an illumination
and knowledge of them that the boy Kendall did not possess; for
a retreat into these far-off clefts and hollows from the disillusion-

ments and sorrows of the world; and from some guilt or 'sin abhorrent' that has overtaken the poet since his days of innocence.

Yet this longing for retreat is contradicted, it seems, by a conflicting consciousness that any such retreat would be a weakness, or unmanly. If we trace the flow of feeling in 'Orara', a poem that seems flawed by its last few stanzas, we see this contradiction and its effects.

The poem begins with the river seen after a storm:

> The strong sob of the chafing stream
> That seaward fights its way
> Down crags of glitter, dells of gleam,
> Is in the hills today.
>
> But far and faint, a gray-winged form
> Hangs where the wild lights wane—
> The phantom of a bygone storm,
> A ghost of wind and rain.

But the scene is now calm: the storm is gone, 'the soft white feet of afternoon' (a typically vague image) 'are on the shining meads', and 'the fierce disastrous flying fire/That made the great caves ring' is forgotten. The poet sees 'a rose-red space of stream . . . a radiant brook, unknown to me/Beyond its upper turn'. The source of the river is 'in the green/Far-folded woods of fountains clear/Where I have never been'. But now he will not attain it; for

> The world is round me with its heat
> And toil, and cares that tire;
> I cannot with my feeble feet
> Climb after my desire.

But the mere source of the actual river is strangely transformed in the next few stanzas:

> But on the lap of lands unseen,
> Within a secret zone,
> There shine diviner gold and green
> Than man has ever known . . .
>
> Yea, in my dream of fall and brook
> By far sweet forests furled,
> I see that light for which I look
> In vain through all the world—

> The glory of a larger sky
>   On slopes of hills sublime,
> That speaks with God and morning, high
>   Above the ways of Time!

But the following stanzas renounce this image of a timeless country:

> Ah, haply, in this sphere of change
>   Where shadows spoil the beam,
> It would not do to climb that range
>   And test my radiant Dream.

> The slightest glimpse of yonder place,
>   Untrodden and alone,
> Might wholly kill that nameless grace,
>   The charm of the unknown.

And the poet concluded that 'perhaps the lot is bright/Which keeps the river of the song/A beauty out of sight'.

A certain confusion and frustration seem to overcome both the poet and the reader in these verses. If, as the earlier stanzas tell us, what Kendall sees at the source of the river is indeed 'the glory of a larger sky . . . that speaks with God and morning, high above the ways of Time', then the Dream cannot be 'tested' by any climbing of the actual range, and it is obviously more than the mere 'charm of the unknown', which any bushwalker may feel and may have dispelled by closer knowledge. The poem, in fact, rises to its height outside the ordinary world; Time cannot be used as a touchstone for the timeless.

So the last stanzas, in which Kendall falls almost defensively back into the everyday standards of the world, are not so much a mere contradiction, as a total denial, of the central theme. The river cannot, within the scope of the poem, be both the river that rises in Eden and the River Orara, unless the poet can fuse his vision of the ideal with his knowledge of the real; and this he does not even try to do. It is as though the poem itself shied away from the responsibility. The poem has not merely not come off—the writer himself has given it up as hopeless. 'Orara', in fact, is a poem deeply flawed by the poet's own inner contradiction.

'Mooni', written later, is a much more unified poem, being wholly a poem of lament and longing. In it the river image, instead of wavering between the ordinary and the ideal planes, is transferred entirely to the ideal, to the sphere of the symbol, and scarcely pretends to any objective particular existence.

> Ah, to be by Mooni now!
> Where the great dark hills of wonder,
> Scarred with storm and cleft asunder
> By the strong sword of the thunder,
>   Make a night on morning's brow!
> Just to stand where Nature's face is
> Flushed with power in forest places—
> Where of God authentic trace is—
>   Ah, to be by Mooni now!
>
> Just to be by Mooni's springs!
> There to stand, the shining sharer
> Of that larger life, and rarer
> Beauty caught from beauty fairer
>   Than the human face of things!
> Soul of mine from sin abhorrent
> Fain would hide by flashing current
> Like a sister of the torrent,
>   Far away by Mooni's springs.

To 'be by Mooni' means here to be, not merely a human being beside an actual river, but to be again in communion with beauty and innocence, 'sharer of a larger life' and of a 'beauty fairer than the human face of things'. Moreover, it is to be hidden from 'sin abhorrent', and, the poem goes on, the dweller by Mooni is 'safe'.

Clearly the poet is not thinking of any ordinary river in the ordinary world; this is an Eden-river, a protective source from which the poet set out but to which he cannot now return. For though he once

> Stood where Mooni's water crosses
> Shining tracts of green-haired mosses,
>   Like a soul with radiant wings,

and though, he says, he then

> resembled
> Lords of light unstained, unhumbled,

he now

> Shrinks before the splendid
> Face of Deity offended . . .

and
>   the loveliness is ended.

The poet can only long

> Just to rest beyond the burning
> Outer world—its sneers and spurning . . .

And the phrase 'the burning *outer* world' is significant, confirming that the image of the river is of an inner, not an outer reality.

This water imagery is always opposed, in Kendall, to quite another kind of image—the 'heats' and 'burning' of the outer world; or, in Kendall's equally significant explorer poems, of the Australian inland, which is depicted as a blazing desert in which the explorer's only hope is to find water, a kind of solitude like that to which Cain was cast out. Several times Kendall refers to his 'sin' which condemns him to exile from his river-Eden, and even from his hopes of becoming a poet. In 'The Voice in the Wild Oak', he writes

> But he who hears this autumn day
> The more than deep autumnal rhyme
> Is one whose hair was shot with grey
> By Grief instead of Time.
> He has no need, like many a bard,
> To sing imaginary pain,
> Because he bears, and finds it hard,
> The punishment of Cain.

This 'punishment of Cain' seems to colour all his poems of inland Australia with a lurid imagination of thirst and heat and exile. For Kendall, the thought of this desert country is unbearable; he even has, in his poem 'Leichhardt', to soften the explorer's real fate (and incidentally, from a more forthright point of view, to sentimentalize it) by imagining for him a gentler grave than the one he really found:

> On the tracts of thirst and furnace—on the dumb blind burning
>   plain
> Where the red earth gapes for moisture and the wan leaves hiss
>   for rain,
> In a land of dry, fierce thunder, did he ever pause and dream
> Of the cool green German valley and the singing German
>   stream? . . .

Down a dell of dewy myrtle, where the light is soft and green,
And a month like English April sits, an immemorial queen,
Let us think that he is resting—think that by a radiant grave
Ever come the songs of forest, and the voices of the wave!

Kendall's explorers, in fact, are seldom triumphant or successful; they are always stumbling through 'the bitter hopeless desert',
through

spheres that no bird knows of, where with fiery emphasis
Hell hath stamped its awful mint-work deep on everything
    that is.

('Christmas Creek')

'On a Cattle Track', 'On the Paroo', 'The Fate of the Explorers'—poem after poem presents the same picture of shadeless
and waterless deserts, without mitigation or saving detail. Kendall's 'Australia' is a place sharply divided between Eden and
Hell—between the lush forested clefts where waters fall forever,
and the pitiless desert.

It is, in fact, no real country, but a country of opposing symbolic landscapes seen in a vision that is almost tragic in its in-
tensity. Its sole figures are the poet who, banished into the 'burning outer world', dreams forever of the rivers and their sources,
and the stumbling explorer in a desert from which he can only
hope to escape by discovering water. We may suspect that the
explorer figure is also Kendall, in another aspect of his poetic
drama.

The explorer theme first appears in an early poem, 'Fainting
by the Way', set in the form of a dialogue between two wanderers
in the outback:

'Oh, across these sultry deserts many a fruitful scene we'll find
And the blooms we gather shall be worth the wounds they
    leave behind . . .'
'Ah my brother, it is useless! See, o'er-burdened with their load,
All the friends who went before us fall or falter by the road!'
'. . . Rise, and lean thy weight upon me! Life is fair and God
    is just,
And he yet will show us fountains, if we only look and
    trust . . .'

The wanderers here were successful in their search; but in later
poems like 'On a Cattle Track' the outcome is not so happy.

Here the thirst-stricken riders, deceived by a mirage, die in the desert, with the epitaph of one of Kendall's poorest stanzas:

> Some men are successful after seasons distressful,
>   (Now, masters, the drift of my tale)
> But the brink of salvation is a lair of damnation
> For others who struggle yet fail.

And that Kendall had himself 'struggled yet failed' he has told us often enough, and mournfully enough, for us to suspect a connection. The mirage that floated ahead of him—whether it was Poetry, Fame, the Harp Australian, or simply relinquishment of ambition and retreat into an impossible Eden—led him into inescapable misery.

If we ask the question whether Kendall's imagined Australia—that contrast between a remembered Eden and a present-enough Hell in which Kendall found himself struggling—issued in any real poetry or any real reconciliation between Kendall and his world: we must, I think, agree that, though this violently divided landscape is Kendall's rather than ours, it has a real relevance to our literature. As for the desert scenes, with their load of guilt and suffering and penance, they may seem exaggeratedly melodramatic; but it is in Kendall that we first find stated the preoccupation that recurs in our literature with that particular theme, the 'death in the desert' theme with which our painters, poets and novelists have dealt so often since.

Kendall knew little of inland Australia, but he did know a great deal about the hells of the outcast and the scapegoat and of the divided mind, and the beckonings of the mirage of peace and the return to mindless innocence. These are his real subjects; these generate the pressure behind his best work, strong enough to force from his minor talent such essential poetry, perhaps, as it contained.

Kendall's talent, in spite of his singing gift and his real dedication to poetry, was minor chiefly because he did not quite know what poetry meant. When he had chosen to sit at Harpur's feet, it was less because he admired Harpur's own single-mindedness and rock-like honesty of poetic purpose, than because he saw himself as 'one of a glorious band', and saw Harpur as a poet dedicated to his own imagined Muse of the Wild. He had few or no demands to make on his audience; he loved praise and popularity (the little he was given went so far to his head that he mis-judged his times and himself, and imagined it possible to make a living by poetic journalism).

Where Harpur had 'given to the Future his heart', Kendall looked for recognition from the present; and when it became clear to him that Harpur was not, in fact, likely to be recognized as the chief of a band of Australian poets, he was disillusioned.

Yet Kendall had a significant relationship with the older poet whom he had once called a 'man of men', and it had its place and meaning in his poetic development and in his life. The two were both working against the current in attempting serious poetry in their place and time. But Harpur was stronger in himself, and moreover, he was capable of deeper insight and a purer res-ponse to his vision than the younger man, distracted from the beginning by problems of his circumstances and personality.

What was remarkable in their first relationship was the rap-turous enthusiasm with which Kendall greeted his discovery of Harpur, and the lack of any apparent jealousy or even criticism with which he accepted Harpur's verse when he declared himself ready to sit at the feet of the Australian Muse's 'first and her fa-vourite child'. Between one generation and the next there is usually—and in a sense there ought to be—a certain distrust; the younger man may acknowledge the mastery of the elder, but it is generally with a mental reservation of 'but I shall do dif-ferently'. Kendall's reaction has about it something a little un-natural, disarming though it is.

It is not straining the possibilities, I think, to suggest that Kendall was looking for what nowadays is called a 'father figure' in Harpur. His family circumstances are probably relevant; his father had died when Kendall was thirteen, and with his twin brother and his mother he had gone to live with his maternal grandfather. He does not seem to have had at all a happy rela-tionship with the old gentleman; and at the age of fifteen he had gone on a hard and difficult trip as cabin-boy in a whaler, with an uncle. He was only eighteen when he was faced with the responsibility of helping to provide a living for his mother and three sisters. His twin brother Basil was of little help, and his family seem to have preyed quite unscrupulously on the poor young poet. It was little wonder that the much stronger poetic personality of Harpur appealed to him, or that he found support in his notion—not wholly well-based—that even in his neglect and isolation Harpur remained 'serene as light, and strong as truth'.

So it is permissible to believe that in his hero-worship of Harpur, Kendall was looking for a masculine strength to balance the weaknesses in his own personality; his longing for refuge, escape, return to childhood and even beyond it. Harpur, even more than Kendall, had found his 'fate and fortunes alien'; but Kendall saw in him a certain quality of unconquerable faith, a 'serenity and strength', that made him a very suitable recipient for the young man's admiration.

After Harpur's death, and the death of Kendall's other mentor James Lionel Michael, Kendall seems to have felt himself more than ever alone. The increasing problems of his life and of his marriage, his financial losses, the failure of his second volume, *Leaves from Australian Forests,* and, in 1870, the death of his baby daughter in Melbourne, formed a succession of blows that finally overwhelmed him. Between 1872, when he suffered a breakdown partly due to alcoholism, and 1876, when he had recovered enough to write fairly regularly again and was reunited with his wife and children, he produced very little.

But his long fight back to health and self-command culminated in his best book, *Songs from the Mountains,* published early in 1880. Its dedicatory poem, *'To a Mountain',* is deeply interesting, because in it, for the first time, Kendall transcends his central and tormenting preoccupation, his yearning for peace and the past and the Eden-rivers of his childhood, and (literally) looks down on his dream-valleys from a new height.

It is clear, from his abrupt ending to 'Orara', that Kendall recognized that his unhappy longings for escape, and his placing of his Eden in the past, could not help to solve his problem. It is, he tells us, as well that he cannot try to follow his Dream. But the constant recurrence of his water imagery, gleaming like a mirage in the desert of the 'burning outer world', tells us that he was still preoccupied with the same problems and difficulties.

He needed, not to escape, but to come to terms with life; and for this, a new and reconciling symbol was necessary. In 'To a Mountain', for the first time, Kendall finds it; and whatever the 'sin and guilt' may be to which he so often and obliquely refers, and however deeply he may be marked by 'the punishment of

Cain', he is at last able to accept and forgive himself from the height of this new manly stability.

The symbol he chose to express this new stage of his life is the Mountain—the mountain from which he can look down on the valleys and rivers of his Dream, the mountain that contains the source of those streams that Kendall had longed to find, and that breeds the storms that feed them, but itself remains unmoved and strong, with its head in the light and its roots 'laved' by the 'sea-streams'. The Mountain, in fact, is the perfect natural symbol for the masculine powers, for the reconciliation with the weaker feminine, for the raising to a higher level of the emotional and intellectual forces of personality.

It is necessary to begin with this interpretation, because no one could possibly mistake Kendall's Mountain for a natural feature of an Australian landscape, as the 'Mooni' poem has been taken to be a poem 'about' an Australian river. This is very clearly a symbolic mountain; if we try to give it a local habitation or a name, we are faced with the fact that there is no Australian mountain which 'shines far above the zone of wind and cloud', and 'round whose lordly capes the sea rolls on'.

Kendall, indeed, addresses his Mountain in terms more suited to a disciple addressing a master, than to an artist apostrophizing his subject. Throughout the poem, the mountain is humanized— or rather, superhumanized. The first lines introduce the ideas of fatherhood and of transcendence:

> To thee, O father of the stately peaks
> Above me in the loftier light—to thee,
> Imperial brother of those awful hills
> Whose feet are set in splendid spheres of flame,
> Whose heads are where the gods are, and whose sides
> Of strength are belted round with all the zones
> Of all the world, I dedicate these songs . . .

He has chosen the Mountain, the superhuman symbol, as having 'the song complete of which my songs/Are pallid adumbrations'; and, he says, he has taken it for his Teacher in preference to 'men and books and all the schools.' For

> in the psalm
> Of thy grave winds, and in the liturgy
> Of singing waters, lo! my soul has heard
> The higher worship; and from thee, indeed,

c

> The broad foundations of a finer hope
> Were gathered in; and thou hast lifted up
> The blind horizon for a larger faith.

This is a new note, for Kendall; but not for poetry. It is a reversion to Harpur's loved, though criticized, Wordsworth; but it is a much more thoroughgoing reversion than Harpur would have approved. As we have seen, Harpur did not accept the idea of Nature as guide and teacher; for him humanity was the higher value, and man, in his spiritual aspect, himself a 'child of that/ In which the world began and hath its end'. Kendall's poem almost out-Wordsworths Wordsworth, if we take it at its face value.

Kendall goes on:

> Certain sounds
> Of strong authentic sorrow in this book
> May have the sob of upland torrents—these
> And only these, may touch the great World's heart,
> For lo! they are the issues of that grief
> Which makes a man more human . . . .

This again is a new note; an acceptance of grief, and a reconciliation with it, that rise above the agonized self-reproach and self-pity of so many of the earlier poems. And he continues:

> But in these pages there are other tones
> In which thy large, superior voice is not—
> Through which no beauty that resembles thine
> Has ever shone. These are the broken words
> Of blind occasions, when the World has come
>
> Between me and my Dream . . . .
> . . . All my days
> Have been the days of a laborious life,
> And ever on my struggling soul has burned
> The fierce heat of this hurried sphere . . . .

This, taken as a whole, is as good an estimate of Kendall's actual achievement as any; and that Kendall had been able at last to see his work in its failures and its successes, quietly and without any of the outcry which his earlier poems of struggle contain, is a measure of the new level of self-understanding he had attained since his dark years of mental and physical breakdown.

The poem continues:

> To thee the noises of this violent time
> Are far, faint whispers; and from age to age,
> Within the world and yet apart from it,
> Thou standest! Round thy lordly capes the sea
> Rolls on with a superb indifference
> For ever; in thy deep, green gracious glens
> The silver fountains sing for ever. Far
> Above dim ghosts of water in the caves,
> The royal robe of morning on thy head
> Abides for ever . . .

Here the obsessive water imagery, for the first time, is subordinated to the rest of the poem; it takes its proper place, as it were, in being seen from above. The source that Kendall had longed to find, in 'Orara', is now seen, not as in the unattainable regions of Eden and the past, but as part of another overriding symbol, the mountain; and the mountain towers above the 'dim ghosts' of water in its caves.

So, the poem represents some kind of triumph on Kendall's part, over his own past self. It is a bridge between the old guilt-laden yearnings for his Eden-river, and his new acceptance of manhood. This reconciliation eases all the old tensions, so that Kendall can accept himself, humbly but without self-reproach; the deserts in which he had suffered 'the punishment of Cain' are now no more than 'the fierce heat of this hurried sphere'. Whatever we may think of its apparent pantheism, it is clear that the poem represents a real change in Kendall's attitude to himself and to the world, a final attainment of the strength that he had always so sorely needed.

The notion of the mountain's masculinity and its symbolic status as a Teacher, and as a Father, are emphasized; and the link, in the poem, with Harpur, the old poet who had once filled the place of a teacher, is an interesting aspect. To begin with, the poem is in Harpur's own favoured blank verse, which Kendall seldom used; he had, however, used it in 'The Glen of Arrawatta', his openly imitative poem on the same theme as Harpur's 'The Creek of the Four Graves'. Moreover, in certain aspects the Mountain reminds us of Kendall's early idea of Harpur himself; where Kendall now kneels to the Mountain, he had once wished to 'sit at the feet' of Harpur; he had thought of him as 'serene as light and strong as truth'; and where the mountain is 'within the world and yet apart from it', Kendall had seen Harpur as 'living his life, untired and tameless',

> And far and free, this man of men . . .
> Had fellowship with gorge and glen
> And learned the loves and runes of Nature.

Whether or not we accept Kendall's description of Harpur as correct, we cannot help hearing it echoed on a new height in 'To a Mountain'.

A new height—for the whole poem carries with it a sense of conviction that is, for the first time, religious. Kendall's Christianity was conventional and not deeply felt; his Biblical poems are wooden and unconvincing. But here, in a poem that seems based on a Wordsworthian pantheism, Kendall for the first time convinces us that he was capable of a depth of feeling, which flows, not back to an impossible Eden, but now towards an image that is strikingly like that of the Father whom Adam once disobeyed.

So we may see this poem as including and transcending all Kendall's former poetic world—the dead poet he had once hailed as his 'Chief', the 'tracts of burning desert' where he had stumbled with his explorers, the rivers of his lost childhood and their unattainable sources, the Christianity that had not greatly helped him, the Wordsworthianism (Harpur's originally) that is here so curiously mixed with it ('God's grand authentic Gospel' delivered in the voice of the Mountain; the 'Light ineffable' that falls in the forest and makes Kendall feel 'as felt the grand old prophets'), and finally, Kendall's own Dream of an unattainable poetry and his final offering, his 'book of rhymes'. We are right to feel that this is Kendall's most significant poem; it is the poem in which he attains to self-understanding and thereby to his proper manhood.

Kendall, in fact, is not, as his admirers tell us, the 'first Australian poet'; looked at hard and honestly, he is scarcely to be called an interpreter of Australia at all. He is, however, something quite as important, the poet of his own desperate struggle and final self-mastery.

CHAPTER III

The Growth and Meaning of 'The Bush'

ᔐ

KENDALL DIED in 1882, and with him died the nineteenth-century attempt to interpret this new country in 'serious' verse. Harpur's adjuration to himself—'Be then the Bard of thy country'—had been heard, beyond his own generation, by no one but Kendall; and Kendall's decision to take over the search for the Harp Australian had, as we have seen, ended at the worst in poems which were time-serving and 'the words of blind occasion', and at the best in poems which, in spite of their apparently objective reference to 'Australia', were given their chief force by a tormented subjectivity whose chief reference was not to the outer reality, not even to an Australia taking shape in the minds of her new people, but to Kendall's own frustrations and search for resolutions of his problems.

After Kendall's death, the split in the Australian consciousness took its most obvious shape, on the one side in the 'bush balladists' who for the first time began to express what was happening to European character in the new conditions of Australia, on the other side in Christopher Brennan's withdrawal from all such manifestations of 'nationalism' and his attempt to rejoin the main stream of European thought.

What exactly, it is now possible to ask, did Kendall's frustrations consist in? Why was it not possible to be an Australian poet during this generation, or indeed for generations after? I think the question requires not only an examination of what was happening in Australia, but of what was happening in Europe too; and more particularly in England.

England, it has been said, is twenty years or more behind the Continent in its thought; it was natural that Australia should be even farther behind England. Yet there are certain large trends of feeling—and of negation of feeling—in which we can see much the same thing happening during the century, wherever the same general conditions applied. Kendall was not a thinker; he was a man of feeling. He did not know much of what was happening during his lifetime; it is doubtful if he took an interest in the current events in his own country, let alone in others. But he *felt,* and he reacted to what he felt. He withdrew from the world the tentacles of his spontaneous feeling, because he recognized that what he found there was hostile to him and to his poetry, even when it pretended sympathy. 'Just to be beyond the burning/Outer world, its sneers and spurning' became his characteristic cry.

Like Harpur's, in fact, his aspirations to be a poet had received a bitter setback. (Understand that I am talking here of poetry— not of Cantatas for the Melbourne Exhibition or of bush sketches —a very different matter.) So the images of Australia that he had 'purposed once to take his pen and write' about, had undergone a subtle change; they had become the symbols of his inner torment, the torment of a poet (however minor) turned back upon himself. If, to the undiscerning, they still looked like images of Australia, and if he was spoken of as a poet of Australian themes and landscapes, that only emphasized the gap of incomprehension between himself and that audience, and the fact that his audience knew very little of what poetry actually was.

Yet poetry is, so we say, the most reliable gauge to the inner life of a people. What had happened—or not happened—to the inner life of the Australian people during the nineteenth century? Harpur had in his despair given up hope of a true inner response being generated among his own contemporaries; 'in the dearth/On every side, of sympathy' he had greeted Kendall as his only appreciative audience.

He did not, however, greet him as an understanding audience. For clearly Kendall's notion of what the possession of the Harp Australian entailed on its holder was a good deal shallower than Harpur's. Kendall's Muse of the Wild, though she bears a resemblance to Harpur's Muse of the Evergreen Forest, had nothing to do with tending Harpur's Tree of Liberty (as Harpur may even then have noticed). Kendall demanded much less of his audience than Harpur had, as he demanded much less of himself; yet he did not, for the most part, obtain even that little, and much of his time was occupied with filling the shallow but exigent demands his audience in turn made on him. The results of these demands are beyond question Kendall's very poorest productions, and those which more than anything else prevent us from considering most of his work seriously as poetry. Harpur's audience was his despair; Kendall's was his poetic ruin.

I now want to suggest that, though we are apt to think of Australian life and thought as spiritually impoverished *because* of its isolation from the main stream of European thought, it was in fact the main stream of European thought and feeling that largely impoverished the life of Australia. It is a commonplace that when the circulation of the blood is poor, the first parts of the body to suffer are the outlying parts, the fingers and toes. This is what happened to Australia, the most distant outpost of Western civilization; the blockage of thought and feeling, the increasing sense of separation from the rest of the universe, and of the 'death of God' that Nietzsche announced with lament and triumph, was felt less consciously here, but its effects were even more devastating. This new colony of an old civilization, so far distant and faced with such forbidding tasks, needed, in order to develop real vitality, a strong and confident sense of the importance of its task, the strength and viability of its race and civilization.

It needed, in fact, a force and unity that could only be given from its European background. The fact that this had been a convict colony need not, I think, have mattered as it has done in the Australian psychology, if there had been any assurance of a possible redemption, of a re-entry into the current of a meaningful and purposeful civilization.

But in Europe the original impulse was fast ebbing from traditional Christian culture. In the year that Kendall died, Nietzsche was struggling from his years of despair into the desperate attempt at some kind of affirmation that led him to write *Thus Spake Zarathustra;* man, he thought, had come to an end, because man had been based on God, who was now 'dead', and only Superman could now take up the burden of a world so profoundly shaken and undermined.

In England, that year, Rossetti died; Rossetti who had represented, however shallowly decorative his rebellion, some kind of stand against the spread of grey industrial ugliness and materialism. Hardy, resigned to the passing of a simply faithful country way of life, was writing his desolate novels; Wilde was cultivating a desperate dandyism and wit against the coming of the deluge. The Established Church was, as T. H. Huxley wrote, 'eking out lack of reason with superfluity of railing' against the eagerly rational exponents of the evolutionary theory, and that very railing served to concentrate attention on its obvious weakness both in argument and in spiritual resources. If in all this scene there was any basis for Nietzsche's announced arrival of the Transvaluation of Values, it was not apparent. Europe was drifting.

If this were so, it was even more obvious in Australia, where not even the shell and structure of European traditional values were available as a refuge for the naked. It was no wonder that Kendall, to find any kind of peace and unity, had had to look backwards to his first master Harpur and to Wordsworth for guidance. There was none elsewhere, until Nietzsche had erected that precarious philosophy by which Man was to raise himself to a new level by dragging at his own shoelaces.

Meanwhile, there was nothing for the heart to feed on in Australia; neither the collapsing values of Europe, nor the yet-undiscovered values of a new country. Australia was, for spiritual purposes, not yet discovered; Europe was, for spiritual purposes, lost.

As always, where a vacuum opens in the heart, action and violence rushed in to fill the space. In England, the new voice that was raised belonged to a young man called Rudyard Kipling, but in Australia, Kipling had been anticipated by more than a decade. Adam Lindsay Gordon had already set free a new current of feeling, and a new surge of writing followed it.

Before Britain discovered her Empire as a subject, Australia discovered 'the men of the Bush'. The attitudes and qualities that the balladists, and in their wake the 'nationalist poets', now began to find in or attribute to the Australian character, still to a large extent (perhaps too large an extent) influence our notion of ourselves and our behaviour.

Independence, of course, had always been a part of the personality attributed to Australians; from the first description of the 'Currency Lads and Lasses', through Harpur's self-characterization as 'a man of the woods and forests', and Kendall's description of Jim the Splitter and his ilk who 'look at God's day in the face'.

But Harpur, at least, thought of himself as more than merely independent; he was, or ideally hoped to be, a man 'spherical, and therefore Godlike'. The notion of the Australian that began to prevail from Gordon's time onward had lost this sphericity; it was a flat and narrow personality that looked out from Gordon's 'Sick Stockrider', from Paterson's 'Man from Snowy River', from the bush ballads and from much of Lawson's work. There was about this new type of Australian scarcely any aspiration, scarcely any emotion or passion wider than can be comprised under the sentiments of egalitarianism, self-esteem and 'mateship', scarcely any ideas beyond the political, scarcely any culture more than could be legitimately acquired from an uninstructed reading of Thackeray and Dickens and perhaps (if we are to believe Furphy) Shakespeare and Goethe and the early socialist writers, under the tail of a bullock-waggon or in a drover's camp. The Australian ideal was a man of action—a horseman more daring than any known before, a spare laconic personality with little time for ideas and a restricted grasp on reality, the other side of whose aggressive masculinity turned out, surprisingly often, to be a soft-centred sentimentality that could amount to mawkishness.

All this had its truth—and its falsity. To discover the basis of fact on which the picture was painted, it is necessary to look at the way in which the country itself imposed its conditions on the men who first went out into it.

There were certain factors in the growth of Australia that were unlike those that operated in the growth of other white colonies and dominions, such as New Zealand and Canada. The most important of them were conditions imposed by the continent itself—by its climate, its soils and its size. The climate was, except in certain favoured parts of the coastal plain, unsuited to farming and unwelcoming to small settlers; the threatening possibility of droughts, floods and bushfires (the Terrible Three which haunt Australian thought and writing) prohibited any constant growth and prosperity of settlement; and very few farms or even large stations, in the early days of settlement, remained in the same hands for more than a generation or two without some form of disaster overtaking the owners.

Slumps and low prices for farming products, and the uncertainty of overseas markets at great distances, made their contribution to this. Even in the richer areas of the coastal plains, the soils were variable; and the poor or sometimes ruinous methods used to farm them (since few emigrants were trained in farming, or even if they were, could make allowance for the difference between Australian and English seasons and soils) contributed to the lack of stability both of the soils and the men who farmed them.

Along the plains and valleys of New South Wales, particularly the once-rich Hunter Valley, for instance, the constant cropping of wheat year after year began a process of impoverishment and erosion which has continued to the present day; the soils cleared of heavy forest were at first rich in humus, but once this had been exhausted, with no return made, farms which once made small fortunes for their proprietors reverted to grazing land, and poor land, often enough, at that. It was not until the 1930's that any important moves were made to prevent erosion, which in Australia's lighter soils was a problem as early as the first clearing of the Hawkesbury Valley's forests; and in the interval much had been lost and many small settlers ruined.

The factors of uncertain climates, bad farming and easily-exhausted soils, with the early alienation of much land to a few men, have meant that there has not been in Australia the kind of stable farming population and prosperous increase in settlement that Canada, America, New Zealand and other newly-established white settlements have been able to rely on. As exploration opened up the inland, large stations and runs were gradually established by overlanding cattle and sheep; in the process there were many casualties in ownership, but the sheer size of Australia has always meant that, even if one district was suffering from slump, drought or flood, others were doing better. So there was always work offering, in the shearing season, on sheep stations, and during the rest of the year in droving camps and as stockmen and boundary riders in the cattle country, or (before the days of fencing) as shepherds on sheep runs.

The small settlers, displaced or ruined by bad seasons, tended to go inland on contracting work or as nomadic workers, so that instead of a stable settled population, Australia tended to have a nomadic and comparatively rootless population of workers, men for the most part, and for the most part (since the inland with its great distances and waterless stretches is dangerous for the solitary traveller) moving in groups, or at least in pairs, from job to job. The sheer size of Australia often meant that from year to year they scarcely saw their homes and families (when they had any), or reached the settled areas, so that instead of being merely one of the conditions of earning a living, nomadism became a way of life to many.

Not all the wanderers were simple uneducated men; some were of the class known (since they were numerous enough to form a class) as 'broken-down swells', men who had failed in larger enterprises than the rest, or men dispatched to the ends of the earth by their families as black sheep, or simply as 'colonial-experiencers', and living on here half-forgotten, like Harry Morant, in the hope of returning to England some day as men of fortune. But the conditions of their lives meant that books and reading were things of the past; libraries, however small, cannot be carried in swags.

So the common currency of the bush workers was verbal; and this is how the bush song and the ballad came to flourish in Australia so much more strongly than in other new countries. Songs were seized on, memorized, altered, parodied, sung in camps and riding round the cattle, at shearing sheds and on the track. They came to mirror the kind of life that their singers led; often hard and crude, almost always womanless, and because of this lack of normal balance, generally naive and sentimental under the tough hide induced by hardship and the remorseless conditions of the Australian outback.

It was this life, and these songs, which set the tone of much in later Australian life. The attitude to women—both wary and sentimental—still persists; so does the unspoken assumption that the male-to-male relationship alone can be trustworthy and un-complicated; so do the horse-worship, the naivety, the tough in-sularity—even the White-Australia policy, instilled as a kind of gospel by the bush workers' dislike and distrust of the Chinese immigrant in gold-field days and their pitying superiority to-wards the Kanakas on the sugar plantations. All these, or their traces, can be found in today's Australian psyche, as in the nine-teenth-century bush balladists and their songs.

Moreover, it is here that another peculiarly Australian dicho-tomy is first found—the emotional content in the conflict ex-pressed in the phrase 'Sydney or the Bush'. This country-versus-city opposition has always been a deeply-involved problem in Australia—more so, it would seem, than elsewhere. The choice has always been more an emotional than a rational matter; it has gone deep into our character. Perhaps the most noticeable thing about it is that it seemed almost a matter of morals, a choice be-tween Virtue (the Bush) and Vice (the City).

Australians have always been deeply and narrowly puritan in temperament (with occasional necessary outbreaks or 'sprees', safety-valves of which on the whole the perpetrators have been secretly ashamed). This puritanism, probably, has attached the notion of virtue to hard work, abstemiousness, monastic loneliness; all these conditions were associated with the strict solitudes of the bush in which the worker earned his cheque; putting up mile after mile of fencing; boundary riding, droving, mustering, shearing. The inevitable reaction came with the cheque itself (usually paid six-monthly or yearly) and with the shoddy enticements of the bush shanties or the towns and cities.

The cheque once drunk and womanized away, the rueful bush worker set his face away from the devilish temptations of civilization, which had once again robbed him of his hard-won money and his hopes of a better life; and as he went he repented and promised himself reformation—a reformation with which the hard bush life was associated.

So the Bush came to stand for chastity, purity, cleanliness and virtue, the town for a kind of self-betrayal.

> I take the Old Man Plain, criss-cross it all again,
> Until my eyes the track no longer see;
> My beer and brandy brain seeks balmy sleep in vain,
> I feel as if I had the Darling Pea.
>
> Repentance brings reproof, so I sadly 'pad the hoof',
> All day I see the mirage of the trees,
> But it all will have an end when I reach the river bend
> And listen to the singing of the breeze.
>
> Then hang the jolly prog, the hocussed shanty-grog,
> The beer that's loaded with tobacco;
> Grafting humour I am in, and I'll stick the peg right in,
> And settle down once more to yakka.

('The Jolly Jolly Grog and Tobacco')[1]

Or, from 'The Stockman's Cheque':

> Thank the Lord I'm back at last, back though wrecked and whisky-logged,
> Yet the gates have not come open that I shut,
> And I've seen no broken fences, and I've found no weak sheep bogged,
> And my little cat is purring in the hut . . . .

So the Bush comes to have various, and slightly conflicting,

---

[1] The songs and ballads quoted in this chapter are taken from Stewart and Keesing's: *Australian Bush Ballads* (Angus & Robertson, 1955) and *Old Bush Songs* (Angus & Robertson, 1957).

emotional connotations. It stands for virtue, certainly; but a virtue distinctly hard and uncompromising, a puritanism of narrowness, harshness, and poverty, from which in the end, however repentantly the bush worker may stagger back from his sprees, he must escape again. This aspect is expressed in what may be called the Perisher ballads, those that lay emphasis on the hardness and danger of the bush life, and the toll it takes of human self-assertion and even human life:

> There is no life on the Deadman's Plain,
> Where the Drought King rules supreme,
> Guarding as spoils the bones that lie
> In the bed of a phantom stream . . .
>
> . . . Then a hat we discovered beside the trail,
> A pint and a billycan,
> A bloodstained shirt that was torn to shreds
> And the corpse of a naked man,
>
> With its face as black as the hell-black crows,
> The left cheek gnawed away,
> The right arm pointing across to where
> The phantom waters lay . . . .

or 'Out from Noonkanbah', with its grimly memorable verse:

> The coolibahs quiver,
> The snakewood moans,
> And bowerbirds play
> With Lin Bower's bones . . . .

And the longing for escape is expressed in many of the ballads, such as Morant's 'For Southern Markets',

> O pale-faced sons of Sydney town, who don't find Sydney gay,
> You should have been where we have been these many months
>   away!

So, if sometimes it seems that the Bush acted as a kind of conscience for Australians (the development of this feeling, I think, is clearest in the twentieth-century poet Furnley Maurice), it was a conscience that, for most, was too puritanical and demanding to be obeyed for long. Men accumulated virtue and money, as it were, in the Bush; but they spent the accumulation of both, with the urgency of guilt, in the City. The contrast between hard virtue and lurid, if shoddy, vice gradually passes over, in the later pastiche balladists, into a sentimental yearning on the part of the city man for an impossibly idealized vision of the Bush, not as a grim symbolic chastity, but as a lost Eden.

For the moral element in our feeling for the Bush has certainly not prevented Australians from crowding into the cities, whose growth has been immoderate. It has, however, contributed to a great deal of almost Rousseauist sentiment in our literature and our character. Virtue, to us, is apt to be a matter of negative rejection of temptation, rather than of positive right-living and affirmative attitudes. It is just this element that has caused the notorious 'wowserism' in our national life, against which Norman Lindsay and Hugh McCrae found themselves fighting at the beginning of the twentieth century; and since this wowserism was in association with the particular brand of nationalist sentiment that elevated the Australian Bushman (tall, rangy, daring, freedom-loving and essentially a countryman) as a type of our national life, the fight against it necessarily also became a fight against the 'nationalist' brand of literature exemplified in Lawson and the *Bulletin* bards, and against the kind of patriotism that infuriated Brennan at the time of the Boer War.

Moreover, this flaunted preference for the enforced virtues of solitude and simplicity in hard but pure surroundings led for a time to a kind of hermit-cult, an anti-social glorifying of the lonely life in contact with the realities of the elements, and a rejection not only of the 'artificialities' of the city, but even of society itself. To this nomad-hermit philosophy of the 'bush-hatters' and permanent swagmen forever on the track belongs, perhaps, the 'gum-tree poet' who left his summary biography on a tree:

> Me and my dog
>   have tramped together
>   in cold weather
>   and hot.

> Me and my dog
>   don't care whether
>   we get any work
>   or not.

For the true bush-hatter rejected not only the vices of civilization, but even so much contact with society as was implied in the notion of hard work. Sometimes this rejection of work was associated (whether in rationalization or otherwise) with a refusal to help enrich the 'squatter'; sometimes, like the philosophy of the bums in the United States during the depression, it was sheer hopelessness and detachment from life that lay behind it; sometimes it was a kind of protest against everything implied by the materialist society; an extension of the attitude that the young Barcroft Boake expressed when he wrote to his father 'Civilization is a dead failure'. For the bush ethos attracted the men hurt by life or unwilling to meet its demands; and during the nineteenth century, with depressions, bank failures and over-optimism about the capacities of the land and climate, there were many such, even without the addition of the 'remittance men' from overseas.

This rejection of human society and its squalors forms a kind of undercurrent in the bushman legend. The 'mateship' that Lawson wrote of, though it may have seemed like the opposite side of this tendency, sometimes in fact reinforced it; as in the old Convict Oath quoted by Price Warung, 'mateship' could be and often was a protection against the hostile forces of society, as of the dangers and loneliness of the bush itself.

This gives an almost monastic, even a semi-religious, quality to some of the attitudes to the Bush that persist even today. There are numberless poems, from O'Dowd's 'The Bush' to Hope's 'Australia', in which denunciation of the people—those 'monotonous tribes'—alters to a semi-mystical anticipation of the emergence from this 'Arabian desert of the human mind' of some spirit which escapes 'the learned doubt, the chatter of cultured apes/That is called civilization over there'. (Notice again the rejection of 'civilization' that seems to form part of the Australian legend.) And the apotheosis of this religious attitude comes in *Voss*, where the Australian Desert is the testing-ground through which the expedition follows Voss in his search for reconciliation with self and society—for the apotheosis of love.

So there is a sense, then, in which the idea of Australia is a central, almost mystic, symbol in our literature. It is a vision of a certain kind of innocence, not childlike but regenerative; a purification which is the result of hardship and endurance, of sacrifice of personal ease, sacrifice perhaps of life itself. (Indeed, death is part of the legend; Australia has always been 'the land where the dead men lie'.)

Visitors who comment on the shoddiness of some aspect of

Australian life, particularly city life, are often told that 'this is not the *real* Australia'. The real Australia is always farther out, farther north or farther west. Perhaps it is known only by the hero of the queer poetic bush recitation, 'Humping the Drum'—a cross between the 'tall yarn' and the song of Tom O'Bedlam:

I humped my drum from Kingdom Come
To the back of the Milky Way;
I boiled my quart on the Cape of York
And I starved last Christmas Day.

I cast a line on the Condamine
And one on the Nebine Creek;
I've driven through bog, so help me bob,
Up Mungindi's main street;

I crossed the Murray and drank in Cloncurry
Where they charged a bob a nip.
I worked in the Gulf where the cattle they duff,
And the squatters let them rip.

I worked from morn in the fields of corn
Till the sun was out of sight,
I've cause to know the Great Byno
And the Great Australian Bight.

I danced with Kit when the lamps were lit,
And Doll as the dance broke up;
I flung my hat on the myall track
When Bowman won the Cup . . . .

I pushed my bike from the shearer's strike,
Not wanting a funeral shroud;
I made the weights for the Flying Stakes
And I dodged the lynching crowd . . . .

CHAPTER IV

Adam Lindsay Gordon and Barcroft Boake

ᔐ

SO THROUGH the overlanding days, the bush songs seem to have established themselves in a kind of undercurrent, seldom heard by the cities, until with the publication of Gordon's ballads the tradition came into open notice and even popularity. The horseman, the stockman and the drover had at last come into their own as Australia's typical native product.

But Gordon not only succeeded in introducing the bush ballad themes 'into the parlour'; he also became popular—deeply and lastingly so—with the drovers and stockmen themselves. The currency of 'The Sick Stockrider' and the racing ballads among the drovers and overlanders is attested by Boake: 'Gordon is the favourite—I may say only—poet of the backblockers . . . There is not a bushman or drover who does not know a verse or two of his 'How We Beat the Favorite' or 'The Sick Stockrider'. I call this fame'.[1]

In fact, Gordon, though not much noticed in his lifetime, became phenomenally well known after his death, and that among all kinds of readers. This seldom happens to poets, whose audience is generally select and predictable; and certainly as a poet Gordon was no more than mediocre. For quality of writing, even minor versifiers like the later Roderic Quinn could equal and surpass him. Why did Gordon attract so mixed and enthusiastic an audience?

To begin with, like that of Byron (on whom he so much modelled himself) his fame was at least partly due to his personal characteristics. In England, he would scarcely have attracted much notice as a poet; in Australia, the fact that he was 'one of the Gordons', had been, in a manner never since clarified, a wild young man, had come to Australia and made himself a certain fame as a steeplechase rider (and a good rider could command the hearts of most men), and chose for poetic subjects not only classical and English themes, but Australian themes as well,

---

[1] Preface by A. G. Stephens to *Where the Dead Men Lie and Other Poems*, Angus & Robertson, Sydney, 1897

went very far. His appeal was dual—with the 'backblockers' to whom both horses and ballads were dear, and with the snob element of the exiled English middle class groups who 'dearly loved a lord' or anyone with aristocratic connexions.

So to the drovers and bush workers, Gordon's was a voice they could understand, speaking of things they knew in swinging rhythms easy to remember and repeat; to the 'cultured' of the cities he was an exiled Englishman of some breeding, condescending, as it were, to endorse the rough uncultured life of the backblocks by using it in his verse.

It was, in fact, Gordon's bestriding of the two sides of the 'split' in Australian consciousness, between Australianism and Europeanism, that ensured his success. He became a kind of secondhand Byron, with modern overtones, a legend rather than a poet; but by glorifying the kind of life lived by the drover and stockrider, and by using the material with which his Australian period provided him, he did more to catch the atmosphere of a kind of life then at its zenith than had been done by any other Australian poet.

Kendall, with all his earnestness, was not in touch with the life of the bush; his proper background was the gentler and more settled coastal country, not the hard life of the horseman and drover; and since this outback life was to provide the popular image of the essential Australia, Kendall remained at the margin of the popular acclaim which raised Gordon to the level of a best seller.

Just how 'original' was Gordon in his Australian verses? The most characteristically 'Australian' of them is probably 'The Sick Stockrider'. It is interesting to compare this with a bush song which appeared in *The Queenslanders' Colonial Camp Fire Song Book,* published in 1865, five years before the appearance of *Bush Ballads and Galloping Rhymes* (in which 'The Sick Stockrider' was printed).

'The Sick Stockrider' is written in a Swinburnian metre of a trochaic eight-foot line followed by a five-foot; the ballad, 'The Stockman's Last Bed' has a four-beat anapaestic line in a four-line verse, with a chorus of two similar lines. But for all the difference of their metres, the Gordon poem being in a then fashionable form (Browning used this kind of metre in 'A Toccata of Galuppi's' and—though with divided lines—in 'Soliloquy of the Spanish Cloister') and the ballad in a more traditional metre, there are certain elements common to both.

The first line in Gordon's poem:

Hold hard, Ned! Lift me down once more, and lay me in the
   shade

may be compared with the chorus of the ballad:

For we laid him where wattles their sweet fragrance shed
And the tall gum-trees shadow the stockman's last bed,

and with its last two lines,

Ride softly the creek-bed where trees make a shade,
For perhaps it's the spot where poor Jack's bones are laid.

These lines, again, may be compared with the last verse of Gordon's poem:

Let me slumber in the hollow where the wattle-blossoms wave
With never stone or rail to fence my bed . . . .

There is also a possible comparison between Gordon's line

With a running fire of stockwhips and a fiery run of hoofs

and the ballad's line

The crack of his stockwhip, his steed's lively trot . . . .

All this may be no more than coincidence; but the mention of 'wattles' near both graves is perhaps more significant than it may seem. For neither balladists nor, on the whole, more academic early poets (with the exception of Barron Field) often mention Australian trees or wildflowers by name; the wattle occurs in scarcely any other ballads or poems written before the early 'sixties.

Even if the resemblances between the ballad and the poem are entirely accidental, each forms an interesting critique on the other. For though it is crude and simple enough, the ballad is (for once) not sentimental; it has a note of sincerity and mourning, and even in certain respects the tone of one of the early English ballads. Here is the first verse of one of the Robin Hood ballads ('A Little Geste for Robin Hood'):

Lithe and listen, Gentlemen
That be of free-born blood;
I shall you tell of a good yeoman,
His name was Robin Hood.

And the first verse of 'The Stockman's Last Bed':

> Be ye stockman or no, to my story give ear,
> Alas for poor Jack, no more shall we hear
> The crack of his stockwhip, his steed's lively trot,
> His clear 'Go a-head, boys', his jingling quartpot.

In each there is the same direct and economical approach to the audience.

Gordon's poem is in the first person, making it more artificial in tone. The lengthy reminiscences of the 'sick stock-rider' which follow are vivid enough, and there is even a legendary quality about some of the verses:

> In these hours when life is ebbing, how those days when life
>   was young
> Come back to us; how clearly I recall
> Even the yarns Jack Hall invented, and the songs Jem Roper
>   sung;
> And where are now Jem Roper and Jack Hall?

But when the poem leaves these direct reminiscences for the moralizing of the last few verses, the tone is one of sentimental cliché:

> I've had my share of pastime, and I've done my share of toil,
>   And life is short—the longest life a span . . .

This is popular moralizing (the next verse is a well-known album-piece), and by the time the stockrider is directing the patient Ned on the location of his grave ('Let me slumber in the hollow where the wattle-blossoms wave') the temporary reality given by the reminiscences has evaporated. The poem has become a sentimental piece for recitation.

Poor Jack of the earlier ballad (who 'while drafting one day was horned by a cow, "Alas", cried poor Jack, "it's all up with me now"') is a figure with far more immediate reality, if less theatrical romance.

Indeed, Gordon wrote little that was truly original and stamped with reality; and sometimes he did some outrageously imitative verses. 'From the Wreck', for instance, is so close to its Browning original that it is practically an infringement of copyright.

But Gordon will always be forgiven his poetic sins for the sake of the legend of his life and for his place in the uncertain growth of Australian writing. Without his recognition of the kind of life that was lived in the outback, and the stamp of approval that was given it by his using it in his verse, it might have taken many years longer than in fact it did to establish certain facets of life here as potentially poetic material. After Gordon came the deluge of 'Bulletin bards', as well as a renewed activity among lesser writers. Australia had begun to recognize itself.

One legacy, however, he left to Australian versifying which did it no good—a certain tendency to a negative despair. Gordon had, basically, brought his problems from England with him; they were bound up with his own life and temperament, and Australian conditions did nothing to help him solve them. The Byronic brooding, the melancholy, the rejection of the world that mark his verse are sentimental and shallowly based, perhaps, but they found a certain echo in the temperament of Australians. Moreover they led to certain effects on Australian writing, if not on the Australian psyche, whose sources need to be recognized.

If Gordon's rather theatrical melancholy roused numerous echoes in later Australian writers, it was because melancholy came naturally to the Australian temperament, at least at the end of the nineteenth century and the beginning of the twentieth. The 'backblocker' was an easy prey to gloom. Marcus Clarke's well-known melodramatic description of the Australian landscape expressed a real reaction to the country's outer aspect; and the loneliness and hardship of the outback life, the poor food, the uncertainty of income or even of work, as well as the climate, and above all the monotony of the inland existence, made life in the inland difficult. Even a cheerful temperament might easily flag at times. If indeed 'from the desert the prophets come', we ought to remember that Jeremiah and Job were numbered among them.

Yet it is noticeable that the early bush ballads, on the whole, were not particularly mournful, and often were both cheerful and forthright in their attitude to the hardships and misfortunes of life. Certainly the immigrants and settlers lamented at times; but the ballad of 'The Old Bark Hut', for instance, with its dismal list of the disadvantages of the swagman's life, is vivid and amusing; and the list of attractions offered to the prospective wife of the owner of 'The Old Bullock Dray' is made to sound quite enticing; while patriotic ballads like 'Sunny New South Wales' give a most optimistic picture.

But in his Introduction to Gordon's poems (the 1912 edition)
F. M. Robb says:

> Gordon left his impress deeply upon men like Paterson, Law-
> son, Farrell, Edward Dyson, Boake and others of what are
> known in Australia as the 'Bulletin bards' . . . and seems
> to have begun a wail of pessimism, cynicism and hopeless-
> ness whose echoes have not yet ceased to vibrate. . . Had
> Gordon learned (Browning's) lesson (of optimism) the whole
> tone of the immediately succeeding generation of Australian
> poets might have been different.

Clearly some of the bards Robb lists are not blameable in this
respect—Paterson, for instance, takes a singularly rosy view of
life upon the whole; but there is justice in what he says, more
particularly of Boake and Lawson.

The story of Gordon's life and death is well known, and that
it should have been elevated into the realms of romance is easy
enough to understand. But the story is not essentially or typically
Australian, just as Gordon is not a typically Australian writer.
The poems with an Australian background are few, and there is
reason to think that Gordon did not consider them his best; he
did not think highly of 'The Sick Stockrider' for instance. He
may have had a higher opinion of his 'fashionable' themes, and
of the poems written under the influence of Byron and of Swinburne, such as 'Ashtaroth' and 'Bellona'; but his weaknesses and
crudities of sense and thought show up more clearly in these
than in the less ambitious action-and-narrative poems that have
made his reputation.

Action, in fact, was a necessity for Gordon. Left to brood and
philosophize, he sank into self-pity and a kind of cynicism that
sprang more from personal frustration and bitterness than from
any depth of thought or feeling. It is hard to tell, at times, how
much this cynicism owed to Gordon's habit of striking attitudes
and how much to his own personality. At any rate, it is of quite a
different nature from the irony of the 'backblockers' and the
bush singers, his predecessors in the bush ballad. More realistic
and direct, the sardonic note of the bush singers derives more
from circumstances than from the mood of the singer; its conditions are particular, not generalized. It has been loosely called
cynicism; but cynicism is darker and emptier than this. Cynicism
is rather to be found in verses like these of Gordon:

Though our future lot is a sable blot,
Though the wise ones of earth will blame us,
Though our saddles will rot and our rides be forgot,
   DUM VIVIMUS, VIVAMUS!

and, from 'The Last Leap':

With the flash that ends thy pain
Respite and oblivion blest
   Come to greet thee. I in vain
Fall: I rise to fall again:
   Thou hast fallen to thy rest—
   And thy fall is best.

This kind of swaggering emptiness—the emptiness that pre-
cedes insanity or suicide—represented in Australia the kind of
moral impasse that was then facing the consciousness of Europe,
in the person of Nietzsche. It was not different in kind, but it
was very different in degree. Gordon had not arrived at it through
an intellectual awareness of the 'death of God', as Nietzsche had;
but it nevertheless permeated his being, and left its poison in his
verse. The voice was the voice of Gordon, but the words were the
words of Europe's own despair.

And Gordon's restless need for action and physical occupation,
which is also reflected in his poetry, was symptomatic of the
same disease. Kipling, with his idolization of violence and authority, machines and armies, his barrack room ballads and his
invocation of the God of Battles, is fundamentally as empty of
faith as Gordon, but his despair was translated into a worship of
violence. Gordon, less capable of self-deceit and more lacking in
resources, turned the violence on himself.

But the fundamental hollowness of his outlook and the darkness at the core of his verse found a certain echo in later Australian writing. The complaint of Kendall was that he was un-
heard, unappreciated, that in order to live he had to betray his
own gift. But Gordon's 'sickness was his soul' (to quote the words
of another English pessimist) and when he 'played the man' and
ended himself, it meant more than that he had merely been
unable to pay his financial debts. He had also been unable to
pay spiritual debts that were far more pressing. The sting of this
he left behind him, poisoning his verse; and traces of the same
poison can be found in the work of some writers who admired
and followed him, in his own generation and the next.

Kendall, as we have seen, regained his own balance and found himself, in a certain kind of peace. In this, he was stronger than Gordon, though he had not thought himself a match for the hard-riding Englishman. And most of the backblock balladists who admired and recited Gordon's verses were too realistic—and too hard-worked—to take his point of view on life very seriously. But there was, nevertheless, a kind of Gordon cult here and there, among the lonely and semi-educated young men of the outback; a cult of hopelessness and a certain Gordonian melodrama and self-pity. His swinging rhythms, his fake-masculine recklessness and flamboyance that lapsed into mournful sentimentality, appealed to young men leading a lonely and deprived life in the bush, as did the cult of horsemanship and action in which Gordon was an obvious leader.

So there was a price to pay for uncritical devotion to Gordon. The first to pay it was a young man named Barcroft Boake.

Boake was born and reared in Sydney, except for two years' voyaging as a young boy, in the Pacific island groups. In 1886, at the age of twenty, he was working with the Survey Office as a temporary draftsman, and went to Adaminaby on the Monaro, as assistant to a Mr Commins. He lived with the Commins family, for two years, which seem to have been the happiest of his life; there is a hint, in A. G. Stephens's introduction to his book of poems, of an attachment to a girl living on a near-by station, the 'Rosedale Station' that figures in one of his bush narrative poems. At the end of those two years, he took work briefly as a boundary-rider; then, with two companions, set out into the backblocks and joined a drovers' camp. The long droving trip that followed, through the winter of 1889, took him from Devonport Downs on the Diamantina up to Cunnamulla in Queensland with eleven hundred head of cattle.

He wrote to his father during this trip:

> Fourteen hours a day I reckon I have in the saddle, straight off . . . Still, this is the only life worth living, that I see . . . this is the only place where a poor man can get a cheque together in a short time.[2]

And, from Windorah, he wrote later:

> If I could only write it, there is a poem to be made out of the back country . . . for there is a romance, though a grim

[2] ibid.

35978

one—a story of drought and flood, fever and famine, murder and suicide, courage and endurance . . . I often wonder if a day will come when these men will rise up—when the wealthy man . . . shall see pass before him a band of men— all of whom died in his service and whose unhallowed graves dot his run.

This letter is the germ from which sprang 'Where the Dead Men Lie'; and Gordon's popularity with the drovers and back-blockers was the chief influence in turning Boake himself into a writer.

He returned to Bathurst with cattle in early 1890; but misfortune sent him back perforce to his old trade of surveying, this time in the Riverina. It was during the following two years that he began to publish in the *Bulletin* the few poems that made up his posthumous volume. They stem directly from his time as a drover and from the influence of Gordon's Australian poems, and, probably, from the bush songs he had learned and heard, as he mentions in one of his letters.

It is worth giving this background for the poems, since Boake was the first of Gordon's young versifying disciples, and in his way the purest type of them. He had served his apprenticeship as a bushworker (as by no means all of the '*Bulletin* bards' did); he seems to have cared comparatively little for any other poet, Australian or English; what he wrote sprang from experience and observation, and crude and unshaped as it was, it had a certain power and even violence about it that makes it more impressive than that of most of his generation of bush writers. 'Where the Dead Men Lie', the title-poem, has found its way into almost all the anthologies that include Australian nineteenth-century writers, even into those from which Paterson is excluded. 'Fogarty's Gin' is a vivid and moving narrative, with its night ride to save the cattle:

Thud of hoofs; thud of hearts! breath of man! breath of beast!
With M'Ivor in front and the rest, heel to flank;
So we rode in a bunch down the steep river-bank
Churning up the black tide in the shallows like yeast.
. . . Staring eyes, swaying forms, o'er the saddle-bow stooping,
With the wind in our shirts, grip of knee, grip of rein,
Losing ground, falling back, creeping forward again,
Behind us the low line of dark coolabah,
Overhead a sky spangled by planet and star;

> And to the left, on our shoulder, the mighty Cross flaring,
> While afoot the quick pulsing of hoofbeats disturbs
> Moist silence of grasses and salty-leaved herbs.

For sheer authenticity and breathless excitement, for handling of prosody and for re-creation of the sights and sounds of the ride, this far surpasses anything in Gordon's Australian verse.

Then there is the long ballad about a cattle-duffer, 'Jack Corrigan', which for its full significance needs to be compared with Paterson's 'The Man from Snowy River'.

Here are a few lines :

> So spoke Long Jack, the boldest mountaineer
> Who ever down from Nungar raced a brumby mob in flight
> Or laid a stockwhip on a stubborn steer.
> From Jindabyne to Providence, along the Eucumbene,
> The kindest-hearted fellow to be found,
> And when he crossed the saddle not a horse was ever seen
> That could make Jack quit his hold and seek the ground . . .

And again:

> Just time to catch old Dandy, where he's munching second
>   growth
>   Of hay; just time to leap upon his back,
> And then the smartest trap who ever swore a lying oath
>   Could never foot me down the River track.

The relevant comparisons from Paterson's verses are:

> There was Harrison, who made his pile when Pardon won the
>   Cup,
> The old man with his hair as white as snow;
> But few could ride beside him when his blood was fairly up—
>   He would go wherever horse and man could go.

> And Clancy of the Overflow came down to lend a hand,
>   No better horseman ever held the reins;
> For never horse could throw him while the saddle-girths would
>   stand—
>   He learnt to ride while droving on the plains.

If Paterson took hints from Boake, it is no reflection on him to point it out, since the bush ballads were all cross-fertilized from each other, and altered and enlarged, very often, as time went on; and certainly Paterson, a much more polished and consistent writer than Boake had time to become, enormously improved on

Boake's rougher verses. But Boake's poems are worth remembering for all that; just as Boake himself, a melancholy sacrifice to the bush-cult of Gordon, deserves to be restored to his right place in the temporal forefront of the '*Bulletin* bards'. This at least is to his credit; he was one of the first to write directly from his experience of the outback, a poem that truly reflects the lives and problems of its people. 'Where the Dead Men Lie' is as burningly concentrated as a heated cattle-brand.

In a sense, in fact, Boake anticipates Lawson as much as he anticipates Paterson. His passionate indictment of the 'absentee landlords' who made their money out of the hardship and death of the men who worked their inland stations, appears to come, not from any political indoctrination, but from pure indignation at what he saw. The story of Barefooted Bob and his mate Bat, in Furphy's 'The Buln-Buln and the Brolga', is the prose equivalent of Boake's poem; but again Boake had anticipated Furphy in important respects, and 'Where the Dead Men Lie', with its power and passion, puts Furphy's case more memorably than does his own circuitous and ironic story.

From many points of view, Boake, even with his different approach to Australia and his lack of interest in 'serious' poetry, was more akin to Harpur than Harpur's own disciple Kendall had been. It was in Boake that Harpur's burning interest in 'liberty' and equality (not egalitarianism) reappeared in Australian writing. (Kendall had cared little or nothing for either.) And Boake, too, might have said, as Harpur did, that he rejected the 'parks and parterres' of literature in favour of a 'rougher' and stronger verse.

Moreover, in Boake we get glimpses of a certain feeling for Australia herself—a feeling expressed in his statement 'this is the only life worth living that I see'. Why was it the only life worth living? Because for Boake 'civilization is a dead failure . . .'—it was the results of 'civilization', of Moneybags, that Boake saw in the dead men who lay 'out on Moneybags' furthest station'. Civilization was exploiting this simplicity that he loved, this country which offered 'the only life worth living'; Boake rejected the city with force and vehemence. 'I should smother if I had to go back to Sydney again; my home is in the bush.'

This was to be the cry of many of the later balladeers; but for most of them the choice was a sentimental one, not a real alternative. For Boake it was a real issue, because his rejection of civilization was a reasoned rejection. If civilization meant Money-bags, meant the exploitation of this country, then Boake condemned it outright; no compromise was possible. He presents in its purest form the alternative between Sydney and the Bush, Vice and Virtue, because for him the alternative is not just a convention, it is vital. Boake took himself with extreme seriousness; for him there was no compromise.

So there is a sense in which Boake is the archetype of the bush poets, and in which his shadow stretches as far as the realm of 'serious poetry'. Not only was he Gordon's most faithful follower, but he was, even with his small and imperfect output, the forerunner of most of the balladists who took up the bush themes; he was the very type of Marcus Clarke's 'Esau, who loved his heritage of desert sand better than all the bountiful richness of Egypt'.

But, through Gordon, the melancholy of the 'failure of civilization' penetrated even into Boake's solitary life and made it seem so little worth living that at the first misfortune, unwilling to change his life, he decided to leave it. Like the Bush itself, he had been despoiled by the touch of materialism and opportunism. What happened to Boake was, in its essentials, what had happened to the much more deep and comprehensive consciousness of Nietzsche. God was dead for Boake in Australia, as he had been for Nietzsche in Europe; and civilization was 'a dead failure'. Accordingly Boake hanged himself.

CHAPTER V

The Reformist Poets

AT THE end of the nineteenth century, the two currents of thought that found their early expression in Harpur—the reformist and the nationalist—are again clearly to be seen. Lawson and O'Dowd represent the first; and there is a sense in which both are also nationalist poets, since both talk a great deal about Australia and her mission, which was, they thought, to set an example to the world as the first Socialist and truly rational nation.

But Lawson is a less pretentious writer than O'Dowd; he confines himself mainly to verse of personal protest, ballad-type verses, and rousing 'battle-hymns'. As a serious poet, he does not really rate consideration; as a symptom of the times, as a short-story writer, and as a man, he is significant. He took up Boake's cry of indignant despair on behalf of the men on whose labour Australia's new-rich were living; and he extended it into the cities where already slums were growing. As for his verse, since he used it either for popular journalism or as a weapon it is of little artistic consequence. He was trying to arouse uncomplicated emotion and reaction in an uncomplicated audience, and subtlety was of no use to him.

Yet there is a poetry about Lawson himself that is for the most part lacking in his verse. It is what makes him memorable as O'Dowd is not memorable. The very clumsiness and sentimentality of his personal verses, seem somehow to underline the Lawson legend. When he looks back nostalgically to

> The golden days when I was one
> Of Nature's gentlemen,

we do not feel embarrassed, as we easily may feel over Gordon's morbidly theatrical cynicism, but sympathetic. There is an inner truth in Lawson's self-pity; we may see him as a representative of the fact that lies behind the cliché, as facts somewhere lie behind all such clichés. A gentleman, in the right sense of the term, Lawson was; no gentler and more sensitive man has lived among us. If his verse is for the most part marred by his conception of its purpose, we have the economy of his stories to show what he could do in a form he understood.

Perhaps the worst influence on Lawson's verse was the spirit of the time he lived in, with its smugness and its hollow patriotism, and its taste for violence and drum-beat rhythms. Kipling and Henley, the Boer War and the *Bulletin* bards, all influenced his writing; he imitated Paterson even while he combated his optimistic view of the Bush and its inhabitants; and though he uses Kipling's verse-forms for other purposes than Kipling had done, the crudeness and the ranting note remain.

At first sight Lawson seems a paradox. Boake had not imagined any possible answer to the injustices he saw done; for him they were simply a proof of his feeling that civilization was 'a dead failure' and that only in the hard work and solitude of the bush was virtue to be discovered. Lawson, on the other hand, was passionately occupied with the notion of progress, of 'civilization', as a struggle towards some form of social justice. It was a narrow aim, and not clearly thought out; and it gave rise in Lawson's verse to a good deal of rather hollow and sentimental talk about 'the lurid clouds of war' and 'the flag that is dyed with our hearts' blood'. But it was at least an aim, and it should, one might imagine, have inspired Lawson with purpose, if not with optimism. His tales, as he says, are 'tales of wrongs that fire the spirit'.

Yet fundamentally, throughout his life, Lawson is one of our most melancholy writers; and to this melancholy his life is a testimony. There is no personal note in his work that is not charged with hopelessness. He and Christopher Brennan both wandered Sydney's streets, in their last years, alcoholic and despairing; but when we think of Brennan it is of the young and middle-aged poet of *Poems 1913,* rather than the sad wreck he later became, while the Lawson of the popular image is already a broken and unhappy man.

It was, from the beginning, as though Lawson's militancy and his reformist zeal were already undermined by a certain lack of conviction—not of conviction of the misery of the life he saw around him, or of the necessity of reform, but of its possibility. Lawson lacked confidence in himself; the note he strikes in the lines

> He was the only gentleman
> that shamed the lout in me

may strike us as ridiculously humble, and we may protest that in Lawson, of all people, the lout was least obvious; but clearly Lawson means what he says. He was (like Kendall) full of a sense of guilt; he was bitterly self-reproachful at the same moment as he was most self-pitying. Hopeless for himself, he did not find it easy to translate his personal problems into a more generalized hope for the world. He is that paradox, a revolutionary writer who is never quite convinced that revolution will bring the Utopia he wants.

It is tempting, and perhaps not too far-fetched, to think of O'Dowd and Lawson as representing two opposite sides of the Australian psyche; the one, a reformist, scraping together for his Utopia what he thought 'the best of the old', but rejecting tradition and authority in favour of an ill-balanced political rhetoric—exemplar of the self-confidence of adolescence; the other, representing its self-doubt; bitter and moody, accepting the role of scapegoat for half-imaginary sins, protesting against the crimes of 'the world' and claiming the right to 'march with his comrades against it', but far more obsessed by its sorrows and his own than by any brash intellectual plan to mend them.

In the end, Lawson remains the poet of the dark streets and alleys that he knew, of the seamstresses and the drovers' wives, of the pale gutter-boys and the tramps. We scarcely think of him as a political poet; his polemics vanish behind the far more human figure, the man who identifies himself with human woe, the man of compassion and sensitivity, the eternal scapegoat who suffers for and with others. It is this quality in Lawson which makes him, if not a poet, then a poetic legend, a figure who remains real to us when more rational and persuasive writers are forgotten.

There is a sense, too, in which Lawson's melancholy seems to stem less from the woes of the slums and the back-tracks and of his own personal life, than from the same root as Gordon's and as Boake's. For Lawson there was, in the end, nothing but human relationships, and these were doomed to failure as the human body was doomed to death. One of his best poems, 'Out Back', traces the wanderings of the swagman who travels the inland plains in search of work and finally dies on the track.

> And dirty and careless and old he wore, as his lamp of hope
> grew dim;

> He tramped for years, till the swag he bore seemed part of himself to him.
> As a bullock drags in the sandy ruts, he followed the dreary track,
> With never a thought but to reach the huts when the sun went down Out Back.

It is a characteristic verse. In practically all his narratives, about people or about human relationships, the end is failure and death. Even 'The Sliprails and the Spur', a romantic ballad, does not have the conventional happy ending; the lover who rode away does not ride back again, but leaves the girl to 'cry herself to sleep'; and we are not even given a reason for his defection.

Lawson was, in fact, deeply pessimistic about human nature and its fate; and since his revolution was to be based on human values, his revolutionary poems never seem convincing or even convinced. They are in fact poems of protest, not of programme; the flag they wave may be dipped in Lawson's heart's blood and that of the people of the alleys, but even in Lawson's early and more enthusiastic days there is something half-hearted about his exhortations to that battle, into which it is to precede Lawson's tragic army.

For his army, perhaps, the battle was already lost, and Lawson knew it; and his inherent pessimism kept him from hoping much for the future. His love for humanity did not prevent him from seeing its weaknesses, and he excuses his own faults by protesting that he too is 'human, very human'. It is this faultiness and this humanity that will keep Lawson always clearly before our eyes, and in our affections.

His contemporary (though Lawson died first) in reformism and nationalism is the far more rhetorical, far more programmatic and learned Bernard O'Dowd. Lawson was drawn into the political arena in his verse, by the depth of his feeling; O'Dowd, Irish, redheaded and intellectual, by the pugnacity of his mind.

His earlier works are largely political and inflammatory. In the book which at that time won him recognition by the young for its rationalist Socialist programme, *Dawnward?* he set out his ideas for Australia's future. They were even more ambitious than Harpur's. Australia, as the youngest of the continents and hence least trammelled by tradition, was to devote herself to the task of creating the new society on purely rational lines. Human thought had now been freed from all traditional claims; the Darwinian theory had done away with the notion of divine sanctions and the old political tyrannies had been broken. At last it was open to man to create the just society. *Dawnward?* was O'Dowd's attempt to point the way.

Where Gordon and Boake and Lawson found in the 'failure of civilization' and the loss of religion a cause for melancholy, O'Dowd welcomed both. Abstractions like Democracy and High Ideals were the natural habitation of his mind; 'that apocalyptic word Evolution', as he termed it, was the Logos out of which his new heaven and earth were to be made.

'All, all', he cried, 'is being thrown, has to be thrown, into the crucible of revaluation, customs, morals, religions, laws, institutions, classes, castes, politics, philosophies, all . . .'[1]

The appalling problems presented by such a wholesale toppling of civilization into the melting-pot scarcely gave him pause. The Millenium was to follow, and it was to depend upon the operations of the Poet: the Poet Militant. 'The function of the poet', O'Dowd considered, was to 'permeate the masses with the high ideals communicated to and communicable by him' (though from where they were communicated O'Dowd does not make clear). 'The permeator poet, the projector of ideals, the Poet Militant', was required especially 'in the present reconstruction of all things beneath the wand of Evolution theories'; and 'in this virgin and unhandicapped land of social experiments, embryonic democracy and the Coming Race, Australia', it seemed to O'Dowd that his function was particularly important.

Moreover, the poet's function was 'to create gods . . . and the mythologies that give them blood and bone and power'. This may seem a little odd, since these gods must also be destroyed by the Poet 'when their hour strikes'. But this is not all; 'another of his functions is the co-ordination of Truth and Goodness with Beauty'. Nor must he continue to neglect 'the fairylands of science', 'the relations of the sexes', or 'Social Reform'.

This comprehensive programme, which might well have daunted a committee composed of archangels, O'Dowd himself attempted to adumbrate in verses composed of what he called, rather oddly, 'fourteeners', that is, couplets of eight-syllable and six-syllable lines. This is a sample verse (from the greatly admired *Dawnward?*)

1 *Poetry Militant: An Australian Plea for the Poetry of Purpose,* Lothian, Melbourne, 1909

D

> Will Sport educe a virile pith?
> Our pulses teach to throb?
> Or weary earth re-saddle with
> A Nika-riot mob?

O'Dowd peppered his verse with miscellaneous references to by-gone religions, philosophies and mythologies; feeling apparently that the new religion of Poetry Militant would be more easily compounded of elements of all the older religions, than by imagining a wholly original pantheon.

In the confusion of his rhetoric and the pedagogy of his half-assimilated information, O'Dowd can be likened to no other literary figure of his time, except perhaps, in some respects, d'Annunzio in Italy. But where d'Annunzio had taken the 'death of God' as a licence to forget the existence of Law, O'Dowd took it as a licence to invent new and more abstract gods, and new and more defined Laws. His lawgiver and godmaker, the Poet Militant, is in the end O'Dowd himself.

The difference between Lawson and O'Dowd is striking and instructive. Lawson seems always to begin from the human, from the specific instance; when his feeling is aroused at this level he moves rather uncertainly towards generalization. O'Dowd begins at the level of abstraction, at the intellect, and uses the specific instance seldom, and only as an illustration. Hence the theoretical, abstract, haranguing temper of his verse and its *ex cathedra* tone. This is why Lawson at his worst can still move us, and O'Dowd at his best cannot convince us.

O'Dowd might have taken to heart the acute observation of his correspondent and mentor Whitman: 'Logic and sermons never convince; the damps of the night drive deeper into my soul'. As it was, all we can find of Whitman, in this loud-voiced versifying, is the habit of rhetoric and of catalogue-making.

Moreover O'Dowd, except in a verse or two of 'The Bush', gives no hint of possessing a pair of eyes and the capacity to use them; his verse is almost the verse of a blind man. He could never have written a poem like 'When Lilacs Last in the Dooryard Bloom'd', for he would not have seen the lilacs with their 'heart-shaped leaves of rich green', or heard the hermit thrush's song, or thought of weaving either into a song written for a dead leader, however revered and loved. O'Dowd in fact was not a poet; Whitman was.

O'Dowd seems to have taken up the practice of verse comparatively late in life. He believed that mythologies and religions, and the world-views to which they contributed, were the work of poets, or at least of the poetic faculty in man; and this seems to have led him to the conclusion that, since it was his ambition to become the creator of a new society or at least a leader in its creation, he must become a poet. His choice of the four-line stanza, which he called a 'fourteener', he explained by remarking that its simplicity was such as to force the poet to 'cultivate his intellect as well as his emotions', and it 'subordinates the call of the verbal music to the more important call of thought-motif and the spiritual theme'.

Letting alone the curious assumption behind this, that the poet can be forced to cultivate his intellect by his own conscious choice of a metrical measure, it is more than doubtful whether O'Dowd ever produced, in this stanza-form, anything that could be regarded as verbal music at all, or that, in fact, he ever gave any real thought to the question of verbal music. The stanza, in his hands, becomes a jerky doggerel, a medium for political rhetoric; its final effect is not that of the early Anglo-Saxons who used a measure which resembles it (though only in syllabic count and never in actual speech-rhythm), but that of 'Yankee Doodle'.

It is perhaps this unfortunate stanza-form, as much as O'Dowd's habit of personification and abstraction, and his total lack of understanding of verbal and consonantal appositeness, or of any kind of verbal felicity, that makes *Dawnward?* now so difficult to read, as well as so uninspiring. O'Dowd's verse in other metrical media does not sound so incongruous and awkward. He was capable of handling the sonnet-form fairly satisfactorily, and its more chastening and demanding rhythms impose on his thought, if not a discipline, at least a sentential nimbleness, which is certainly lacking in his 'fourteener' stanzas.

In the ten-line stanza of 'The Bush', too, he gave up the awkward and un-English syllabic-count method, in favour of a freer rhythm that allowed some flexibility, almost approaching speech rhythms.

Yet, in fact, O'Dowd's verse sounds always much less like speech than like a public speech—a very different matter. There is never, even in the more human stanzas of 'The Bush' or of 'Alma Venus' (his two most admired achievements) a hint of man speaking to man; it is always orator addressing audience. His crowded and hortatory volume is itself a demonstration of the difference—which O'Dowd never learned—between poetry and oratory.

His long poem, 'The Bush', however, has been generally acknowledged as a landmark in Australian development. It is something like a public monument erected over the achievement of the nationalists and the reformists in the two or three decades before it, and it is also a distant tribute to Nietzsche's cycle-theory of history. Nietzsche, who had, as it were, dared mankind to accept his notion of Eternal Recurrence—himself evidently appalled by its implications—had reckoned without O'Dowd, who accepted it blithely and used it with the utmost carefree optimism. Yet the modern reader of 'The Bush' may find himself appalled all over again. A mitigating feature of the poem, however, is its appealing sincerity.

O'Dowd has practically no sense of humour; but there are times when, as F. T. Macartney puts it with a fine instinct for the *mot juste,* he is 'playful'. The well-known stanzas of 'The Bush' in which his Australian contemporaries are identified with Recurrences of figures in ancient Greek history are possibly classifiable as, at least in part, 'playful' in intention; and if they remind us of the playfulness of an emu imitating a wagtail, they still lighten the otherwise enormous seriousness of O'Dowd's works.

And, without doubt, this is the representative poem of the whole reformist-nationalist movement. After O'Dowd, the deluge; Australian poets have never been able to take themselves quite so seriously since.

What is, and remains, interesting about O'Dowd's programmatic verse is not the verse itself, but the response it seems to have aroused at the time. The lecture on 'Poetry Militant', when it was delivered early in the century, 'made such an impression', says one of his hearers (K. S. Prichard: *Meanjin,* iv, 1953) 'on those of us who were beginning to think seriously, that upon leaving the meeting, we were almost too exalted and exhilarated to speak'. And it appears that there were a number of people who agreed with this reaction. We have the word of several contemporaries that O'Dowd served as an inspiration to many of the young writers of the time.

Clearly 'Poetry Militant' is, as it were, the expression of nineteenth-century demagogic rationalism in the face of the situation summarized by Nietzsche as 'the death of God'. It was the optimism, the air of accepting the challenge of a universe suddenly become the sole property of man, that roused the enthusiasm of the youthful. But it was an optimism which was merely the obverse of the pessimism which Boake and Gordon had felt in the face of the same mental situation.

At the same time, in England, the young Bertrand Russell was expressing the rational opposite of O'Dowd's programmatic glee:

> That man is the product of causes which had no prevision of the end they were achieving, that his origin, his growth, his hopes and fears, his loves and his beliefs, are but the outcome of accidental collocations of atoms . . . and that the whole temple of man's achievement must inevitably be buried beneath the debris of a universe in ruins—all these things . . . are so nearly certain that no philosophy which rejects them can hope to stand.
>
> ('A Free Man's Worship', from *Mysticism and Logic*)

Russell's propositions here are basically exactly the same as those of O'Dowd. The difference is that the one chooses to emphasize the 'inevitable' end of man's achievement, the other chooses to emphasize the necessity of revaluing that achievement. Clearly, once the basic similarity of their positions is seen, it is merely a matter of temperament which statement of the situation is accepted.

Both views are melodramatic reactions to the notions of evolution and 'the death of God'; neither is truly rational, in that it follows inevitably from that notion. The basic error of both, it may be, is in imagining that from the contemporary success of the idea of evolution, anything at all necessarily follows.

But at that time, in Australia, the O'Dowdian optimistic reaction was most popular, just as, in England, the Russellian pessimism was fashionable. It may be that the first, though no more reasonable, is slightly more endearing; but it is clear that poets were hardly to be drawn into O'Dowd's grandiose plan for the revaluation and remodelling of a universe once proved so untrustworthy, without some kind of guarantee that their own labours in turn would not be immediately outmoded. This guarantee O'Dowd, of course, could not give; he offers the Poet, however, the further enticement of being allowed to pull down the gods and mythologies he is to erect, when 'their hour strikes'.

Gods and mythologies, however, have now in fact become ideologies, and poets have been rather engaged in shoring fragments against the ruins of the old mythologies, than in erecting new. The O'Dowdian notion of a grand new world has itself suffered certain basic revaluations since the end of the nineteenth century. For if, as O'Dowd put it, all the achievements of the past had become 'mere tyrannies' the moment man had diagnosed himself to be a higher animal rather than a child of God, there was surely little point in inventing new gods and mythologies which, in turn, would become mere despotisms to be overthrown. The sand on which O'Dowd built his house was so shifting that already the house has almost disappeared into it.

Nevertheless, if one accepts that exhilaration, however unsoundly based, is better than pessimism, O'Dowd and his followers seem, if no less naive, at least less unattractive than Russell and his disciples. It was not merely unsophistication that fed their hopes for the future; it was also their environment, less sceptical than that of Europe and less commercial than that of America. In Australia, political reformism was then more at home than it is now; and though jingoism and the stupidity and violence fed by Kiplingesque patriotism were at home also, they did not sit quite so oddly on a raw young country as they did on the older country that led the movement.

There was a sense in which O'Dowd and Lawson were nationalist poets; but there were also plenty of nationalist writers—notably the *Bulletin* balladist Paterson—who did not subscribe to their reformist aims. Still, even the conservative Paterson felt the pull of the spirit of 'egalitarianism' that Lawson expressed in his notion of mateship, and that Furphy had expounded in *Such is Life* (though that long and complicated novel had a very slight success in its time).

Paterson, along with numerous lesser writers, was exploiting the vein of the bush ballads; and, as often happens, in doing so he marked the end of the period in which those ballads had flourished. The kind of life that had produced them was now becoming conscious of itself, and changing in the process. It was the life that Boake had spoken of as 'the only life that I see', the life of the men who were opening up and broadening the frontiers of pastoral and mining settlement. By its nature it was opposed to any consciously literary appreciation of its qualities; when Paterson began to exploit it, when it became at last a popular stereotype, it had already almost ceased to exist as it once had done.

The cities began to see Australia in terms of these more sophisticated versions of the bush ballad; and with the cult of the independent sun-tanned bushman, of mateship and self-reliance, of egalitarianism and the outback and the 'droving days', the outback legend became less real and more formalized.

There had been much in that life that was never translated into balladry—the silent war with the blacks, the change that had come over the country itself with the invasion of hard-hoofed creatures into the vast plains that had never felt hoofs before, but only the soft pads of kangaroo and wallabies and the naked feet of the aborigines; the erosion and the dust storms that followed, the slaughter of animals, birds and forests. So when the stereotype was set, and the picture of the hard-riding independent bushman became almost as formalized as that of the American cowboy, much of the real truth of the 'droving days' was left forever outside the cult. It still remains to be rescued. But Australia had found her idealized hero-pattern, in 'The Man from Snowy River' and 'Clancy of the Overflow' and the rest; and few looked farther.

In fact the nationalist-reformist movement among the writers has left behind it a paralysing uniformity. Much of the later revival of the 'Australian legend' is traced through them; they gathered together the threads of the more innocent, more various life of the previous century, and popularized and generalized it.

The immigrants of the early years, of the gold-rushes and of the 'seventies and 'eighties, had brought with them their own variety and their own aspirations. The life traceable in old memoirs such as the books of Mary Gilmore, of Nehemiah Bartley and of de Satge, and many others, set against the unsubtle generalizations of Paterson, O'Dowd, McKee Wright and even Lawson, seems strangely unfamiliar.

We have our stereotype of Australia and of her life and that of her inhabitants—the toughness, the sentimentalism, the loyalty, the mateship. It seems that this is what we want to believe of ourselves; and while this is so, and while we dismiss all other notions as somehow a betrayal of the 'Australian legend', it will be of no use examining farther into the various and treacherous reality. So what was begun in the comparative naturalness of the early bush ballad is capitalized on by twentieth-century writers pandering to the natural desire for some simplification, something recognizable and familiar, a predictable hero typifying a predictable country.

Indeed, Australians have to some extent grown into the pattern they imposed on themselves, as usually happens when subtlety and variety are rejected in favour of generalization. We have become a kind of caricature of the Australian outback hero we once set up. His qualities survive in our writing, which is apt to be 'tough', colloquial, matey, political in a simple black-and-white sense that excludes the nuances of policy and all issues that may seem to cloud the direct choice or introduce the possibility of deeper considerations. We like to believe, still, that life is at bottom a matter of easy alternatives; that right is right and wrong indubitably wrong. At the back of most of our observations of the foreigner, the misfit, the coloured man or the person who refuses to submit to our categories, there is a more-or-less-hidden sneer. That sneer was built-in in the early days of the century.

It comes from the apotheosis of the outback hero, and of the political good-mate; and it comes, too, from the never-questioned picture of Australia as the Land of the Dawn, the egalitarian paradise—the picture which a New Zealand poet has described as the Australian 'cynicism and softness—the two sides of a double-headed penny in a two-up game'.

O'Dowdian rhetoric, Lawsonian and Patersonian colloquial heroics, while we may overtly reject them, seem to have built themselves slyly into our characters; they are traceable in Hansard reports, at public dinners, in newspaper leaders and letters, at Anzac Day services. The nationalist and reformist writers, by so drastically simplifying the issues for us, left us a dubious legacy that it seems we may take another century to outgrow.

The proliferation of political demagogy and the cult of the unreal bush-hero nationalist hid the beginning of the twentieth century in a kind of mist of bad writing. Behind the mist, however, another writer was taking his own doomed eccentric path, in complete rejection both of the nationalists and of the reformists. He had turned back, away from the English influence (which at that moment, with few poets in existence and the crudity and arrogance of Kipling in the ascendant, was doing Australia nothing but harm) to the subtler and more complex thought of contemporary Europe. This writer was the almost unknown Sydney librarian and academic, Christopher Brennan.

CHAPTER VI

Christopher Brennan

∾

IT WAS in the 'nineties that Australia's first real contribution to international literature began, with the poetry of Christopher Brennan. A man of intellectual grasp and deep capacity for understanding the important problems of his time, Brennan was drawn into real involvement with what was happening in Western thought and literature. His contribution to that development, though it remained for many years little known and imperfectly understood, was none the less real for that frustration.

The very scope of Brennan's work, and his impatience with local limitations, have made his poetry in some sense irrelevant to the immediate growth which was going on, in the lower levels of Australian poetry. Brennan looms far out of focus in any survey of what has happened here, both before and after the publication of his *Poems 1913*. The terms in which he must be judged are not local, but universal; so that he must of necessity throw off balance any criticism which attempts to include him in a local frame of reference. He was not influenced by his Australian predecessors, and he has had little influence, in his turn, on his successors here.

So, for the most part, criticism has had to treat him on a level rather academic than immediate, and the chief concern of his expositors has often been less with what he was saying than with the way in which he chose to say it. The theory of correspondences, taken by Baudelaire from Swedenborg, and farther elaborated by Mallarmé, was the basis of Brennan's poetic practice. He spoke in symbols drawn from the whole history of Western man, and the sources and connotations of these symbols, their linkages, associations and implications, have necessarily occupied a great deal of his critics' time.

The fact that Brennan's symbolism was already at one remove from direct experience—that the figures and images with which he chose to work were already loaded with human significance—carries his practice a step from that of Baudelaire, who used his own intensely-experienced life as material, and even from the remoter Mallarmé, who was still capable of translating the glow of a cigar-end into a powerful poetic image. This lack of immediate temporal or local reference is one of the things about Brennan's poetry that make it seem at times too inhumanly elevated, too much at a remove from life—as indeed many of the other poets of the 'nineties also were.

In fact, Brennan was perhaps forced by his lack of immediate contact with other writers, and with the stream of thought in which he felt himself to be working, into a certain over-elaboration and intellectualism. He was, indeed, in a somewhat ambiguous position; almost sole representative, here, of the Symbolist school, he had early seen its importance and its bearing, and had given much thought to aesthetic theory. If he had been in England at the time when Symons's book on the Symbolists was published, and when Yeats and his friends came under Mallarmé's influence, it is likely that his personal insights and interpretations would have been recognized and acknowledged by his peers, and that in turn they might have been altered by other cross-currents of thought.

As it was, he found, in effect, a very small audience of initiates here, while overseas, as was natural, his work was largely disregarded. For many years he remained a poet without a properly appreciative audience, and until recently, his work was practically unobtainable except by students in the larger libraries.

Perhaps the greatest ambiguity Brennan presents lies in himself—an ambiguity that was crucial for his poetry and for his life as well. Brought up as a Catholic, he chose, instead of the priesthood he had once intended, to become a student, and was caught up in the currents of late nineteenth-century thought, particularly that of Herbert Spencer. But though he was at that time apparently an agnostic, his nature and upbringing seem to have required, if not a religious dogma, at least a religious outlook on the universe; he can scarcely be said ever to have abandoned the search for a ground of faith, even though he denounces the temptation to set up systems, to take refuge in certitudes.

Brennan's chief poetic preoccupation was with the relationship between man's thought and his universe, and hence with the supposed dichotomy between mind and matter. His statement of the philosophical position as he saw it is to be found in its most condensed form in his paper 'Fact and Idea' (p. 3, *The Prose of Christopher Brennan*). This was given in 1898, when Brennan was twenty-eight years old. Most of his other writings, like the important 'Philosophy and Art' (1903) (p. 39, ibid.) deal with aspects of the problem as it relates either to the practice of the artist, or to literary or artistic judgements. An understanding of his early position, though it altered over the years, is necessary for any critic of his poetry as such.

In 'Fact and Idea', Brennan's conclusion is that consciousness 'has broken up its own unity, that it might become more fully aware of its interests, each by each, and use them in turn as means to remodel the world'. This fragmentation or analysis, however, is 'just so much preparation to some greater synthesis—the complete humanization of the Universe . . .'

> Our negative consciousness of the infinite, the void . . . has for emotional aspect the aspiration, or more than aspiration; *I, the Human, ought to be there*, to fill that void; or, since in the Infinite we can only live Here and Now, to feel that we stand in some satisfactory natural relation with Eternity . . . What we fear is that the Idea of the Infinite may be found incompatible with the Idea of the Human.

Only, then, in the final 'Unity of World and Human' that the journey of consciousness implies, can that journey find its end. This state, 'where thought would be like quivering flame, inseparable from sense, emotion and imagination', is Brennan's foreseen Eden, the second Eden in which God and man, mind and matter, flesh and soul, and all dichotomies, are reconciled.

Since it is only the increase of consciousness that can lead to this apotheosis of man-in-world, Brennan's position here might seem to point him rather in the direction of philosophy than of art. But, in his paper delivered in 1903 and titled 'Philosophy and Art', he states his view of the function of the artist in the world-process. In this paper, too, a number of ideas important to his poetry are to be found; especially his statement of the dilemma of thought deprived of any absolute basis. For Brennan, only the increase of knowledge, i.e. of consciousness, could lead to the union of man with his universe; but knowledge is seen to be founded, not on absolute referents, but on human experience and human consciousness itself, and, says Brennan, 'all concepts (are) teleological instruments, the creatures of attention and of attention obeying the hest of interest . . .' 'Here was the whole foundation cut away from under all the splendid shrines erected on the eternal rock of reason and its ideas: ideas were man's tools and eternal only if he found them most fitting.'

This is the very crux of his 'Lilith' series, in the poem from 'The Watch at Midnight', 'The plumes of night, unfurl'd', and the point on which Brennan himself seems to have been finally impaled. But in the paper 'Philosophy and Art', it is not over-emphasized. If his chief figure, Lilith, is to be discovered in the notion of the 'infinite, the void' that beckons man to humanize it, the Wanderer, the figure of the final sequence, is to be seen, though with a somewhat more positive air, in Brennan's answer to the dilemma. 'If all our thinking is teleological and anthropo-morphic', he says

> and if the world has obediently taken the stamp of our thought, what better argument in favour of teleology as a whole? . . . We are turned out on the road . . . but we have received our stick and our crust and it would seem that the road does lead somewhere . . . Man the wanderer is on the way to himself . . . That vast region of the unconscious or subconscious must also be in process of becoming con-scious . . . A goal lies before us then—the state in which man shall have taken up into himself the whole world that lies outside him, and the whole world that is within . . .
> (pp. 45-6)

This process, the making conscious of the infinite, the void, and the unconscious, was for Brennan the field in which art operated. 'Philosophy can adumbrate to us, intellectually, the theory and possibility of a harmony. Art makes that harmony a living thing to us, by its power of symbolizing.' (p. 47)

The road, for him, thus led not only toward the reality of the world and the self, but also to the conquering of all possible areas of the unconscious—to 'the state wherein man shall have taken up into himself the whole world that is outside him, and the whole world that is within'. The Absolute that Brennan felt humanity to be in search of was, in fact, not to be known by intellect alone, but by the fullest possible power of human experience, deployed in the function of imagination and 'media-ted by the symbol', the point at which inner experience and outer reality find their expression and unity.

It is at this point that Symbolist theory becomes crucial for Brennan. Yet there are important differences between his use of it, and that of Mallarmé. Brennan's notion of the symbol is as a form through which a dynamic current flows in two directions; from the inner toward the outer, and back again. The symbol itself may cease to mediate one particular current (the Rose's meaning changes with time, but the form of the Rose remains and may be reanimated by new insights). What is important is that meaning though it may alter, is a real relationship between inner and outer—that the 'correspondences' between inner and outer which are mediated through the symbol form a guarantee that human experience is truly connected with, and can assimilate, a true reality: 'our spirit is adequate to the whole outer world, and . . . the whole outer world is a perpetual corroboration of spiritual fact'. (p. 160, *The Prose of Christopher Brennan*)

There is a sense, in fact, in which Brennan's whole exploration and achievement stem from his religious upbringing—it is an attempt at reconciliation and reanimation of his early religious experiences. And, if there is one note in his writing that is unmistakable, it is the habit of mind and even of diction that his early experience left in him. His mind is not secular; his vision and the imagery he used are constantly coloured by, and refer back to, his early training. And it may be that the somewhat *ex cathedra* tone of many of the poems, the assumption of a kind of timeless experience in the speaker (as though, like Eliot, Brennan were assuming a Tiresian mantle) is traceable to Brennan's early ambition toward the impersonal authority of the priesthood.

Yet the import of his chief work, *Poems 1913,* is far from the Christian viewpoint. Brennan is never a poet of redemption, in the ordinary sense. Whatever redemption was possible for man, he felt, must come from his own struggle towards full consciousness. The Eden he had lost was an Eden of primal unconscious innocence, pre-knowledge and almost pre-perception. The Fall was a symbolization of the entrance of consciousness into that Eden; man's history since then was that of search for what had been lost, but this time on a new level and with new demands to be fulfilled. This second Eden cannot be achieved until consciousness has accomplished its task of knowing; until, that is, the challenge of Eternity has been met and the universe has been humanized. No less than complete self-knowledge and complete knowledge of the corresponding outer reality is the necessary condition for the re-entry into Eden.

The central symbol of Brennan's Edenic myth is the Rose. In 'Towards the Source', it is the symbol of the original innocence of the flesh, of youth and joy; but it is also the 'perfect hour' of fulfilment, the nuptial 'rose of all fulfill'd delight'. But its appearance in the next section, 'The Forest of Night,' heralds a change of mood. Its second poem, 'Liminary', originally entitled 'The Year of the Soul', traces the story of the fulfilled soul and its 'summer-bride, new life from nuptial lands', through the joys of that fulfilment into an autumnal scene, in 'some dark pass that leads into the west', 'some eve whose dragon-dying hides the sky'. The new element here is of change, doom, 'the death of kings'; and the sunset evokes

> The unslaked caravans of vast desire,
> seeking in furnace-sands some fiercer rose
> with deadly heart . . .

This is the signal for the resumption of the soul's journey towards solitude, winter, the House of Contemplation, 'the fixed light that charms the fields of death'.

The next section is 'The Twilight of Disquietude', and in this section Brennan most clearly sets out the terms of what he saw as the human task and doom—

> the pangs that guard the gates of joy
> the naked sword that will be kist—

It is to be the exploration of the unconscious:

> The mother-deep, wise, yearning, bound,
> I feel it press beneath my heart,
> the deep where I were free and crown'd
> o'er mine own realm, alone, apart . . .   (41)

And the only road to it is through the self and the extension of consciousness:

> What do I know? myself alone,
> a gulf of uncreated night,
> Wherein no star may e'er be shown
> save I create it in my might . . .

> What do I seek? I seek the word
> that shall become the deed of might
> whereby the sullen gulfs are stirr'd
> and stars begotten on their night.   (42)

In this section the Wanderer sets out on his journey away from 'those days of sweetness and content', through the darkness of the seas 'where good and evil merge'.

Out beyond good and evil are we blown:
then wait not that the dark One lift his scourge.
Shake out the sail: somewhere his face is shown. (43)

In the next section, 'The Quest of Silence', the search for Eden
leads the seeker to the heart of the Forest—the worship of Earth
herself, the legendary romance of pantheist innocence, the
Rousseauist dream and the chivalric legend. But no revelation
comes: the knights of romance found death instead of the Lady
of the Forest, and Pan has become senile; there is no return to
this particular kind of innocence and mythic unity with the
world, except at the expense of decay and self-betrayal. Only the
elements themselves persist. As for the old religious certainties,
the rose symbol of the church window is now empty, the rose is
shattered, and the grey indifferent stare of the daylight looks
through its 'petal-ribs'; henceforth its emptiness is only to show
us the old illusion of the spring and the 'traitor roses of the
wooing dawn'.

But the rose image appears again, this time in a new guise; it is
now 'the rose that bleeds unseen, the heart of night'. The fleshly
rose, Eve's 'dower that Eden lent', is now the 'limbeck where the
enamour'd alchemist/invokes the rarer rose, phantom descent'.
It is Lilith who works this change; for she lies at the heart of the
rose, as of all man's symbols. The rose will be hers, its centre 'the
fleeting centre of the abyss', until man conquers her and under-
stands her beauty. Only then, out of the death of 'old delight',
can the new rose be born, and then it will be changed to a
'deathless rose of gold'.

From one point of view, the whole structure of *Poems 1913* is a
personal testament to Brennan's own 'fall' from the Church in
which his youth found fulfilment, and from the love that symbolized Eden to him in later years, and to his search through the
whole recorded conscious history of man, from the Cabbala to
Swedenborg and beyond, for a rebirth of faith. But if it is in
essence the story of Brennan's spiritual movement away from
Catholicism, it is also a great deal more. It is also a history—a
symbolic history—of the whole movement of consciousness
through recorded time, and its successive attempts at embodying
itself in absolutes that themselves become lifeless and give way to
other absolutes, whether religions or systems of thought.

For Brennan, all such systems (pantheism, sun-god religions,

the Mars-worship of empires, even the pursuit of ultimate wisdom)
are themselves no more than symbols—symbols of man himself
and of his never-ending search. This is why the section 'The
Forest of Night', which deals with this search, is dense, difficult
and cyclic: it is an attempt to deal symbolically with the history
of consciousness seen as a succession of symbolic embodiments. It
is like a series of Chinese puzzle-boxes, but the series is infinite—
Eden is as far off at the end, as at the beginning.

And yet it is not, after all, as far off. The history that Brennan
tells is a history with direction; the search is, seen rightly, a search
for self-consciousness. This self-consciousness, this knowledge of
the self and of its correspondent harmonies in the reality of the
universe, is nearer at the end than at the beginning of the poem,
because man has at last become conscious that this is what he
seeks, and that the search is a human search for full human
stature. The gods, the religions, the attempts at absolute systems,
that strew the path behind us, can at last be seen, according to
Brennan, for what they are—symbols, forms, which man has used
to mediate his own experience—crystals that he has used to
polarize the universe. Now he is sufficiently conscious to discover
the reality of his own humanity; he can cease to dream that he is
a king for whom the universe has been created, and can realize
that the creation is his own—that it is for him to accept responsibility for his own journey towards consciousness and for the
'humanizing of the universe'.

For until ye have had care of the wastes there shall be no truce
    for them nor you, nor home, but ever the ancient feud . . .
go; tho' the going be hard and the goal blinded with rain
yet the staying is a death that is never soften'd with sleep. (95)

Accordingly the last section, 'The Wanderer', is almost bare
of those symbols and images that crowded the lines of 'The Forest
of Night'. The Wanderer (Ulysses, the bereft Lear, Brennan himself, Adam) is in a cold grey landscape, lashed by winds and seas;
he is haunted by longing for the 'hearth with its glow and the
roof that forbids the rain', the old security of which knowledge
has stripped him, and the comfort of the unthinking, but he
knows that there is no retracing the path that has led him away
from his 'old dream of kingship'. Consciousness once won cannot
be renounced, for if there is a way to Eden it can only be through
increased consciousness. Yet 'The Wanderer' series ends on a note
of almost hopeless scepticism—

> no ending of the way, no home, no goal,

and only acceptance of this hopelessness brings peace.

This final denial of everything except the way itself seems to go farther into despair than Brennan's prose exposition of his theme had taken him. In his lecture 'Philosophy and Art' to which I have referred, he had said:

> Here we have the wandering given, and perhaps are struck with dismay: but I think, if we look more closely we shall find the goal of the wandering given too . . . We are turned out on the road, it is true, and our house and home is broken down: but we have received our stick and our crust and it would seem that the road does lead somewhere . . . Man the wanderer is on the way to himself.

If some of Brennan's assurance had left him meanwhile, and he had begun to doubt the possibility of human achievement of the goal of complete consciousness, it may have been the encounter and wrestle with his Lilith-figure that had caused the change. She so much dominates the poem, and is so presented, as to leave us with a deep doubt that Adam can ever grow to her stature— as he must do if he is to find his way beyond her. She represents Brennan's deepest exploration into his own psyche, and into the concepts of death, eternity, and evil; at the same time she must stand for the eternal allure of the unknown, of the feminine, of the maternal, of the abyss of the past and the undiscernible distance of the future. To embody all this, and more, in one figure was task enough to exhaust the vision and invention of any poet, and leave him doubtful of human ability and achievement.

The presentation of Lilith is terrifying enough to the reader; to the poet faced with so ambiguous and unfathomable a task, it must have been a crucial experience. For it is a condition of Lilith's being that the poet must perceive her everywhere—she is the negation in the heart of all achievement, the 'fleeting centre of the abyss', she is present by implication in all situations and in all thought. Each assertion implies its opposite; every positive exists by virtue of its own negative. In fact, the farther Brennan explores this terrible symbol, the less possible it seems that the exploration can ever be completed, since exploration itself contains the seed of its own negation.

After the last line of Lilith's own speech—

> Go forth: be great, O nothing. I have said.

Brennan finds, in fact, no convincing reply. The Lilith series belongs, not to Brennan, but to Lilith herself. It is possible to feel that Lilith herself is the reality of the poem, Brennan no more than the symbol, 'the meeting-point of many analogies'.

However, when the momentary illusion is over, we can recognize the greatness of Brennan's achievement. It is undeniable that he owed much to earlier and contemporary ideas; but there are few figures in literature so convincing, so deep in their conception and so towering in their realization, as Brennan's dreadful and ambiguous figure of Night.

This ambiguity has as one of its human aspects the so-called death-wish (though Freud had not yet announced his 'discovery' of this aspect of human personality); the deep attraction of life towards its opposite. It was this recognition which took Brennan deep into the chief problem of human knowledge—the solipsism of thought, when it is seen as a wholly individual and human product, the impasse posed by Hume and never answered. Brennan's statement of it is one of the pivotal points of the series and also one of his own best poetic achievements. Its five verses convey a despairing inevitability, a vertigo, that Brennan had himself clearly experienced—the poem is (as can by no means be said of all these poems) a product of experience rather than of theory.

> . . . O weary realm, O height
> the which exhausted flight
> familiar finds, home of its prompting ill!
> here, there, or there, or there,
> ever the same despair;
> rest in thy place, O fool, the heart eludes thee still.
>
> Rest—and a new abyss
> suddenly yawns, of this
> the moment sole, and yet the counterpart:
> and thou must house it, thou,
> within thy fleshly Now,
> thyself the abyss that shrinks, the unbounded
>   hermit-heart . . .

This (from 'The Watch at Midnight') is, for Brennan's own statement of the theme of *Poems 1913,* a crucial point. If no reply can be found, then the wanderer's search is indeed directed to 'no ending of the way, no home, no goal'. No man can, in fact, 'house the abyss' within his fleshly Now, and remain both conscious and human, unless he has some form of faith that there is more than his fleshly Now to oppose it. I suggest that Brennan does not, within the framework of the poem, solve this problem of the individual faced with the solipsism of human knowledge seen as individual knowledge; and that the uncertainty of the last poem in 'The Womb of Night', and the apparent loss of hope in 'The Wanderer' series, are reflections of this lack of a solution.

It is no disgrace, however, to be unable to master a conception that is by definition all but unmasterable, or to be unable to take the measure of the unmeasured. Brennan's real achievement was to look his terrible vision full in the face. She presents herself to our day perhaps even in a more final aspect than to Brennan's, but there are still very few of us who dare so fully to acknowledge and confront her, in her inescapable meaning, with our own humanity.

'To humanize the Universe'—and the challenge is extended by Eternity. It is no wonder that in spite of the bravery of his attempt, Brennan fell so far short of a task that, if it is possible of achievement, means no less than the conquering of time itself.

In the final section, 'The Wanderer', the rose image has disappeared. What is left is only the bleak light of consciousness and the winds of time. 'The deathless rose of gold'—the final fulfilment, the realization in full consciousness of man's own unity with the universe—was glimpsed only as a vision, no more than momentary; the final poem of the Lilith sequence marks its disappearance. The poem is one of Brennan's most ambiguous and negative statements:

> Because this curse is on the dawn, to yield
> her secrecy distilled of nuptial tears,
> and day dismantles, casual, nor reveres
> whate'er august our brooding dream'd reveal'd;
>
> because that night to whom we next appeal'd,
> no more gestation of inviolate spheres,
> shameless, is mimic of the day, nor fears
> the scant occurrence of her stars repeal'd:
>
> Therefore, if never in some awful heart
> a gather'd peace, impregnable, apart,
> cherish us in that shrine of steadfast fire,
>
> be these alone our care, excluding hence
> some form undesecrate of all desire,
> the wings of silence, adamantine, dense.

The whole sonnet, in its hesitating movement and its repetitive negations, seems to close off the Lilith-experience, almost to dismiss it as meaningless. The long wrestle with that subtle and ambiguous figure seems to have ended not even in defeat, but in inconclusiveness. At the end of 'The Forest of Night' we seem no nearer the 'deathless rose' than at the beginning, even less so. The wanderer seems even to have lost his belief in its possibility. Perhaps by now Brennan believed that the fight was indeed 'foredoom'd disastrous'.

It seems as though, in spite of his glimpses of the positive side of his night-goddess, Brennan was never in fact able after his encounter with her to give full credence to his earlier assertion that 'the road does lead somewhere'. She is his Muse, but she is also his Medusa, and his poem was not shield enough to protect him against her.

He had written in the dedication of a sonnet (p. 268, *The Verse of Christopher Brennan*) that to see her 'in her secret beauty' is the poet's eternal task, 'and particularly mine'. But in the end, for all his temporary possession by her image, he was not able to live up to the vastness of his own conception. He emerged from it, in 'The Wanderer' sequence, still convinced of the necessity of the search, but no longer convinced of the possibility of an end to it.

'The Wanderer' sequence, though it has been greatly admired, and with justice, has in fact a note not only of uncertainty but at times of hollow vaticination. It is where the Wanderer is most clearly speaking through Brennan's own experience that it is at its best, and perhaps only here is it really convincing. Where, in the persona of 'The Wanderer', Brennan addresses 'the souls that serve', or cries 'Dawns of the world, how I have known you all', it is right for the reader to feel a little uneasy. It is too like Brennan's own voice under the prophet's mantle; it is somehow inflated, hollow, not sufficiently human. The 'I' who speaks is not intended to be personal: this is the voice of the figure from the Cabbala: 'man is a wanderer from his birth . . . his house is builded upon the winds, and under them upon the storm'. But it is dangerous to assume too far a symbolic and universal persona— and I cannot help feeling that Brennan in this series identifies himself a little too closely with this vast generalized archetype of man—that this is less the Wanderer speaking through Brennan's lips than Brennan speaking with the voice of the Wanderer. The individual should not assume the universal; it is a dangerous expansion. The personality can disintegrate under the strain.

It is possible, I think, to argue that this is in one sense what happened to Brennan. His long and involved struggle with his Lilith—which ended inconclusively—perhaps stretched his powers beyond their limit, and allowed an over-identification with his Lear-like protagonist. In an essay he speaks of Lear as a form of the Cabbala-figure, himself a Wanderer. Shakespeare, however, who was so often right in these matters, was clear enough that Lear's wanderings were too much for his humanity: Lear was, after all, mad. To humanize the Universe is only a step away from the attempt to universalize the human; and the individual, however great his capacities, cannot become Man. If he tries to do so, he assumes an impossible burden, and loses in the end his own humanity.

Perhaps this is the explanation of the fact that during the years after the publication of *Poems 1913* Brennan so curiously failed his own vision. The war poems published as *A Chant of Doom* contain some of the most unpleasant and inflated verse produced by any war. In them Brennan's worst weaknesses come to the fore—indeed, they seem for the time to take over the whole of Brennan's carefully built-up poetic personality.

> DOOM we utter, doom we will;
> Head shall judge, and hand must kill
> —Whom? Behold him: eye in eye
> Mark him, ere we bid him die.

> Yon self-righteous bulk, 'tis he,
> The world's giant Pharisee . . .

> Pharisee, thou whited tomb,
> Mankind hath decreed thy doom.

No abuse, no condemnation, no hatred seemed enough; these poems hurl every possible curse at the German 'monster-birth of man and fiend':

> Quicklime for the felon's pit,
> Pledge of fires his forfeit lit!
> Earth nor Hell yields this no grace:
> Where shall be his resting-place?

To be in fact a great poet, certain virtues are necessary; and perhaps the basic virtue (if we remember Chaucer, Shakespeare, Dante and many others) is a kind of humility that makes the

poet capable of true sympathy with all that is human. This does
not mean permissiveness, nor even necessarily tolerance; but it
does imply a depth of understanding of oneself and of the human
possibilities of good and evil, which is the first necessity if the
poet is to pass beyond himself and see both self and world as
one. It was precisely this that Brennan had—apparently—understood as the poetic task. His Lilith was not to be blindly opposed
—the road to Eden led through understanding, not through
opposition.

'Out beyond good and evil are we blown', when that journey
is undertaken; not because good and evil no longer exist, but
because the poetic task is one which comprehends both as human.
Brennan had seen this: 'We have no right . . . to judge, to condemn, or punish, for we too are imperfect', he writes, in his
treatment of Blake (p. 93, *The Prose of Christopher Brennan*),
and again,

> Good and Evil . . . are no more ultimates than that dis-
> tinction of body and soul: in the eternal they are invalid.
> But just as we cannot yet perceive, but only believe, that
> body is a portion of soul, so we are yet caught in the draw-
> net of good and evil. In the meantime we must not set up
> to be 'holy' and sin against life.

But it is scarcely possible to read *A Chant of Doom* without
feeling that here Brennan is indeed 'setting up to be "holy",'
judging, condemning and punishing without appeal. The question whether or not the German nation indeed embodied Evil at
the time is irrelevant; what is relevant is that Brennan, of all
men, was inexcusable in the wholeheartedness of his condemnation, in his renouncing of all considerations but his own hatred.
Evil and guilt are real enough; but to attribute them wholly to
the 'other side', when that side also is human, is itself a betrayal
of the Edenic vision. It would have become him, as poet and even
as man, to have made a proper distinction between the 'eternal
foe' and its temporary and partial objectification.

The role of hanging judge is dangerous for any man; that is
why the judge is appointed by society as instrument, not as
person. Here Brennan takes it on himself, without appointment,
and without qualms. This is distasteful enough, even in those
too ignorant of moral responsibility to know what they are
doing. But we cannot believe that Brennan was ignorant of
the issues involved. We can only watch in horror while he pulls

the whole structure of his own thought about his ears. This is no abstract judgement on the principle of Evil (and even that he would once have disowned, with Blake); this is a personal judgement on a human foe.

It is just here that I think the nature of Brennan's failure to measure up to the demands of his own vision becomes clear. He has fallen into his Lilith's most obvious trap; he has made the mistake of identifying the eternal foe with the temporary wrong, as he identified the Eternal Wanderer with himself.

If there is truth in this explanation, if in his attempt at 'humanizing the Universe' Brennan faces an antagonist far too strong for him, and succeeds only in making himself inhuman, it ought also to be an explanation of the sense we have that his poetry is at too far a remove from the real immediate world of happenings, things, and persons. In effect, his Symbolism is not really symbolism at all; it much more resembles allegory. For the symbols with which he is working are already symbols before he reaches them; they are not transformations of Brennan's own, they are already one step beyond the perceived world and are conceptual. Brennan escaped at a bound from the first poetic necessity—that of seeing, hearing, feeling and undergoing the immediate flow of personal experience, before the transformation process can begin. His process of thought led him, logically and correctly, to the belief that 'the progress of art is the continual victory over matter which had been rejected as ignoble and unfit for art' (p. 171, *The Prose of Christopher Brennan*). But his choice of the 'Edenic myth', of the figure of Lilith, and of the figure of the Wanderer, as the symbols through which he sets out his theme, was a choice not of the intractable matter of his personal experience, but of what had already been tamed and made 'noble and fit for art' by other artists; his poem is a synthesis of already-existing symbols, through which Brennan expounds his philosophy of man and the universe. The poem that he writes has, in a sense, already been written; the transformation has already taken place. He has inherited its riches, he has not worked for them.

This is not to deny that the great figures and the great myths have their continual part in our temporal circumstances; nor that they need to be re-experienced, re-embodied and reinterpreted by every poet and every age. This is a very obvious truth about art. The figure of Lilith and the figure of the Wanderer are part of the whole human inheritance; the myth of Eden never loses its meaning. But such myths and figures ought never to be used as pieces in a kind of poetic chess-game, or an illustration in a philosophic history of man-versus-universe. They must be come upon by the poet—not seized upon; they must be rediscovered, always in a new and revelatory form, if they are to act as true transformers of experience. They must never be plot-characters; they must grow of themselves out of the struggle with raw experience. And I think that in an important sense *Poems 1913* is a plotted poem, a chess game, with symbols whose meaning Brennan already knew, or thought he knew.

In this context, I quote from Brennan's lecture on Mallarmé, delivered in 1904, where he speaks of Mallarmé's projected, but never completed, great poem:

> What now is the form of that art-work which is to satisfy all our spiritual needs?
>
> 1. It is a myth. Not a particular legend, but a myth resuming all the others, without date or place, a figuration of our multiple personality; the myth written on the page of heaven and earth and imitated by man with the gesture of his passions.
>
> 2. It is a drama; for nature is a drama and as Novalis had said, 'The true thinker perceives in the world a continued drama'; 'In the people all is drama'. It is the assimilation of our inmost passion to the tetralogy of the year. But a drama again, as it was a myth. There is no limited fable, no individual hero. We, who assist at it, are each of us in turn and all of us together, the hero. (p. 145, *The Prose of Christopher Brennan*)

And later, (p. 156)

> . . . poetry is not dead yet. Some time or other the great genius will come who will take up and finish what they (i.e. Mallarmé, Blake, Novalis) began.

It is hard to avoid the conclusion that here we have a backstage glimpse into the writing of *Poems 1913*, its motivation and its plot, and perhaps even into Brennan's secret opinion of its writer too.

This is no denigration of Brennan; if his opinion of himself was high, it was rightly so. His insights into literature, his scholarship and his powers of synthesis were far—very far—beyond those of many of his contemporaries. But short-cuts to a great work are treacherous. 'The myth written on the page of heaven and earth and imitated by man with all the gesture of his passions'— the *grande œuvre,* the absolute poem—there can be no short cuts to that, no plotting, no by-passing of the original struggle with sense, perception, emotion, life itself; all must be sacrificed, and first of all, perhaps, the secret conviction that the poem is in one's grasp, or can be.

This is not to say that Brennan plotted the poem with its protagonists as little more than dramatis personae. Clearly his imagination had been deeply involved in recreating the figures and the landscape of the Great Myth; and clearly too, he had a much wider and deeper grasp of their implications than might have been expected. Rather, it seems to me, the poem began in Brennan's conscious intelligence, but as it progressed took him farther and farther from his own intentions, into regions he had not foreseen. The disproportion of the Lilith sequence (which is both longer and much more complex than the other sections), and the unexpectedly hopeless note that rings through the Wanderer sequence (unexpectedly, when we remember Brennan's comparative optimism in his earlier lectures) seem unambiguously to point in this direction.

In the last of his six lectures on *Symbolism in Nineteenth Century Literature,* summing up the implications of earlier lectures, Brennan makes use of the philosophy of F.C.S. Schiller as a demonstration that 'philosophy is driven in the same direction as poetry'. Comparing Schiller's 'principle of postulation' with the Symbolist theory of correspondence, he says:

> But if the principle of postulation has any meaning at all, it means that the process has a goal. Man . . . is on a way but not an endless one: he is on the way to himself. In the second lecture it was laid down as a fact implied in all knowledge and in all poetry, that there is in us a self transcending our manifested self, and that this transcendent self is . . . a reality in dynamic relation with our imperfect but none the less real life. Well, the essence of all our experimenting is to bring this self from its latency, to make it explicit, and thereby to introduce more harmony into the world and into our consciousness . . . . (p. 165, *The Prose of Christopher Brennan)*

It is reasonable to conclude that 'The Wanderer' series was

intended to symbolize this task of man, the wanderer 'on the way to himself', and that the Wanderer himself, as symbol of the search, might be expected to have had at least a glimpse of the possibility of the way's not 'being an endless one'. In fact, however, the whole tone of 'The Wanderer' series is that man's fight is 'foredoom'd disastrous'; that man is

> the wanderer of the ways of all the worlds,
> to whom the sunshine and the rain are one
> and one to stay or hasten, because he knows
> no ending of the way, no home, no goal . . . .

Whatever may have happened to alter Brennan's attitude, between 1904 when the lectures were delivered, and 1913, it does seem clearly to have altered in the direction if not of actual despair, at least of pessimism; the Eden vision seems to have been swallowed up by the encounter with darkness. All that seems to be left of it is the search itself; and the searcher, the Wanderer, so far from being identified with man himself, seems now to be visualized as a somewhat arrogant, somewhat overweening figure, whose task apparently is that of arousing the less enlightened from their comfortable ignorance and driving them forth on a journey that even the Wanderer acknowledges to have 'no ending' and 'no goal'.

There is no overt mention at all of the 'transcendent self' which is to be made explicit and to introduce harmony; man is not even given that hope and consolation for his loss of hearth and home. We cannot help feeling that the Wanderer is not merely a somewhat uncongenial and rhetorical figure, but that he is sometimes even an over-inflated preacher, with little more than a sense of superiority over others to prove him an eternal and archetypal symbol.

It seems to me, in fact, that the poem, taken as a whole, represents a second loss of faith, this time in the possibility of man's attaining, by his own powers, the realization of self and the humanization of the universe, to which Brennan had turned as a substitute for his early Catholicism; and that this second disillusionment has something to do with the violence of his later reaction to the German aggression.

The poems written between 1923 and 1932, first under the influence of his brief and tragic second love affair, later from the depths of his unhappiness after 'Vie's' death, and his own personal poverty, are much more immediately human and even lyrical than *Poems 1913*. Few as they are, they make Brennan much more real to us as a man, and more sympathetic, than do the earlier poems. The final brief 'A Jingle or Drowsy Chime', written in 1932, not long before his death, closes the circle that his whole work draws, in a gentleness and quiet acceptance of both 'the antient woe' and its transcending. It is a final note or epigraph perhaps, to a life whose dominant note was of recurring attainment and loss, but which seems to have closed, if not in happiness, at least in all-embracing peace.

Note: Number references on pages 85 and 87 are to poem numbers in *The Verse of Christopher Brennan* (Angus & Robertson, 1960).

CHAPTER VII

The Affirmation of Hugh McCrae

AT THE same time that Brennan was working on his poems—those poems which for the first time proved that Australia was part of Western civilization and could afford poetry in place of nationalism—quite another kind of assertion of this fact was being made by quite another kind of poet. It was in the early years of the century that Hugh McCrae began to publish the poems which Slessor, nearly a generation later, was to call 'blossoms wrenched from sweet and deadly branches'.

McCrae himself observed later in a letter to a friend that 'when I began to write, Poetry wore petticoats'. Certainly in Australia, except for Brennan's verse, this was the case. Moreover, Australia's poetic history was one of solemnity. Harpur had taken his poetry seriously; Kendall had tried to do the same; Brennan most certainly took the same high view of the function of the poet that Harpur had done. Gordon's ballads were popular, certainly, but even Gordon's reckless devil-may-care attitude was a response rather to despair than to joy. Now, for the first time in Australia, with McCrae and with Neilson, a carol began. Rhyming for rhyming's sake, phrase-making out of pure joy or love, broke through the nineteenth-century conventions, the solemn nationalism, the political protest and the ideal utopianism.

McCrae's first book, *Satyrs and Sunlight,* was published in 1910, Neilson's not until after the war. But though McCrae perhaps reached his peak sooner, both were writing at the same time; from the end of the nineteenth century (Neilson's first poem in the *Bulletin* appeared in 1896) until the end of the 'thirties. The two voices together—one so robust and resilient, one gentle and even vague, but sometimes so piercingly beautiful—make for us a chorus that is the springtime of Australian poetry; that might be thought of perhaps as the equivalent here of the Latin medieval lyricists, in European literary history.

Yet their lives were very different, and it is not recorded that they ever met or corresponded, though each admired the other's verse. Alike in certain things—each an irrepressible rhymer, neither a philosopher, each more adept in feeling than in thought, and neither a sophisticate, there is a sense in which each of them complements and counterpoints the other's faults and weaknesses.

McCrae, the son of a poet (as Neilson himself was), was a man of sufficient education, though he was not, like Brennan, a scholar, and would have rejected with horror the notion of being considered one. Perhaps the most significant happening in his youth, apart from his decision to give up studying to be an architect, and write poetry instead, was his coming into the ambit of another young man who, though not himself a poet, could be struck into enthusiasm by poetry, and could himself strike sparks from poets—the youthful Norman Lindsay.

Just how much Lindsay's ideas gave to McCrae, how much McCrae gave to Lindsay, it would be interesting but probably immaterial to know. What Lindsay did for McCrae, was, as it were, to go before him with a fiery sword of conviction and pugnacity, attacking the wowsers, and clear a space in which McCrae, the singer, could produce his poetry.

One of McCrae's most important early poems, 'The Deathless Gods' (*Lone Hand*, 2 Aug., 1909) (which is not republished in the 1962 edition of his poetry) seems to be a source poem for much of Lindsay's own painting and for a good deal of the poetry that followed:

> O, often I have seen in these new days
> The deathless gods, all naked, without hoods,
> As some old carving, pregnant with the rays
> Of noon . . . alive, and singing in the woods . . .
> Syrinx, to me, unfolded in my hands,
> And, once again, became a laughing girl . . .
> Within my bosom I have felt the strands
> Let down by Daphne from her forehead-curl . . . .

But though it is a poem that anticipates and includes, and thereby makes redundant, some of the theories of the later *Vision* movement (it was included in the *Vision* anthology of 1923), McCrae was still unsure of his poetic way. Another poem published in the same year, 'Faithlessness', has all the melodrama and shoddy romanticism of an imitation Swinburne—

> Heaven curse your inmost soul
> And take and keep from you, all peace and happiness,

And may your days be burdened with long weariness
Until your death-bell's toll—

to quote one verse. It would not be worth referring to this early poem, which was not perpetuated in later collections, except that it shows something of where McCrae's weaknesses lay and gives a clue to how the Lindsayan ethos strengthened and pruned his imagery and feeling. For McCrae is never at his best in dramatic moods or in dealing directly with experience. Between the poet and his world some kind of disciplining system, some order of imagery through which experience could be translated, was interposed by the Greek legends, the fauns and satyrs and nymphs and goddesses, of the Lindsayan pantheon. So the poem 'Ambuscade' —one of the most vividly seen and muscularly phrased of all McCrae's poems—though it was published almost at the same time as 'Faithlessness', marks a poetic advance, not only in McCrae's work but in Australian poetry itself, that amounts to a wholly new level of expression.

What makes 'Ambuscade' such a surprising poetic achievement is the visual and sensual element that carries it from the first line to the last. Like so much of McCrae's best work, it seems unfinished, part of something larger: it begins with the conjunction 'Or'; it ends with less than a half-line. But from the first image of the 'black centaurs, statuesquely still' to the last violent irruption of the stallions who come to the rescue of their mares, 'A roar of hooves, a lightning view of eyes/Redder than fire, of long straight whistling manes . . .' all is seen, all is felt, as though it happened under our eyes; we share in the very sensations of the centaurs as they 'feel their hearts—besieged with blood— stagger like anvils when the sled-blows rain/Shower on shower in persistent flood . . .'

Nothing so vivid, so immediate, so urgent in its imagery, had yet broken into the earnest but not sensuous scene of Australian poetry. It must have looked as though this extraordinarily powerful poet would burn his way through all the conventions, the limitations, the littlenesses of the society he was born into, and go on to write some of the most splendid poetry ever written.

It did not happen. In McCrae we have a poet, sometimes of extraordinary beauty and joy, sometimes of incorrigible carelessness and airiness, sometimes of brilliantly decorative imagery, sometimes of almost domestic whimsy and tender self-mockery.

We have a poet to love and admire and be proud of, but not a
great man. The springtime of his verse remained a spring; it
somehow did not mature into the full compass of summer,
autumn and winter. Even in his latest poems, McCrae still gam-
bols, rhymes for the sake of rhyming, makes his delightful
arabesques of language for the sheer joy of making:

> Pretty pittosporum,
> Drowsy with nidor,
> Haunt of the wasp or em-
> Broidering spider . . .
>
> ('Scentimentaliste')

Yet it is this joy that makes McCrae a poet ('Poetry, an art
practised by the ancients'), and in the most characteristic of his
poems it leaves its track in every springing line and sentence; a
kind of caracoling glee quite physical in its effect on the reader.
This is a quality that cannot be imitated or faked by any amount
of technical accomplishment or concentrated hard work; either
the heart sings or it does not, and McCrae is an incomparable
singer.

> Water-brooks dance through the meadows,
> Little fishes
> Have their wishes,
> Shadows kiss their fellow-shadows.
>
> Ponies shake and leap for pleasure,
> Turning over
> In the clover,
> Fat, and full of summer treasure . . .
>
> ('Song for Pierrot')

And even, in perhaps the most sincere and moving poem he ever
wrote:

> She looked on me with sadder eyes than Death,
> And, moving through the large autumnal trees,
> Failed like a phantom on the bitter breath
> Of midnight; and the unillumined seas
> Roared in the darkness out of centuries . . .
>
> I seek her in the labyrinthine maze
> Of stars unravelling their golden chain,
> And, from my cavern, mark the lightning blaze
> A pathway for her down the singing rain.
> In vain, in vain; she cannot come again.
>
> ('Never Again')

—even here where McCrae, for once, feels deeply and convinces us that he feels deeply, he cannot help making phrases, following on the track of rhymes, decorating the simple basic utterance with garlands of stars and singing rain.

This quality makes McCrae's books a delight to read—a ride on the swings and merry-go-rounds of youth, with fireworks exploding round and the gayest of companions; a companion, too, whose invention and delight seldom fail, and in whose company sordid realities vanish and Life with a capital letter becomes the only value to be regarded.

> Why should I philosophise?
> Being happy, I am wise . . .

There are disharmonies in this music, certainly. Even satyrs must die; there is darkness outside the fair-ground, and beautiful women are in the end one of death's perquisites. But on the whole McCrae retains his balance and serenity. Few of us are lucky enough to be able to write poems on our seventieth birthdays; and surely very few can still praise their youth in such youthful lines as McCrae uses in 'Happiness';

> So strong; so fresh; and wild with joy;
> This morning's bird wings round his tree,
> His tree:
> > then, throated like a boy,
>
> High treble clef—tra-lee! tra-lee;
> Awakes his darling back to life
> To be, another day, his wife.
>
> O happy, happy, handsome boy;
> Through whom I live young times anew;
> A married child, once more—like you!

If we call McCrae a limited singer, we might well wish such limitations for ourselves and most other people.

Nevertheless, his limitations do prevent McCrae from being, what once he seemed likely to be, a great or even a finally impressive poet. He was perfectly right, in a certain sense, to refuse to 'philosophise' and to prefer the wisdom of happiness; but happiness, of the senses at any rate, does not take him very far along the poet's road. When he tries to take his stand outside his mythologies and fertile inventions, as now and then he does, nothing much comes of it. His poems—his attempts at serious poems—are then generally about women ('The Phantom Mistress', 'Metamorphosis', 'The Wedding Ring', 'The End of Desire', 'The Bridegroom'); but about McCrae's women there is something curiously unreal. They are thought of only as objects, not as subjects; even in 'The Phantom Mistress', which is supposedly told by a scorned wife, there is only just enough reality in the teller to keep the story alive.

And since his women are objects—generally objects of desire—the emphasis is always on external attributes, richly and splendidly described, so that all the woman is there except the woman herself. One cannot help feeling that any of them, put to the test of reality, would vanish like the temptress in 'The End of Desire',

> I took her closely, but while yet
> I trembled, vassal to my lust,
> Lo!—Nothing but some sarcenet,
> Deep-buried in a pile of dust.

Here, I think, lies the curious disharmony we sometimes hear in the music of the fairground, the sudden harshness that disturbs the tender notes. Women are either kissed, or killed. When something happens, in McCrae's poetry, it is something violent; knives are drawn on the other side of the rose-trellis. Examples are 'Mandragore', 'The Murder Night', 'The Phantom Mistress', 'Now Do the Entering Trumpets Sound', 'Gallows Marriage', 'Rescue',—even 'Morning', with its tender and lovely recollections of a light love . . .

> Ah frail and sadly beautiful—

ends with the couplet:

> But I must end this play and go—
> Or choke you with your pillow-lace.

These are the limits of McCrae's gamut—tenderness and a kind of destructiveness, both of them physical in their source, so that sensuousness in his verse seems to equate itself rather too much with sensuality, and joy with unthinking egoism.

Perhaps it is just here that McCrae's failure, in the end, to be a great poet, in spite of his remarkable gifts, becomes most explicable. Great poets contain this sensuality and destructiveness,

ɪᴅ

but in great poetry both are subservient to other ends than themselves; they are transmuted and related to their opposites, spirituality and creativeness. McCrae's range is not so wide; it is as though he escaped from the responsibility of humanity and chose instead the satyr-dream of the young man he never ceased to be.

> I love to lie under the lemon
>   That grows by the fountain;
> To see the stars flutter and open
>   Along the blue mountain.
> To dream that the mythic wood-women
>   Each brown as the honey
> The bees took their toll of from Hybla
>   On days that were sunny,
> Come parting the hedge of my garden . . .
>
> ('Fantasy')

But the dream, however vivid McCrae's imagination may make it, is not in the end real enough to last very long.

> So I wake, and eagerly listen—
>   But only the fountain,
> Still sleeping and sobbing, complains at
>   The foot of the mountain.

And so with the poetry itself, which charms and delights and sometimes troubles us, but has not the weight of meaning to attach itself to life. It troubles us, perhaps, most because in its affirmation of life it seems somehow to deny life. The wood-women, the centaurs, the fauns, the medieval ballads, even the love-songs ('The Elves o' Spring', 'Sensual Love', 'The Secret House', 'Below the Moon', 'The Return') for all the splendid immediacy of their imagery, seem somehow neither more nor less real than the wild spring procession of his poem 'Bacchanalia', with its satyrs and cupids and panthers and eunuchs and women following their fat Silenus,

> Into the night I saw the rabble float,
> And there remained not one, or man or beast . . .

Yet it is true that McCrae is both an important and a climacteric figure in Australian poetry—that, almost in spite of himself, he has meant a great deal in our poetic history.

To read McCrae's poems against the background of what was

being written in Australia in the early 1900s, is to begin to understand both the necessity for just these particular poems, and the
pressures which, it may be, prevented McCrae from writing more
and greater poetry. No society can be as cruelly narrow and conventional as a small and isolated community intent on respectability and the acquirement of wealth; and it was against just such
a background that Norman Lindsay began his fight for freedom
and McCrae his production of poetry. The violent opposition
and disapproval that was inevitably aroused, Lindsay diverted
mainly to his own head by his fearless diatribes against the parochialism that he saw everywhere round him.

Unfortunately, like many other controversialists with a fundamentally good cause, he spoiled it by rejecting everything that
did not tend entirely to confirm his views, and in particular he
cut himself off from the school of writers represented by Lawson
and O'Dowd and Furphy—the school he dubbed 'nationalist'.
In doing so he rejected—and McCrae with him—a great deal
that might have served to anchor McCrae more firmly to
some kind of rock-bottom, and to give his work a basis broader
than McCrae was ever able to find. For McCrae was too airy and
too elusive a personality to do his anchoring for himself.

As 'Ambuscade' and a few other poems proved, the mythology
and imagery that Lindsay helped to provide did form a channel
through which McCrae's gifts of visualization and pure song
flowed into poetry. But even then, the poetry was fragmentary—
brief glowing splintered visions of a world that never became
quite real.

Indeed, it scarcely could become real, since for Australia it
had never been so, and for Greece and Italy its reality was long
past. And even for Greece and Italy it had not been real in the
sense in which it was now being used; it had been a product of,
not a stimulus to, a way of looking at the world. Lindsay and
McCrae, and later the whole *Vision* movement, were in fact
putting the cart so far before the horse that the two had even
lost contact. A culture is not initiated in any country by imposing
on it the incidental products of the culture of another country
and another time. What is produced is only a decoration, beautiful perhaps but in the end forced, unnatural and unsuitable for
its time and place.

The value of Lindsay and McCrae was, however, greater than
the value of the notions they tried to impose, at least during the

decade of their best work, that leading to the beginning of the
Great War. It was a time when any kind of vivifying and affirmative influence would have been doubly important; the days of
pioneering were over, the cities were growing, Australia was becoming self-important and the pieties of convention and respectability were strengthening. Against this background McCrae's
poems shine like jewels, and Lindsay's affirmations of the beauty
of sex and the necessity for artistic freedom are as stirring as a
bugle-call.

But once the decade had ended and the Great War had begun,
something new had entered Australian life, even though except
for a few poems by Leon Gellert, Vance Palmer and Furnley
Maurice, and a few novels, little came of those years for Australian writing. What happened then did in fact make an enormous
difference in the minds and hearts of many. Australian jingoism
during the Boer War had sickened the intelligent, including
Brennan, whose poems *The Burden of Tyre* fiercely denounced
it; but Gallipoli and the losses in France brought home to many
people more sobering truths. Australians for the first time had a
chance to realize that their country was part of a world and
shared its perils, and should also share its responsibilities. The
tragic sight of Brennan, betraying his own insights and art in
violent invective against the German enemy, was a warning
against easy patriotism, even for those whose imaginations were
not strong enough to 'besmirch blood all over the soul', as Owen
put it; but merely to withdraw from the war, as Lindsay did,
was only the other side of that patriotism, and led him into as
frustrating a cul-de-sac as Brennan's.

Perhaps it was Lindsay's attitude to the war that led to Mc-
Crae's also taking no notice, practically, of what happened in
those years. There is very little poetry of the war years, either by
soldiers or civilians, except for the few I have mentioned; but
it is noticeable that McCrae's post-war poetry is progressively
lighter, more flippant, more domestic in its note, and that he
more and more disclaimed any involvement with the world
around him. The epigraph to 'The Ship of Heaven', that airiest,
most impossibly delightful of operettas, is characteristic:

> Obscurantists find no rebus here; play-field only for butterfly
> nonsense dreamed by Jeremy Jessamy below a haycock, 'all
> on a sommer's dae'.

For McCrae, perhaps, the 1914-18 war was a decisive watershed; if he had ever hoped to influence his world or change its puritanical cruelties and pomposities by his own sensuously joyful poems, that hope must have been put away during those years of unprecedented fury and hatred. So he went ('retreated' is not the word, for no poet has remained so undefeated by time) farther into his own world, the world of the poem.

> Here will I lie
>   Under the sky,
> Green trees above me,
> All birds to love me . . .
>   Nature and I.
>
> Wish me good den
>   And leave me then . . .
> This sweet forest wind
> Is more to my mind
>   Than cities or men . . .

And *Satyrs and Sunlight* remained his main, as it was his first achievement.

Perhaps his most characteristic production is the series of fragmentary scenes collected under the name of 'Joan of Arc'. It is his only large-scale attempt at construction in poetry, and splendid and vital as the separate passages are, they are disunited and (except for the first long poem, 'Introduction') unfinished. Moreover, the only completed scenes are scarcely to be called dramatic. The speeches by Orleans and Isabelle are wholly poetry, descriptive, discursive, passionate, but probably barely playable on stage. The first scene contains, besides, some passionate love-making which in itself would make the scene quite unpresentable in public. The second scene contains an impossibly complicated part for a dog (the King's hunting-hound) and ends with Orleans's hands being cut off by his enemies. The third scene is brief but terrible (*Enter the mad King, carrying the bleeding hand of Orleans*) is the first stage- direction; the last (*He knocks upon the door with the Duke's hand*). The fourth scene appears to have nothing to do with the first three or the Introduction, and is unfinished.

It is—in a sense—true to say, as Slessor does in his appreciation of McCrae as a poet, (*Southerly*, 3, 1956) that the fragmentary nature of McCrae's achievement does not interfere with the quality of the poetry. But in another sense it is not true. We may admire and enjoy what McCrae has given us; but we ought to admit that the very splendour and achievement of the fragments we have make the failure to complete them more deplorable. This is a case where it is excellent to have a giant's power, but tragic not to use it like a giant.

The unplayable nature of the play is not a relevant excuse; McCrae must in any case have realized that it was never likely to be acted, before he began to write it. What is relevant is the fact that McCrae abandoned it. What is never completed cannot be judged; and however much admiration 'Joan of Arc' deserves as it stands, it is in the end a signpost to McCrae's limitations.

So with advancing years the poems become briefer and more momentaneous.* More and more they become epigrams, quatrains, scraps. McCrae's felicities are perhaps even more felicitous for being as frail as passing butterflies, but less and less with the years do we find the marvellous visualizations of the early poems.

But there is one poem of these later years (and, sadly, it too is called 'Fragment') which in itself sums up and magnificently contains the essence of McCrae. It has the haunting strangeness, the visual quality, the sensuous splendour, and in addition a tautness and perfection of diction that makes us sigh afresh that McCrae achieved so much—and so much less than might have been.

> As if stone Caesar shook
>   His staff across the wet
> Black passages, and took
>   With marble eyes a yet
> Unconquered gaze of Rome;

—what more satisfying image of the petrification of authority? And a strange depth is given to it by those 'wet black passages' that catch at one's attention like a clue in a mystery story.

And a mystery story the poem is; for the movement continues from Caesar to the cypress boughs that still

> Stood thick about his home
>   As when he bent his brows
> Three centuries before
>   Across some Gordian knot
> His civic business wore—
>   *Hic jacet* the whole lot.

* I admit to inventing this word. However, it is made in accordance with the rules, I think, and has a meaning that isn't conveyed by 'momentary'; what I mean about these poems is that they *spring from* the moment, not that they only occupy a moment, and the suffix '-an' conveys this.—J.W.

Now enters the image of violence that is never far from Mc-
Crae's surface:

> What hammer fell? And whose
> The crushed white paper skull
> Mixed in the side-bank ooze
> Of mighty Tiber? . . .

But the image is rejected in one of the most extraordinarily
perfected and sustained sentences in the whole of McCrae's work:

> . . . Dull
> The mind and hand that first
> Wrought sparth and sinker-blade
> Knobbed clubs and spikes to burst
> The fairy spirit from the shade
> He entered in, when through a mesh
> Of aching tissues, blood to blood
> And flesh on softly folding flesh
> Man with his woman made a flood
> Of kings and weavers, so the world
> Might fling about in sunny ways,
> Some to the hunt, and some, up-curled,
> Stung silent in the martyr's blaze.

This whole poem is an example of the sudden firing as it
were, upward from level to level, that can only take place when
in a poet his major life-preoccupations suddenly fuse into their
inevitable relationship, in images and poetic sentences that are
forever unalterable and eternal. Nothing more haunting has been
written in Australia than this.

Goethe, that bridge between two eras, once told Eckermann
that the modern critical-analytical attitude to literature was
destructive of creativity.

> Daily criticisms in fifty different places, and gossip caused by
> them, prevent the appearance of any sound production. He
> who does not keep aloof from all this, and isolate himself by
> main force, is lost. Through the bad, chiefly negative aes-
> thetical and critical tone of the journals, a sort of half-culture
> finds its way into the masses; but to productive talent it is a
> noxious mist, a dropping poison, which destroys the tree of
> creative power . . .

What was great in McCrae, I think, was fragmented and frustrated by just this anti-creativeness around him. He was above all
a creative poet, a singer, rare and somehow medieval in his attitudes as in his poetry. Theory was anathema to him; and it may

be that he chuckled ruefully at the theorization that went on around his own songs, even as he took cover from it. There is little place in our world for sensuous joy and its carolling; the world and the critics soon sour the blood of youth into a political or academic vinegar.

McCrae refused to be soured; but in the result, the price he paid was a frustration of his personality and of his poetry, a kind of inability to grow beyond his own youth. To the end, it is the values of youth he asserts, and though 'being happy, [he is] wise' it is the wisdom of rejection, not of affirmation. He knew what he did not want, with a true instinct; what he did want remained the same at seventy as at thirty—

> Friended by the great Creator,
> Through his fingers glad to run
> Among the flowers in the sun
> All my day; and then, at e'en
> Die for joy that I have been.   ('Oy! Oy!')

This was indeed to 'isolate oneself by main force'; but not in the sense that Goethe meant; it is not isolation in order to meditate, create and work, but to live to and for oneself. So it was not, in the end, a creative isolation, but a selfish one.

Well—charm is selfish, though selfishness is not always charm; and bound to our wheel of responsibility, we love and respond to the spells of McCrae's airy song. How much good it would do the 'sorry lads' of literature to spin off on one or two such butterfly flights with their psyches! Perhaps it does not matter, after all, that McCrae never became a great poet—he was a poet, and that is much more than we can say of many writers with a greater sense of responsibility to their fellows, yet who in the end maybe serve them less.

For music is the greatest gift, perhaps, that can be made to the world; and as McCrae recedes into the distance his perfect cadences still hang on the air:

> Faint through the fluttering
> Fall of a flute divine
> Softly the cellos sing:
> 'Colombine, Colombine'.
>
> . . . . .
>
> Softly the 'cellos sing
> 'Colombine' . . .
> 'Colombine' . . .

CHAPTER VIII

John Shaw Neilson

∽

FOR THE poets before Brennan, their Australianism was inescapable, a straitjacket. It meant that they had no poetic terms of reference, since the English terms no longer applied, and since until they were invented (which is the same as to say, discovered) there could be no Australian terms at all. It meant also that a writer's very existence, as writer, was so questionable as to make him fair game for any critic, literate or illiterate, and to make his champions, if there were any, fair game too.

It was certainly that crippling pressure that forced the special note of Australian writing, the rhetoric and selfconsciousness that marked Harpur, Kendall, Brennan, and even in our own time the earlier work of FitzGerald and some of the poets who followed him. Rhetoric need not be a fault in poetry, in spite of our present bias against it; but the rhetoric of Australian poetry has been of a special kind. Harpur set its key, with his vocal awareness of responsibility, isolation and dedication; Brennan widened its reference to include the whole of the poet's attitude to the universe. It came from opposition, loneliness and defiance, and led more often than not to personal tragedy. Harpur died in distress at the neglect of his work; Kendall, Lawson and Brennan were each in their own way made miserable by unreconciled opposition to their personal or spiritual circumstances. Selfconsciousness was basically, in one way or another, the theme of each, and few of us are strong enough to stand a great deal of that.

But in the early part of the century there appeared a new note in Australian poetry. A late spring seemed to break out in a literature which had never had a youth. If ever there was a time when poetry here has been not 'literature', not 'culture', but simply song, it came and went briefly in the work of two poets, McCrae and Neilson.

But even here a reservation at once appears. The achievement of Hugh McCrae, which looks at first glance as joyously simple and sensuous as that of the medieval Latin lyricists, becomes less simple when it is examined. We begin to feel it more and more as an artefact, involving a deliberate rejection of certain attitudes in favour of others. Certainly it is not the outcome of a pose, but rather of a stance taken up in full knowledge of what McCrae wanted and what he chose to leave out of the reckoning. McCrae knew more of the world than he wished to tell, and his cry

> This sweet forest wind
> Is more to my mind
> Than cities or men—

was rather a rejection of one side of life, than an affirmation of life itself.

Perhaps this is why, in McCrae's verse, he himself is so inescapably present: why even the best of it leaves us feeling the faint undertone of insistence and invention. The bonhomie of the later verses in particular seems to be the bonhomie of the charming and successful confidence man. However delightfully fashioned, the verse *is* still fashioned; it does not lift us beyond ourselves, as Shaw Neilson does in poems like 'The Orange Tree'.

Neilson, unlike McCrae, believed wholly in his own poetry, and this allows him to speak, at his best, with the simplicity of such writers as produced 'The Maid in the Moor', or 'It was a lover and his lass', or 'The Echoing Green'. The more we read of his poetry—even though at first, knowing that it was written in our own century, we may reject it as childish or naive—the more its special note, the particular clarity of its inner truth, rings clear and unmistakable.

Written in our own century, yes; but it would be a mistake to imagine that poetry of this kind is tied to time. A famous psychologist once pointed out that in any age only a very few minds can be called truly modern, the great bulk are half a century or more behind them, and a few are almost untouched by the happenings of their own time—much as the peasant's life is still lived near the industrial cities of Europe. Neilson's mind was of this timeless order. The words 'sophisticated' and 'unsophisticated' have no meaning if we set them near his poetry.

Yet in spite of this, there has been a curious clash of opinion among critics about Neilson's poetry, and what it is and does. Douglas Stewart voices the more popular notion of Neilson as a natural rhymer, a kind of survival from the days when poetry was a matter of course among the uneducated (if such days ever really existed): that he sang 'as the birds sing', almost unconscious of his art. His gift, says Stewart in *The Flesh and the Spirit,* 'comes from the sky, a natural purity and simplicity of style, and all the poet has to do is to take down the words as they arrive'. Yet another critic, A. D. Hope, reviewing Neilson in *Southerly* VI, 4, 1945, calls his poetry 'literary', 'studied', 'mannered', 'with rhythms of epicene delicacy'. Neilson, Hope says, 'employs self-conscious and artificial literary idiom . . . charming, feminine in its sensibility, exotically poetical'.

Making all allowance for the difference in approach between these two critics, this remains an extremely odd opposition of views. How can Hope and Stewart be talking about the same poetry? Yet anyone who has read Neilson thoroughly cannot help feeling that while both critics miss the essential point, yet both have hold of a part of the truth. To reconcile them, it is necessary to go beyond both criticisms to a larger view of Neilson and his work.

The fact is that Neilson finally escapes from all summary attempts to catch and label him. One verse may do to show how maddeningly difficult it is to find him—the verse about the lizard in the poem titled 'The Bard and the Lizard' (a title, incidentally, probably foisted on the poem by A. G. Stephens, since Neilson seldom, if ever, used the pretentious term 'bard', preferring 'singer' or 'poet').

> As green as the light on a salad
> He leans in the shade of a tree:
> He has the good breath of a ballad,
> The strength that is down in the sea.

The similes here spring straight from a perception as unclouded and unselfconscious as that in a child's picture. They sound so odd that at first we think they make no more adult sense than such a picture might. But 'as green as the light on a salad'—that is caught exactly from the green glow of the lizard's scales; the word 'leans' gives us the angle of the lizard's body; and the last two lines are pure Neilson, vaguely 'romantic' at first reading but luminous when looked at carefully. The ballad is old and simple and unchanging; it has the strength of primitivity, of simplicity and age, as do the scaled fish, the scaled lizard, persisting in their old primeval shapes into a world of far more complex beings. The comparisons are true and meaningful, but they do not sound so. They sound, as Hope puts it, 'literary', 'mannered', 'poetical'; they sound invented, but they are the simple record of a perception.

This illustrates the quality in Neilson that frustrates and confuses the intellectual critic, and takes his poetry beyond the region where snap literary judgements apply. Such a vision, such similes, are neither a gift from heaven to a receptive soul, nor a 'self-conscious and artificial literary idiom'. They spring from a level on which the selfconscious writer cannot work, a level to which Cézanne sought patiently all his life to return, or to attain: the level of unsullied contact with the object, of a vision, not indeed childish (for Neilson was a man who knew very well the pains and penalties of adulthood) but unclouded by the demands of the ego.

I think this is Neilson's real secret—the unshieldedness of his inner eye. Lacking what almost all men require to drive them on—an idea of self and its importance, to which everything must be referred to test its value—he was free to accept his perceptions and use them without betraying their immediacy. The light fell on him unfiltered. From that fact, perhaps, comes his chief fault, his lack of self-criticism which led to occasional banality; but from it also come those phrases and cadences which strike home with so surprising a twist of the knife, or touch off a flare of light by which we see again something we have not seen since childhood.

> An evil time is done.
> Again, as someone lost in a quaint parable,
> Comes up the Sun.
>
> ('Break of Day')

Or, of the violet,

> Shy one, I said, you can take me away in a breath,
> But I like not the coat that you come in—the colour of death.
>
> ('I Spoke to the Violet')

Or, of the parting friends,

> Dimly we taste the old,
> The pitiless meal of Death.
>
> ('The Hour of Parting')

If this is the central fact about Neilson, it is also the explanation of our curiously double-sided reaction to him—sometimes patronizing, sometimes over-praising, sometimes merely scornful, but always tacitly uneasy. The capacity to be naked to life, to meditate rather than judge, to respond rather than to choose, is something from which in our noisy and dangerous civilization we recoil in anxiety. Neilson lacks a sense of self-preservation; and this is something that the man of today begins to develop so early in life that he no longer knows how much of his true self this sense is walling off from experience, or how difficult it is to step outside it.

It is from this elusive difference between Neilson and ourselves that our difficulty in 'placing' his work arises. If Neilson is a man without a mask, without an ego to be defended or to defend, then everything we say about his poetry tends to be a half-truth, because it is not in our arena that his poetry operates. We can hear what Neilson is saying—our difficulty is to understand it.

For this reason, the intellectual critic will always remain uncomfortable with Neilson. The critical approach to a poem implies that the poem has been constructed by someone who knows what criticism is and is working with that knowledge, however sub-consciously, in mind. It is therefore a useful if not perfect tool when we are dealing with almost any poet from Ralegh onward for whom the element of craft and intellect plays an important part in poetry; but it can scarcely be applied to, for instance, 'Clerk Saunders' or 'The Cherry-tree Carol', which work on a somewhat different level.

There is, too, something disconcerting to intellectual pretensions in a poet who so firmly refuses to be discussed in ordinary terms. There is something about him which reminds us of the difference between the child's outlook and the man's (children, too, can be disconcerting, showing up adult self-esteem). It is almost in self-defence that we call his poetry sentimental and immature, and say that the love he sings of is that of an adolescent, who has yet to learn the real problems and fulfilments of human love. If we think, in comparison, of Hugh McCrae's far robuster and more precise love-songs:

> Her heavy hair, as smoke blown down
> Athwart the fields of plenteousness;
> Her folded lips, her placid frown,
> Her insolence of nakedness—

it is easy to mistake Neilson's gentle mistiness for impotent abstraction. We miss the deeper note of the body, in his poetry, and do not see that the love he sings of is not of the same order as the physical and sensual love hymned by McCrae.

If we do not realize this, our hasty judgement betrays us into further mistakes. We may even go on to deny Neilson a mature attitude to his art, imagining that it springs from the same source as the art of children, which charms us, not by its solution of difficulties, but by its innocence in not knowing that the difficulties exist. Or, seeing that in fact there is both art and labour in his work, we swing to the opposite error and call it epicene and mannered. The swing from one misjudgement to its opposite is due to our failing to understand that it is possible to be truly adult yet lack selfconsciousness, to be an artist yet retain the vision of a child.

Neilson's life story as we know it seems to lend colour to this kind of patronizing view of his work. The poverty-stricken selector's son, the clumsy labourer so short-sighted that he could not even read, riding his cart-horse to work on neighbours' farms, wearing cobbled incongruous clothes, working willingly for a pittance and sharing it uncomplainingly with his family—the picture is as comically rustic as we can imagine. He grew old at his work like a plough-horse, and was only rescued by friends who found him a job little higher than that of an office boy, in the detested city. His poetic ambitions might never have carried him farther than the columns of the local newspaper, if the journalist and critic A. G. Stephens had not backed and encouraged him. As for Stephens's judgements on his work, though he knew them to be sometimes unsound, he accepted them with gentle humility.

That is the obvious picture of Neilson the man; but like most other assessments of him, it leaves out something important, the core of the poet Shaw Neilson. He was a man as dignified as he was shy, as self-assured as he was awkward—a man who could write with perfect conviction:

> Good fellow of the song,
> Be not too dismal; it is you and I
> And a few others lift the world along.
>
> ('Speech to a Rhymer')

It is a most Neilsonian paradox that, though he was almost an archetype of the downtrodden labourer, and though he has written indignant and pitiful poems about the human misery

that results from greed and oppression ('The Long Week-end',
'The Poor can Feed the Birds') he has never been claimed with
any assurance by the writers of the 'class-struggle' as one of themselves. Perhaps they are as little at home with him as any. Hatred
was not in his gamut, though he was too clear-sighted to love the
human race as such; and he was hopelessly undoctrinaire.

Yet it was not that Neilson lacked pride—of a certain kind. In
spite of his courteous deference and gratitude to Stephens, he
often had a clearer perception of the worth of his verses than his
mentor did: he seldom allowed any falsity to creep in with
Stephens's criticisms and amendments. Of 'Song for a Honey-
moon', for instance, he says:

> He gave me many valuable hints, and in one or two stanzas
> put in lines of his own. Most of these I threw out . . . We
> argued a good deal over these lines, and taking into account
> our lifelong friendship, I gave way in several instances.
> Honestly, however, I think that I would have put in a
> better line myself.
>
> One stanza of 'Sheedy' was altered very considerably with-
> out me being consulted. Had I been consulted I could have
> done the alterations much better. Many years after this A.G.
> complained about this particular stanza. He did not like it.
> I pointed out that he had himself altered this without asking
> me.[1]

Not even Shelley had a higher notion of the poet's value to
the world than Neilson did ('chief messenger of light')—though
Neilson's basis for it was not the same as Shelley's. Nor did he
lack a clear vision of the greed, spite and ignorance of the world;
he was never a sentimentalist about his fellow-men, though he
was occasionally so about their accidental qualities. But, setting
poetry above politics, he seems never to have been betrayed into
the erosive attitudes of hatred or bitterness, preferring—even too
much preferring—the quietness in which his perceptions most
easily flowered and his songs were made. He hovered in certain
respects on the edge of what is called 'real life'; and perhaps the
fact that his point of view was always a little marginal, a little
short-sighted, gives his perception of truth its curious angle, its
revealing lights and blurring mists.

The light by which he saw and the truth he sang of were the

1 James Devaney, *Shaw Neilson*, Angus & Robertson, 1944, p. 86

simplest and most elemental light and truth, and the most rhymed-over. His was the age-old poetic starting-point, the rite of spring—the recurrence of love and birth, and the dark background of death beyond them. That is such old stuff that to the ignorant eye it is better left alone, for nothing new can possibly be said about it.

How, then, does Neilson so often manage to make it new?— new, in a few of his poems, as though the world had really come full circle, shed its winters and its disillusions and begun over again; as though love had become possible, not as a repetition of an old story, but as a revelation and a meaning?

Here we return to that paradox, that Neilson writes always of love and the lover, yet without any of the fleshly immediacy of a writer like McCrae. Surely it is not possible to speak of love with any conviction if one has not been deeply and violently involved in love's human implications, burned by its flame and scarred by its withdrawal? Yet, as with the rest of life, Neilson seems always to have stood a little aside from the personal involvement of love. What gives him the right to speak of it is not experience, but vision.

For the love that Neilson celebrates, like the spring that is its physical correlate, is neither individual nor mortal. Both, to him, are in a sense symbolic rather than actual; yet they are such basic symbols that they cannot mean anything deeper than themselves. Neilson's spring is not a season, a month, or even a part of time; it is

> Youth's emblem, ancient as unchanging light,

it is a 'divine speech' set against the 'dark season' of death ('Heart of Spring'). Love is the frail word of creation itself—creation which, seen against the forces of inertia and self-destruction, seems impossible, yet has happened and happens forever.

So love, spring, the return of the sun, are not ordinary foreseeable statistical occurrences in Neilson's world. In each instance they are a new triumph, an infinitely strange assertion, never accepted without a sense of the fabulous:

> Again, as someone lost in a quaint parable,
> Comes up the Sun.

'Lost in a quaint parable'—that is perhaps as close as Neilson ever came to defining his vision of life. One could easily dismiss it as only a phrase: like other sound-intoxicated rhymers, Neilson does sometimes make phrases for themselves alone, troubling little about their sense. But, elastic and precise, the line snaps back into place in his poetry and cannot be dismissed. It embodies the whole strangeness of Neilson's vision—the view he sometimes opens for us on ourselves and the world we live in, seen in a light like that the young girl saw falling on the Orange Tree.

Neilson's basic themes, in fact, are chosen not out of naivety but out of knowledge, and not from boyish immaturity but from a point, beyond our self-involved view, which perhaps only a certain kind of acceptance and humility can attain. Neilson sees life, in his moments of truest insight, as forever new, forever strange, sprung from a meaning we know nothing of and constantly renewed from sources beyond itself in a round of miraculous repetition. The Lizard—that ancient symbol of life-wisdom —tells the poet 'We live by the folly of spring'; and the news is joyful, not ironic. The parable of life is guaranteed, as to its final meaningfulness, by its very renewal.

That kind of acceptance is not unquestioning nor childish. It comes of an attitude much more difficult to attain. Neilson's symbolic spring and love are set against a dark background—a background that he knew well in his own life, of death, winter and poverty. Many of his poems are concerned with death. 'Deep is the dark; it drinks the day', he says in 'The Lover Sings'; and he asks, in 'To the Thick Darkness',

> I have been questioning long: Is Death
> But a poor journeyman for you?

Neilson was no easy optimist. For him the destruction of life, 'the black season', was as real as its renewal.

But there is no question, for Neilson, which is the more meaningful. The poet's task is to make part of that renewal, to be

> Chief messenger of light, to cheer
> The brown earth and that bides thereon.
> ('The Lover Sings')

That is why the song must be 'delicate', tender as the spring itself.

> Let your song be delicate.
> Sing no loud hymn:
> Death is abroad . . . oh, the black season!
> The deep—the dim!
> ('Song be Delicate')

It is this insistence on the shadow-side of life, the imminence of death, that gives his poetry its real depth.

> Old jester merciless with the dead,
> That as a hastening child I knew,
> In the impatient deeps ahead
> How shall I make a friend of you?

he asks in 'To the Thick Darkness'. His affirmations are never wholly unclouded, his acceptances are made in full knowledge. In fact, read attentively, he is one of the most melancholy as well as the most joyful of poets, because of his trembling awareness of the odds against which the creative spirit—that which is manifested in love, in spring and in poetry—makes itself known, and the nature of the forces which oppose it—

> The Bat, the deep-fallen,
> Who craves mankind:
> Who puts out his evil on
> The opening mind.
>   ('The Power of the Bells')

It is this quality of frailness, of breathless tenderness, in youth and love, that his poems catch for us again and again.

> The moon did seem as music spilled
> Upon her spotless gown,
> And at her height of happiness
> The summer tear came down.
>   ('The Eleventh Moon')

For the poet, that 'suckling of folly', reason is the negation of creativity, the bleak encroachment of inevitable death. Neilson clearly saw (as Blake had done before him) that for reason the creative impulse is incomprehensible and outside all logic. He never ceased to emphasize this anti-rational stand; it is a necessary corollary of his choice of life and creation against the cold and darkness of an uncreative rationalism. Beauty is 'folly-fed'; 'we live by the folly of spring'; and the very return of spring and life emphasize more sharply the darkness of winter and of the waiting death that 'craves mankind'. Indeed, there is at the back of a few, at least, of Neilson's poems what in any other poet would sound like despair at the diaphanousness of life and creation against that black background: as, for instance, in 'Say Summer Shall not Die':

> Though Reason in the cold
> Sits as an emperor,
> Say loudly it is gold,
> My thoughts are gossamer;
> With loveless lips and dry
> Say to that emperor
> That summer shall not die.

This poem, found among his unpublished manuscripts, is certainly central to his feeling—one reason, perhaps, why it did not appear in his lifetime. In it he speaks of spring and love as 'the beloved lies'—a phrase which almost too terribly reveals his own struggle as a poet to hold his vision.

Again, in a late poem, 'I Spoke to the Violet', this note returns:

> The silence you come with is sweeter to me than a sound,
> But I love not the colour—I saw it go into the ground.

> And, though you haunt me with all that is health to a rhyme,
> My thoughts are as old as the naked beginning of Time.

His anti-rationalism thus has the deepest of roots; the reign of reason, for him, closes the gate against the irruption of the divine impulse of creation, and is the end of 'all beauty folly-fed'. In his passionate unreasoning opposition to Reason, Neilson followed a true intuition; he is more logical in his own way here than many of the poets who have paid lip-service to that analytical goddess. Like his Lizard,

> He tells me the paramount treason,
> His words have the resolute ring:
> 'Away with the homage to Reason!
> We live by the folly of Spring!'

This is not the note struck by an immature poet. If we persist in thinking of Neilson as the child who never grew up, who never discovered what life is all about, we have not heard a word he is saying. He knew very well—well enough to reject it on higher grounds than most of those who blindly rebel against it—that world in which laws, abstractions, arguments are brought in to reinforce the reign of greed and stupidity, and in which even God is seen as vengeful and justice merciless. He turned from it all his life, with gentleness but with finality. He would return to Stony Town, (which is a city in the heart as well as the city of Melbourne) only with his train of fantastic clowns and dancers.

> If ever I go to Stony Town, I'll go as to a fair,
> With bells and men and a dance-girl with the heat-wave
>   in her hair . . .
>   ('Stony Town')

But that Stony Town is real he understood only too clearly.
Poverty and the ugly nonconformism of his mother's religion
first introduced him to it. His inner way led beyond it (as his
brother said, he was always able to 'live in a world of his own'),
but in his physical circumstances he spent all his life there; first
as a labourer in the country, constantly battling misfortune, low
wages, bad seasons, family illness; later in the city he hated for
its materialism and for its physical qualities of iron and stone,
rough textures, noise, and above all for its abstractions ('the
straight line and the square') which seemed to him a denial of
life and a triumph of detestable rationality.

His way into his inner world was through his own creativity.

> My riches all went into dreams that never yet came home,
> They touched upon the wild cherries and the slabs of honey-
>   comb,
> They were not of the desolate brood that men can sell or buy.
> Down in that poor country no pauper was I.
>   ('The Poor Poor Country')

Those dreams, and the sensitivity to colour, sound and image
that accompanied them, were never to leave him. In 'The Flight
of the Weary', one of the most characteristic of his poems, he
offers them as solace to the crippled child with whom he felt a
compassionate kinship:

> You cannot go out to the blossom:
> You cannot contend in the play:
> I call you the little white maiden,
> The moon that is out all the day.
> The lights in the leaves are of scarlet,
> The colour that comes to redeem:
> The winds are all painted with honey,
> And we can escape in a dream.

But his dream was not of the common kind. It had nothing to
do with the vulgar fantasy, the Hollywood drug, through which
the wounded ego seeks to reinforce itself with lies and falsities.
It was in fact a new and different vision of a world no less real
than our own, of the world as a parable, a tale invented to show

men where truth really lies. In Neilson's visionary world, 'the
leaves are as words in a fable', and God 'shall be drowsy, and
think out His thoughts like a beautiful tree'—not, as Neilson's
family religion had seen him, a God who is 'terrible and thunder-
blue', but the God of the 'gentle waterbird', the God of whom
Neilson wrote

> Sometimes, when watching in the white sunshine,
> Someone approaches—I can half define
> All the calm beauty of that friend of mine.
>
> ('The Gentle Water Bird')

Like Traherne's, Neilson's world is not a mere contradiction
of reality, but a new vision of the real; the eyes that see are
changed, so that they see a different kind of truth.

The particular quality of Neilson's view is beyond that of our
everyday capacities. He speaks a simple, though elusive language;
he writes in simple quiet metres, he does nothing to attract attention. If we cannot see beyond all this, he strikes us as impre-
cise, misty, even banal, not only in subject, but even in metre
and choice of words. No poet is easier to dismiss, or less likely to
reassert himself.

So his mentor, Stephens, complained that he was not 'bold'
enough, that he did not grip firmly enough his 'backbone of
ideas'. 'Your sweet sounds must make sense we can perceive without struggling to grasp a cloud. More firmness! More speed!' The
criticism is true enough on a certain level; but it lacks insight.
It is the mark of Neilson's best work that it does, in a sense,
melt into air, and leave us with only a haunting tune or a sense
of something half-seen—that it seldom, in the immediate context
of life, 'makes sense'. Emphasis, firmness, speed, are qualities
foreign to Neilson's view of life, as they were foreign to his
nature. When the shrillness of a visitor's voice disturbed him,
Devaney tells us, he left the room and returned with his ears
blocked with cotton wool. He shrank from loud sounds and
dazzling lights—'the morning was too loud with light', he wrote
in 'The Evening is the Morning'—and he could never have used
the shock-techniques of modern writing, which are meant to
penetrate the mists of custom that blur our perception of words
and meanings.

Much twentieth-century writing, in line with the Crocean conventions, is wholly personal, the poetry of a single ego in combat

with its environment; and I have suggested that the lack of ego is Neilson's very note. He does not look for the unusual phrase, the different word; when they come to him they come naturally, because they express what he truly was and saw. In fact, because the vision was his natural habitat he often tried, as Stephens observed, to make a word express too much, or packed into a phrase something which might take another writer many words to convey:

> When schoolboys build great navies in the skies . . .
> Sunlight has strange conspiracies above . . .
> > ('The Sweetening of the Year')

> Earth is upon me tedious mild . . .
> > ('For a Little Girl's Birthday')

> Too well they know the tremble
>   Of the hollow year . . .
> > ('Song be Delicate')

His verses can be as elusively suggestive as some of Mallarmé's:

> How should a singer of the cold
> Seeing strange holiness in air
> In his blue famine seek to hold
> Vainly your paradise of hair?
> > ('For A Little Girl's Birthday')

Again and again his favourite words blur the edges of his thought and feeling—'faint', 'dim', 'lavender', 'deep'—but the blurring is intentional; it is integral to Neilson's vision, which is of the frailness, the evanescence of light and spring and love. The passive voice, the present participle, falling rhythms and trailing phrases, all help to convey his effects.

> Fear it has faded and the night:
>   The bells all peal the hour of nine:
> The schoolgirls hastening through the light
>   Touch the unknowable Divine.
> > ('Schoolgirls Hastening')

> I was impelled by the white moon
>   And the deep eyes of the Spring,
> And the voices of purple flutes
>   Waltzing and wavering.
> > ('The Girl with the Black Hair')

Inglis Moore has remarked in *Six Australian Poets* that there are few strong verbs in Neilson's poetry. This is certainly true; and even where they do seem to occur, examination shows that they are not always used as such. Moore quotes as one instance of a 'strong verb', the word 'demur' in 'Ride Him Away':

> The clouds come over, the lights demur—

but I think that a second glance makes it clear that Neilson was using this, not as a verb at all, but as a descriptive word, almost as a piece of music, or as a slur in music. It becomes a hybrid word, something between 'dim' and 'blur', which describes the fading change of sunset light:

> The red goes into the lavender—

and as such, of course, it is almost robbed of its function as a verb in this context. This is characteristic of Neilson's attitude to words, which become for him at times like the strokes in a painting: for example, in 'The Song and the Bird':

> He telleth all his mad
> Manoeuvring to the morn—

where the word 'manoeuvring' follows the line of the bird's lilt, and has no other connotation at all. (This recalls Hopkins's thrush—'he does so rinse and wring the heart . . .')

One of the most interesting features of Neilson's poetry is his use of colour words. As with some children but very few adults, Neilson 'saw' sounds, emotions, qualities, seasons and so on in terms of colour. In this he has been compared to Rimbaud—but Rimbaud exclaimed 'j'inventai les couleurs des voyelles', while for Neilson his colour perceptions simply existed. Rimbaud never succeeded in systematizing his vowel colours; for Neilson systems were alien; but nevertheless there is consistency in his use of colour words, as well as a delicate sensitivity.

In his chromatic scale of perception, as it were, green is the colour of spring, youth and young love. Red is used to signify strength, passion, the height of summer; it is 'the colour that comes to redeem', but at the same time in its darker manifestation it is also danger, heat, a colour of warning. It merges into purple, 'the colour of death' worn by the violet, 'the voices of purple flutes' of which Neilson said: 'That's the deep sounds of the flute . . . that seem to go along the ground. Anything bellowing or deep like that is of the ground, just like violets are of the grave.' Yellow, or gold, is more ambiguous: it can be joyful ('the gold world trembles in a shower,' 'sipping the gold air', 'whites and yellows defeat the gloom'), or mournful and autumnal, like the yellow rose in 'Roses Three', or even connected with death: 'Wrapt in the yellow earth' ('From a Coffin'). Blue also has two aspects, that of the sky (connected with spring) and the 'thunder-blue' of a vengeful God; a greyed blue Neilson conects with twilight, calm and his water-birds, but a cold wind is also blue, and the 'singer of the cold' in 'For a Little Girl's Birthday' speaks from a 'blue famine'. White is unequivocal, the colour of innocence and childhood; so is black, 'the thick darkness' that threatens all creation. The summer sun, in 'The Flight of the Weary', 'apparels the day' in 'moods of unmeasured magenta'—a word which, however, may be used partly for its music and onomatopoiea in this line. Very few of Neilson's poems contain no colour references; and though sometimes they are used with the ordinary denotation, they can be as eccentric as this:

> You were of Love's own colour
> In eyes and heart and hair,
>
> ('You, and Yellow Air')

or, in 'The Gentle Water Bird',

> Creeds the discoloured awed my opening mind.

In 'The Scent O' The Lover', which is one of the most characteristic of Neilson's poems, he tells us:

> I am assailed by colours
> By night, by day:
> In a mad boat they would take me
> Red miles away . . .

—a verse which has also recalled Rimbaud to some critics.

But, though it is not impossible that Neilson had heard references to Rimbaud's work, through Stephens or through Brennan's *Bulletin* article published in 1899, it is at least unlikely that he knew more of it than a few such articles or references might have given him. (Incidentally, Brennan translates the title of Rimbaud's poems as 'The Drunken Ship' not 'mad boat'.) And his obscure life as a labourer, his poor eyesight which made it difficult for him to read at all, and his dislike (recorded by Devaney) of having poetry read to him, led to his being almost cut off from contemporary enthusiasms and influences. Certainly his curious colour perceptions are his own, and not an adopted affectation. In his poetry, they add iridescence and clarity as well as strangeness to the best of his work.

The form of his poems was largely dictated by his necessity to keep them 'in his head', as he said. His only opportunities to write them down, or to have them written for him by an amanuensis when his eyes did not allow him to write or read, were after his day's work. 'Short stanzas are the best for me', he told Devaney. 'I can remember the rhyming better. I don't have it on paper to help.' But the actual design of the poems is not often logical or linear. Much more often Neilson begins with a statement of the theme in the first verse, followed by variations and repetitions, with the last verse possibly repeating the first, or at least recurring to it, so that the poem is circular in its motion. ' 'Tis the White Plum Tree' follows this pattern, with its five verses of which the first and last are identical, the other three embroidering the comparison of the plum tree to a bride.

But the circularity may be less obvious, as in 'Schoolgirls Hastening':

> Fear it has faded and the night:
>   The bells all peal the hour of nine:
> The schoolgirls hastening through the light
>   Touch the unknowable Divine.
>
> What leavening in my heart would bide!
>   Full dreams a thousand deep are there:
> All luminants succumb beside
>   The unbound melody of hair.
>
> Joy the long timorous takes the flute:
>   Valiant with colour songs are born:
> Love the impatient absolute
>   Lives as a Saviour in the morn.
>
> Get thee behind me Shadow-Death!
>   Oh ye Eternities delay!
> Morning is with me and the breath
>   Of schoolgirls hastening down the way.

This poem was written after a particularly hard period of Neilson's life, when his father's death had left him with the responsibility of supporting his young stepmother and her children, and he had been working as a navvy for many months. He told Devaney that it had been written when on a short visit to Melbourne 'every morning I used to meet the schoolgirls coming up to the old High School . . . I used to think those girls were remarkably beautiful. I don't suppose they were any more beautiful than they were before or are now, but a man sees things different at different times in his life . . .'. My point in quoting the circumstances of the poem—which, Neilson told Devaney, was written 'rather quickly'—is that they illustrate how immediate was Neilson's visionary translation of his particular circumstances into his second or parabolic world. Here the parable is to be seen in its entirety: the poverty-stricken navvy and the high-school girls are lifted from the everyday to the universal in a moment, not by an act of Neilson's will, but rather by an inrush of perception.

To express this sudden vision, which most of Neilson's best poems describe, the circular,—one might even say, the flower-shaped—design of the poem is the ideal form. The central illumination—the vision of the Divine light—is contrasted with the night of fear that is its background, in the first verse; the contrast is repeated in the last verse, which at the same time reverts to the 'real world' aspect of the vision, as against the divine: the schoolgirls are, in the end, no more than schoolgirls, and the light of the Divine is the light of the morning. But in the interval the vision has taken effect, reawakening the poet from the heaviness of night ('leavening' his heart) and (this is the poem's real source) setting him again at the point of creativity where 'Valiant with colour songs are born', and where love can reassert itself.

The movement of the poem, from the first word 'Fear', which is immediately negated, is, first into almost unbearable illumination which seems external to the poet; then inward, where the poet recognizes the effect on him and its immediate source; outward again to the schoolgirls' 'unbound melody of hair'; inward once more to the birth of the poem itself in a joy that has long been suppressed by fear (this reverts again to the opening word). The central reconciliation of inner and outer world, vision and fact, is contained in the last two lines of the third verse. In the last verse the poem frees itself from death (and fear) and is able to recognize the simple reality of its starting-point—morning and the schoolgirls. It is the continual movement from outer to inner, from reality to vision, around the central absolute of love, which traces the design; the background of darkness is allowed its reality, but against it the vision, however momentary, is even more real.

Examined in this way, the poem shows that Neilson's apparent simplicity of form is in fact nothing of the kind. It may, in fact, be partly unconscious art that shapes such a poem; but though Neilson's own comments on his work often sound naive, it is necessary to remember that he knew better than most of his critics—including Stephens— what was best in his work, and where it failed; and that such a poem as 'The Orange Tree', for instance, went through a number of drafts, and took four years to complete to Neilson's own satisfaction.

Nevertheless, it has to be admitted that Neilson's lack of self-consciousness was as often a handicap as an advantage. He was not always able to distinguish between whimsy and incantation, nor, in a very few poems, between sentiment and sentimentality. He is constantly being saved from banality only by innocence.

But above all, his simplicity and other-worldliness form the most effective barrier between modern readers and his poetry. We cannot feel with Neilson, for there is nothing in him of the everyday joys and tortures of individual consciousness: the joys of possession in love, or the tortures of frustration, are wholly alien to Neilson's love poetry, in which the worst that can happen to the lover is the absence of the beloved; all here is impersonal, related to eternity. There are no agonies of thought or decision; no doubts or mental crises; no mention of the responsibilities of our solitary selfhood. In his gentle and lovely songs, we miss some muscularity and tension, some immediacy to our own personal lives, that is part of our conception of poetry today. For us, perhaps, selfconsciousness is a measure of capacity, and a necessary ingredient of poetry, if we are to recognize the poet as one who shares in our own preoccupations, and our struggle with our own selfhood.

Perhaps, in fact, this increase in self-consciousness and separateness from society, in the modern poet, is the most significant thing that has happened to poetry since the Romantic Revival. As late as Coleridge's time, the idea of 'inspiration' as something which overwhelmed the poet from outside himself—a holy breath from Olympus, a kind of possession—still survived. Nowadays the notion has changed, in so far as the source and direction of the impulse is now seen as from within, not from outside. Like the rest of the 'divine influences' which once swayed man, inspiration has retired into our own inner recesses, and become something in the nature of man and not the nature of the universe.

Today the poem is thought of as emerging from a more or less unconscious combination of elements—images or ideas, feelings or reactions—in answer to a specific need or problem in the poet himself. The poetic process is seen as a kind of crystallizing or polarizing of the elements of the poem around some formal axis; conscious mental criticism and technical skill come into play only as the poem emerges into consciousness. On this theory, such an emergence takes place at the cost of a momentary lessening of consciousness, an abeyance of the process of censorship which Freud postulates as a main part of the conscious mind; this 'lowered threshold' in the poet allows the poem's material to force its way into the foreground, overcoming his other pre-occupations and imposing itself in their place as it takes shape.

If we are to take this idea seriously, it ought to follow that the stronger and more developed the poet's consciousness, his intellect and will and ego, the more condensed and forceful the poetic images must be, in order to force their way against it. Certainly there is a kind of poetic pleasure which is specifically modern—Miltonic and post-Miltonic—in the counterpoint of metre and thought, struggling against each other rather as a stream struggles against a rocky bed. It is a pleasure quite different from that aroused by such poets as Herrick, Burns or Wyatt, and certainly not at all like the effect produced by the early Scots balladists with whom Neilson has much in common.

The pleasure of opposing tensions, of muscularity and struggle, is something Neilson could never give. Perhaps his constant cultivation of the dream and the vision resulted in a conscious 'threshold' too low to offer much resistance to the flow of the poem. The compensation for Neilson's lack of tension and strength is his sensitivity of perception, his delicacy, his effortlessness, the light and transparency of his vision and its pervading and iridescent colour. These are not qualities with which the modern poet is at all concerned; the writing of poets as diverse as Frost, Eliot, Auden, Lowell and even Yeats is usually a kind of struggle against the poem, the emotion, the language itself. Modern poetry seems to be shaped by its own difficulties. In contrast, Neilson's language seems half-formed, its edges are blurred, melting into air; the poem's movement is all fluid, its rhythms sway subtly and gently on. It is as though, in writing the poem, there was no difficulty to be overcome, except—and that in the best and most haunting of the poems—the difficulty of conveying a vision as delicate and cloudy as that of 'The Orange Tree', or 'Schoolgirls Hastening'.

So Neilson can never satisfy the appetite of the sad modern self, which mourns over its separation from the world and over the problems to which it cannot—perhaps will never, on the level of selfhood—find a solution. His voice is as hard to hear as the sound of running water, against the voices of our inner argument; and his songs are almost as elemental as that sound. His world is a world, not of facts, but of meanings, in which the image is itself reality, as he expressed it in 'Julie Callaway'.

Death is abroad in it, 'waiting with a watchful eye'; but love and spring and sunrise are the other persons in the parable the world presents, and the lover and the poet are messengers of light as well as mourners of the passing. The song Neilson sings is founded on the oldest of tunes, the nursery rhymes of our childhood, made various and strange:

> Almost I fear her low, low voice
> As one may fear the moon,
> As one may fear too faint a sound
> In an old uncanny tune.
>
> ('Pale Neighbour')

We think we are too grown-up to listen. But perhaps we have not yet grown far enough. The child's first task is to acquire an ego, a mask, a shield against the world; but the task of the mature man is different.

CHAPTER IX

Vision

∽

AT FIRST glance, the Great War and its aftermath had remarkably little influence on Australian poetry. Of poetry written by servicemen there are Vance Palmer's *The Camp* and Leon Gellert's *Songs of a Campaign* (which contains probably the best war poem ever written by an Australian, the terse and wry 'Before Action'). At home, 'Furnley Maurice' wrote his series of poems, 'To God—from the Warring Nations'—stumbling, sometimes naive, but urgently sincere pacifist poetry, and Brennan wrote his violently anti-German patriotic verses. Not much else remains of overt war poetry.

In the 'twenties, the first resumption of experiment and assertion came when Jack Lindsay and a few others brought out four issues of a journal named *Vision*. The *Vision* movement is one of the most thoroughly described and documented of literary events; Jack Lindsay has given an analytical and historical account of its genesis and its end, in his two autobiographical volumes, particularly in *The Roaring Twenties*. Essentially it began as an attempt to continue and to broaden the work Norman Lindsay had done before the war in attacking Australian wowserism and parochialism in life and art, and to encourage the growth of a robust and sensuous kind of art that would reaffirm what Lindsay thought of as the true art-values—Beauty, Life and Courage (according to the Nietzschean canons). It was to Hugh McCrae that *Vision* tacitly owed most of its notions of what poetry ought to be, and it published or republished several of McCrae's poems, both in the journal and in the anthology of Australian contemporary verse which the *Vision* group collected.

Vision was much concerned with its theory of art, and both Norman Lindsay and Jack Lindsay wrote articles, polemical and aggressive, laying down what was and what was not acceptable as art, from the *Vision* point of view. McCrae, however, who was their chief exhibit, had little to do with the journal or the theorizing. As Jack Lindsay writes (*The Roaring Twenties* p. 100):

Hugh hated abstractions and generalizings with all the intense 'negative sensibility' (in Keats' sense) that made him the poet he was. He loved Norman as man and artist, drawing deeply from both aspects, but Norman's theorizings made his hair stand painfully on end and increased intolerably his itch to bolt into the green places of intuitive thought . . . But though Hugh was a thousandfold right in sheering off from our domineering ideas, there was that in him which shrank from any conscious effort to grasp the principles of art. Therein lay both his strength and his weakness.

This is probably a true insight into McCrae. But in fact, examining the 'domineering ideas' of the journal, it is clear enough that the poetry that *Vision* imagined itself to be seeking to encourage in the present and the future had already been written by McCrae, and that the Lindsays were in fact theorizing after the event. Their prescriptions for poetry lead irresistibly back towards the poetry of *Satyrs and Sunlight*. 'Sex must return to Art' (wrote Norman Lindsay in the nineteen-twenties) 'by the roads of Laughter, Tragedy and a beautiful imagery in all its forms;' (*The Sex Synonym in Art*) and Jack Lindsay writes, 'How then is the Greek to come to life in Australia? . . . by a passionate sensuality, by the endless search for the image of beauty, the immortal body of desire that is Aphrodite . . . Thus we may found a genuine Australian literature . . . There is something in the realistic atmosphere of the actual conditions that surround one that stultifies the free and *concrete* movement of emotion . . .'. (*Australian Poetry and Nationalism*).

But McCrae himself was already the poet that *Vision* wanted, and perhaps the only one to whom its prescriptions could have applied. He is in himself Lindsay's Australian Renaissance, and his poetry embodies not only all the positive qualities of that Renaissance, but its negative qualities as well.

For poems like 'Ambuscade' and 'The Deathless Gods' had contained both the affirmation and, implicitly, the criticism of Lindsay's dicta. To Lindsay, James Joyce and D. H. Lawrence, van Gogh's painting, the poetry of the Sitwells and many other contemporaries were anathema, part of the modern movement which Lindsay saw as 'the proclaiming of Chaos as the governing principle of Modernity'.

This reaction was clearly a refusal to understand the principles behind post-war European art and the necessary development which led up to, and was carried on through, the artists whom *Vision* anathematized. It was a bidding of the waves to stand still, and naturally contained its own doom.

In Jack Lindsay's own work the result of this refusal was clear enough; the heavy emphasis on wenching and wining, the unconvincing roistering and unreal Bohemianism, make most of the verse influenced by *Vision* an obvious cardboard fake. McCrae could write this kind of verse because it so happened that McCrae was this kind of poet; as a prescription for other writers it was laughable.

The laying down of a certain kind of approach to verse was bad enough (since no one can tell poetry what it ought to be); the denial of practically all current European writing and art was clearly impossible to maintain. It led the younger *Vision* writers, their early enthusiasm once spent, into a kind of repetitive impasse where no advance in any direction was possible. Jack Lindsay quotes a letter from Hugh McCrae to R. D. Fitz-Gerald, written much later in reply to a review in which Fitz-Gerald had referred to his centaurs as 'rocking-horses':

> My rocking-horses too, which you imply stop in one place, while flesh-an'-blud nags flash like Hell to the post . . .
> The worst is, the bastards keep on rocking . . . They keep on rocking millions of hours after the race has been won. How would you, loathing them, like to see them tippetty-upping and downing all thro' your life, in sunshine and rain?

But I think it is permissible here to believe that FitzGerald had made an attributive error. It was not McCrae's centaurs that were rocking-horses; it was the theories that *Vision* based on McCrae's practice that actually stopped in one place, and FitzGerald, having at one time been involved, if not actually engaged, in *Vision's* stationary race, may well have been thinking of this staticness when he reviewed McCrae's book. McCrae had already drained from the Greek imagery all that for him was drinkable; *Vision* insisted on re-offering him the empty cup.

What was lacking in the *Vision* creed was any kind of understanding of what was actually happening in the development of European and Western art; and, worse still, any kind of human depth of relationship, either between man and man or man and woman. The rejection of the nationalist trend in Australian art, of Henry Lawson with his bush ballads and his 'mateship' creed left over from the days of the bush working brotherhood, was valid enough in itself; but an attitude of rejection can only be justified by what is affirmed instead.

The 'mateship' ingredient in Australian tradition was always and necessarily one-sided; it left out of account the whole relationship with woman. The Lindsays replaced it with an equally one-sided exaggeration of the sexual relation, but still wholly from the male point of view. Woman in the *Vision* hierarchy, and also, alas, in McCrae's own poetry, is no more than the foil to the man's physical robustness, the object, rather than the partner, in a sexual act which is seen as creative only from the male point of view. Woman, as in the Nietzschean philosophy, is no more than the 'soil' in which creation and renewal take place.

Jack Lindsay points this out in *Life Rarely Tells* (p. 208):

> The uëbermensch . . . whom Nietzsche saw as the revaluer of all existing values, the man in whom a new centre of living had been born, we interpreted wholly as the hero-artist, the bearer of the creative image . . . Earth, the woman, became only a passive material or object for the plastic and vivifying embrace of the hero . . . By a lonely tour-de-force we wanted to create the realistic and concrete image of beauty which could in fact be born only out of a popular culture with a vital relation to nature.

There is no need to embrace a Marxist interpretation of life, as Lindsay did, to see the fundamental incompleteness of this ethos. It is obvious in McCrae's poetry, and it springs from that curious egoism that makes us at times uneasy even in the loveliest of the poems he left us. It may be strange that this can be said of a poetry which seems to occupy itself so much with the assertion of the beauty of the sensual relationship between man and woman. But the emphasis on the sensual too often clouds and obscures the human fact behind.

The poems are full of an often exquisite sexual imagery. Even the apparent decoration in the best of them is drawn into the current of passion and made one with it:

> I kissed her breasts; and she, with golden eyes,
>   Like the hot panther leaning to the brook,
> Bloomed into passion, while her thirsty cries
>   Throbbed through the night till all her body shook.

> The wandering deer upraised his beetling crest,
>   And took the moon to be his diadem;

F

> And 'mid the sedge the silent firefly presst,
> Or filled the lily with his lustful gem . . .
>
> ('Sensual Love')

McCrae takes his obsession with femininity so far as to speak, in the long narrative poem 'The Phantom Mistress', in the character of the woman who kills her unfaithful husband. But of all the women who appear in his poetry—Colombines, Venuses, passing mistresses, nymphs or wives—none, except perhaps the glimpse of Joan in his Introduction to 'Joan of Arc', has any human reality. Only the poet, and the poetry, are real.

So though McCrae kept outside the entanglements of theory and controversy, he nevertheless acted out, in his art, all the theory's implications. In McCrae we find the demonstration of the Lindsay ethos—its affirmation of the physical and sensuous, its emphasis on the 're-creation of new imagery in Beauty, while mounting an eternal guard against the encroachment of ugliness' its anti-intellectualism, and alas, its retreat from any kind of involvement in larger questions either of principle or action.

Yet the *Vision* movement, with Norman Lindsay and McCrae, had a deeper effect on the work of some of our most influential poets than its shallowness and bluster might seem to warrant. It was, in fact, true that *Vision* was in the end an attempt to impose and extend a view of life and art which had had its value in the chokingly smug atmosphere of pre-war Australia, as a protest against that smugness, but had by the 'twenties, when the magazine began publication, been far outdistanced by events. In 1913, Brennan had published his *Poems;* a poet of far greater scope and insight than McCrae had formally lodged his claim to a place, not only in Australian literature, but in the currents of European poetry. It is doubtful whether Norman Lindsay was ever quite clear about what Brennan was doing; certainly he did not regard Brennan highly as a poet.

Jack Lindsay, while paying his formal respects to Brennan in his autobiography, evidently is himself rather bewildered by the implications of the book, and seems to regard Brennan as an unconscious Marxist in his early poetry, and a lost leader in his later work. But the fact was that *Poems 1913* already stepped so far beyond Lindsay and McCrae that after its publication the Australian scene was forever altered.

And in 1914-18 it was even more far-reachingly rearranged.

Australia's whole relationship to the world fell into a new focus; she was now decisively a participant in the issues of Western culture. It took a number of years for this truth to become clear to Australian writers; but perhaps it would have made an earlier impact if the barren reiteration of *Vision's* Nietzschean and anti-intellectual notions had not occupied so much of the time of her young poets.

The result of this withdrawal from the real issues of Australian development was, oddly enough, a bitterly partisan reinforcement of the very parochialisms that Lindsay had set out to break down. *Vision* attacked the work of almost every British and European writer and artist of note who had emerged during the war years and after. Lawrence, the Sitwells, Joyce and many others joined the French Impressionists in the Lindsayan gallery of villains who were undermining the true development of Western culture acording to Nietzsche. (This resulted in a curious double-take attitude to Lindsay on the part of the bourgeoisie whom he had taken such delight in shocking; for them he did not cease to be a Mephistopheles, but became a demon with some very sound ideas.)

The most important of the young poets who were published in *Vision* and its anthology *Vision* (1923) were Leon Gellert, Jack Lindsay, Kenneth Slessor and Robert FitzGerald. Leon Gellert had already published his *Songs of a Campaign*; the best of them, in their stark simplicity and irony, were very good indeed. Invalided home from overseas in 1917, he published in 1919 a rather poor poem series called *The Isle of San,* with an introduction and illustrations by Norman Lindsay, and with a theme that significantly echoes Lindsay's preoccupation with the betrayal of youth and sexual love by shame and the notion of original sin. After this Gellert published no more poetry until 1928 (*Desperate Measures*) and these poems were comparatively slight.

Jack Lindsay, the moving spirit of the magazine, was soon divided not only in his personal allegiance to Norman Lindsay's ideas, but in his poetic development. His discovery of the facilely dismissed poetry of the Sitwells is described in *The Roaring Twenties* (p. 126):

> Here, I was forced to realize, was sensibility tuned in the same key as my own, the key I sought. In *Vision* we had con-

demned the Sitwells as well as Van Gogh, anything that
N.L. had labelled disintegration or primitivism, on the
scantiest of investigations. But now I was driven to admit
that if I were to be at all true to my own senses and their
poetic impulsion, I must learn to drink at the spring I had
placarded as muddy and polluted . . . I declared to N.L.
that there were many elements after all in contemporary
experimental verse that could be used for our purposes. He
took my word for it, as he wouldn't if I had come to say
the same of Van Gogh or Picasso. But a split had been born
in our concepts that was later to have important effects for
me.

Jack Lindsay's subsequent departure for Europe meant, not
only the end of his own connection with Australian growth and
development, but the end of the *Vision* experiment. The magazine itself had already ceased publication, and its former group
of poets were already beginning their independent investigations
into technique and poetic thought. Jack Lindsay, when he sailed,
was experimenting with a purely imagic poetry, in which his old
preoccupations with the world as presented in his father's pictures were being gradually transmuted into more general and
more abstract images. The long poem he quotes and summarizes
at the end of *The Roaring Twenties*—an attempt to put into
words the emotional line of the Beethoven C sharp minor
quartet—has still the bosoms, girls, and flowers, but they are
transmuted, abstracted; the simplicities of sense are renounced
for a deeper and lonelier search.

The poem with its abstract words and its still rhetorical approach to poetry—

> Did I then leaf with ghosts of fear the night
> and in the cauldrons of the sun
> venom with pain the fumes of light,
> horror and beauty clasped in synthesis
> of the creative kiss . . .

is still far from the angular colourful poetry of the Sitwells; too
vague to be memorable, too full of the names of things instead
of their impact. Lindsay wrote little more poetry; nor did he
ever return, as he had intended, to Australia.

The third of the poets involved in the production of *Vision*,
Kenneth Slessor, was the most remarkable. Like McCrae, he was
then writing poetry whose surface was richly decorated; his

sensuous preoccupation with words, their intricate echoes and re-echoes in the poem, their suggestiveness of sound and texture, was the most striking thing about his early verse.

McCrae seems to begin from the thing imagined and marry his words to it; in such poems as 'The Satyr's Lass', in spite of their sheer inventiveness, he seems to have *seen* the satyr drawing his net 'to take the blind white woman of the brook' and

> when all the little reach was clear again,
> And she within the shallow fairly lain,
> Thrust out his hoof and marked her milky flank
> With two cleft toes . . .

But Slessor, on the other hand, in poems like 'Pan at Lane Cove' and 'Earth-Visitors', seems to create his pictures through his preoccupation with words: he is from the beginning actuated, not as McCrae was, by the song element in versifying, nor, as Fitz-Gerald is, by the struggle to confine an idea within poetic form, but with the sensual and textural qualities of language.

So Slessor's path away from the naiveties of the *Vision* episode was in the direction of technique. He too, like Jack Lindsay, looked a second time at the *Wheels* anthology. Lindsay had found in it 'sensibility tuned in the same key as my own'; it was not the sensibility which attracted Slessor so much as the form, the experiment.

In an address to the Australian English Association in 1931 (*Union Recorder*, 1 October 1931) he qualifies this: 'For the fruit of some of these experiments I feel a violent distaste. None the less, I welcome them more readily than the harvests of stagnation . . . '. But in an article by L. I. Shepherd (*Australian Book News*) Slessor is quoted as saying on a later occasion that on reading the anthology 'I was enabled to see why my own poetry was not moving forward'.

It was clearly not from the subject matter of the anthology that Slessor borrowed so fruitfully. In the lecture quoted above, Slessor goes on to repudiate Gertrude Stein's and Joyce's experimentalism, to praise Eliot's 'Waste Land' as 'filled with the most splendid and haunting rhythms of anything written in our century', and especially to mention the 'remarkable poetry' of Wilfred Owen. 'I regard Owen's experiments as easily the most promising of this century, but no one has yet carried them on.'

Slessor, however, was attracted by them into experiments with rhythm and with various gradations of off-rhyme, half-rhyme, 'analysed rhyme' and formal contrasts.

In these experiments, and the poetry to which they led, Slessor became an original exponent of textural expression in language. In a radio talk published in *Southerly* during 1948, he says, 'The colour and texture of vowel sounds, the infinite rhythm of consonants, the emotional effects obtained by avoiding a rhyme, approaching a rhyme or by subtly altering it—all these are experiments in anarchy of which poets today know very little except by intuitive feeling.' He might have added, except for Slessor. This technical path led Slessor, in his turn, away from the original canons of *Vision*; but in a sense, his subject matter was always influenced, if not by the *Vision* prescriptions, by the episode itself and its final breakdown.

The fourth poet, R. D. FitzGerald, though in many respects he grew away from *Vision*'s narrow ambit, did in fact continue and broaden certain of its ideas. Interestingly, however, his poetry also takes up and modernizes the qualities and even the outlook of the nationalists and balladists against whom Lindsay and McCrae were reacting during the first decade or two of the century. In a sense, FitzGerald remains an exponent of Nietzscheanism; but his emphasis is significantly different from that of Norman Lindsay.

Beyond these three, the ripples of *Vision*'s influence, or rather of the influence of the ideas of Norman Lindsay, continue far beyond the death of the journal itself. There is the poetry of Kenneth Mackenzie (particularly the earlier book); there is the work of Douglas Stewart; and there are various lesser marks made on the work of lesser writers through the influence of the more important. Though much was altered from the first brash exaggerated statement of the aims of the *Vision* group, the current in Australian poetry that is coloured by its influence is still detectable. An emphasis on action rather than intellect, on the physical rather than the emotional, a rejection of subtleties either of thought or feeling, a tendency towards statement rather than suggestion, a certain lushness of imagery and perception, are the traces left on certain writers by the Australian Renaissance that never happened.

CHAPTER X

Kenneth Slessor — Romantic and Modern

∽

IN THE early 'twenties Slessor was beginning to publish poems; and the magazine *Vision* offered him a channel for publication. This, Slessor would probably prefer to say, was the chief reason for the liaison between himself and the Lindsay group. In recent years he has tended to dismiss the notion that he was in any way 'influenced' (an ambiguous term) by the equally ambiguous group whom Jack Lindsay in his books *Life Rarely Tells* and *The Roaring Twenties* calls 'we'. Slessor prefers, it seems, to regard himself as from the first a separate phenomenon.

When we read the few poems Slessor has preserved from the *Vision* era, certainly two conflicting impressions are left with us; the first is of a Lindsayan lustiness and decorative excess where image jostles image and texture is crusted with over-richness; but the second, which seems, as the poems succeed each other, to move nearer and nearer into the foreground, is an emptiness that underlies these feverish sensuosities, a lack of inner solidity, a perception of the abyss that increases gradually into terror.

It seems that in Slessor's poetry two conflicting forces meet— the Nietzschean cry that man must learn to suffice himself, must increase his capacities, must become physically and spiritually superior to himself; and the Nietzschean perception which underlay that demand, that when God is 'dead' nothing can protect man from the malice of the universe. While O'Dowd interpreted Nietzsche with the help of the Bradlaughian rationalist-optimists and the political meliorists of the late nineteenth century, and remained naive and insensitive enough to be able to ignore the deeper implications of Nietzscheanism which finally drove its first exponent to madness, Slessor, after the First World War, was scarcely able to give credit to the notion of a new Renaissance in Australia. The Lindsay group, clearly, was saying either too little or too much.

So, though in the poem 'Earth-Visitors' he salutes Norman Lindsay in his 'one lonely chamber', opening his door to Venus, the last earth-visitor from the lost Olympians to her last votary;

and though in 'Nuremberg', with its rich impasto of description, he celebrates the joy of the artist, in the person of Albrecht Dürer, it is not long before the essential godlessness and shallowness of the modern world, as Slessor saw it, seeps into his poetry. In the poem 'Marco Polo', his glittering visual imagery (Slessor can at times be even more pictorial in his effects than Norman Lindsay's own paintings) is pinched to a bitter end in the last couplet:

> I'm sick of modern men. I wish
> You still were living, Kublai Khan!

From here it is a short step to the poem 'Heine in Paris', in which a bitter rejection of the whole of humankind is put into the mind of Slessor's Heine:

> Men crumbled, man lived on. In that animal's face,
>   'Twas but a squirt aimed at the moon, to fling contempt.
> Meyerbeer, Borne, and Klopstock vanished, but in their place
>   New Klopstocks, Meyerbeers blown again, and Bornes
>   undreamt
> Sprang up like fungi . . .
>
> . . . Heine looked out, and gazed at the world below,
>   Thick with old chemicals, breaking far out of sight
> With ageless tides of man—ah, granite flow,
>   Eternal, changeless flux of humanity,
> Undying darkness and light!
>
> Not treading those floods could save him—not striking stone,
>   Not damming the world could serve—only to fly,
> Careless of men and their shouting—untouched—alone—
>   Snatched by his own gods from a falling sky,
> And singing his own way—clutching his own, his own . . .

It seems significant that Slessor, then a comparatively young man, should have chosen for his subject the embittered and paralysed old age of Heine, rather than his gayer and more productive youth.

So in the poem 'Winter Dawn', Slessor himself rejects the city:

> O buried dolls, O men sleeping invisible there,
> I stare above your mounds of stone, lean down
> Marooned and lonely in this bitter air,
> And in one moment deny your frozen town,
> Renounce your bodies . . .

And when in poems like 'Thieves' Kitchen', another mannered and decorative pseudo-Elizabethan evocation of tavern life, and 'A Surrender',

> (When to those Venusbergs, thy breasts,
> By wars of love and moonlight batteries,
> My lips have stormed . . . .)

Slessor seems to be echoing McCrae's celebrations of the physical without reference either to mind or heart, the tone rings hollow.

In 'Stars', also a comparatively early poem, we meet for the first time the whole horror of a universe from which godhead has been drained away, and in which man is reduced to meaninglessness:

> But I was beating off the stars, gazing, not rhyming.
> I saw the bottomless black cups of space
> Between their clusters, and the planets climbing
> Dizzily in sick airs, and desired to hide my face.
> But I could not escape those tunnels of nothingness,
> The cracks in the spinning Cross, nor hold my brain
> From rushing for ever down that terrible lane,
> Infinity's trapdoor, eternal and merciless.

Once this poem had been written, the whole solipsist problem of modern man (which Brennan had stated so clearly) was already present in implication, and Slessor, essentially a much more lightweight thinker than Brennan, is from now on battling against odds too big for him. The reader cannot help remembering, whenever Slessor again (as in 'Adventure Bay' or 'La Dame du Palais de la Reine') uses a light and cynical manner, the abysses that lie behind it. In fact, there are few of Slessor's later poems in which we cannot see the gaps that lead out into the hollow universe.

It seems that about this time Slessor began to feel dissatisfied with his own poetry; the rich and luscious illustrative vein of the early poems, which seem immediately translatable into Lindsayan paintings, was no longer capable of expressing what he had to say. About 1927, he turned his attention from decoration to technical experiment and accomplishment. In *Vision,* the Lindsays had chosen for one of their chief objects of derision the anthology *Wheels,* brought out soon after the Great War and containing much of the experimental verse of the Sitwells, Pound and Eliot and other leaders in English contemporary verse. But Slessor now began to feel that somewhere in the direction of verbal experiment which *Wheels* indicated, his own way must now be found.

'The old vein had been worked out', he said later (*Australian Book News*, article by L. I. Shepherd), 'and a new lead followed up.' And in an address to the Australian English Association (*Union Recorder*, Sydney, 1 October 1931), while he continued to condemn the work of James Joyce, Gertrude Stein, and others, he acknowledged his debt to Wilfred Owen and to Eliot, and stated his belief in 'experiment in rhythm . . . as a sort of hypnotic agent which will urge the mind to vibrate at a deeper level of consciousness than that of the superficial world'. He quotes his own experiments in rhythm changes and in 'analysed' rhyme and syllabic rhyme, 'The Country Ride', and 'Fixed Opinions' (a title altered in his latest collection to 'Fixed Ideas') to illustrate how he has attempted to carry on the experimentalism of Owen.

But experiment, he says, did not interest him for its own sake. In a radio talk (published in *Southerly* in 1948) he said: 'The practical considerations that have guided me for many years have been those of form and experiment', form being defined as 'that shape of a work, whether in music, words or design, which seems most nearly to reflect the shape of the emotion which produced it.'

It is interesting that, in his choice of Owen as a master, Slessor took a path that English poetry, on the whole, during those years, rejected. Owen's poetry was a more natural outgrowth of previous English developments (harking back as it does to certain early English poets, such as George Gascoigne: 'My wittes be wearie, and my eyes are dymme,/I cannot see who best deserves the roome./Stand forth, good Peerce, thou plowman by thy name . . .) than Eliot's, with its echoes of French writers, or Pound's, with its Italianate and Provençal influences. Clearly, in his admiration for Owen, Slessor's chief reason was that, in Owen's work as nowhere else, he saw the emotion behind the verse working to alter the shape and sound of the verse itself. 'The emotion of a poem', he says in the Address quoted earlier, 'must make the experiment, not the experiment the poem.'

This interest in experiment not only provided a fresh channel for the verbal virtuosity of his early phase, but gave him a new impulse for his poetry. The last section of his earlier work, the

sequence called 'Music', provides a bridge from his earlier to
his later manner. Here he mingles the descriptive with the experimental, using variations in rhythm to convey the variations
in musical mood, as in the country-fair scene from 'Petroushka':

> In and out the countryfolk, the carriages and carnival,
> Pastrycooks in all directions push to barter their confections,
> Trays of little gilded cakes, caramels in painted flakes,
> Marzipans of various makes and macaroons of all com-
>   plexions . . .
>
> Gently the doctor of magic mutters,
> Opens his puppet-stall,
> Pulls back the painted shutters,
> Ruffles the golden lace.
> Ha! The crowd flutters . . .
> Reddened and sharp and small,
> O, *Petroushka's* face!

The first poem in the 1927-32 section of his *Poems*, 'Captain
Dobbin', while it lacks none of the descriptive dazzle of the early
poems, puts it to a new and more serious use: the re-creation,
no longer of the imagined splendours of Marco Polo's day, but
of the retirement of an old sea-captain. And, after the brilliant
and, for once, thoroughly light-hearted series 'The Atlas', we
come on the ironical 'To Myself' ('After all, you are my rather
tedious hero . . .'). 'Elegy in a Botanic Gardens', with a bitter
symbolic significance, records the change of vision that comes
when youth and love first go, and the building in the Gardens
where once 'that was no time for botany', is seen at last as

> . . . no Georgian Headlong Hall
> With glass-eye windows winking candles forth,
> Stuffed with French horns, globes, air-pumps, telescopes,
> And Cupid in a wig, playing the flute,
> But truly, and without escape,
> THE NATIONAL HERBARIUM . . .

The next important poem—probably the most important poem,
for its later influence, that Slessor has written—was his 'Five
Visions of Captain Cook'. It was the first of many later treat-
ments of the theme of early sea-explorations. Other Australian
poets took up the subject gladly, for its historical and rhetorical
bearing on Australia's nationhood, but no one has treated it
either with Slessor's inventive brilliance and lightness, or with his

intrinsic melancholy. It is like Slessor to end the poem with the
Vision seen of the Captain by his old shipmate, blind and dere-
lict, pensioned on half-a-crown a day—

> This was the creek he'd run his timbers to,
> Where grateful countrymen repaid his wounds
> At half-a-crown a day. Too good, too good,
> This eloquent offering of birdcages
> To gulls . . .

—the vision of his death,

> with . . . a knife of English iron,
> Forged aboard ship, that had been changed for pigs,
> Given back to Cook between his shoulder-blades . . .

The half-farcical, half-ironical note makes us recall Slessor's own
disillusion and his denial of the city of humanity.

The note continues in Slessor's later poetry, growing in fact
sharper, bitterer, more unendurable; as in 'The Castle of Glubb-
dubdrib', where the vision is of all the great minds of the past
reduced to the status of mere slaves of the Glubbdubdribians,
the cohorts of stupidity and greed; as in 'Crow Country',
one of the first and most memorable attempts to use a drought-
stricken Australian landscape as a symbol of the desert of the
modern mind:

> Over the huge abraded rind,
> Crow-countried graped with dung, we go,
> Past gullies that no longer flow
> And wells that nobody can find,
> Lashed by the screaming of the crow,
> Stabbed by the needles of the mind.

And in 'Gulliver', a shudderingly exact transcription of neurotic
human misery—

> One hair I break, ten thousand hairs entwine me.
> Love, hunger, drunkenness, neuralgia, debt,
> Cold weather, hot weather, sleep and age . . .
> I could break my teeth on a chain, I could bite through
>   metal,
> But what can you do with hairs?
> For God's sake, call the hangman.

In this poem Slessor probably discovered the most precise and
eloquent image of the plight of modern man that Australian

poetry is ever likely to produce. Like his 'Stars', it is a pivotal poem. Where 'Stars' apparently marked the watershed between his earlier and middle phases of writing, 'Gulliver' seems to point forward to Slessor's last long poem, 'Five Bells', with its quieter acceptance of annihilation.

But before 'Five Bells' is reached, there are the poems in which Slessor gives us his most incisive and characteristic portraits: 'The Nabob', 'Metempsychosis', and 'Vesper-Song of the Reverend Samuel Marsden'. All are portraits of men, lusty and eccentric and aged; but the two whom Slessor evidently prefers—Samuel Hickey and John Benbow—are both seen from outside, while Samuel Marsden, the 'flogging parson', is made to deliver a piously sadistic address to his Lord, in a first-person poem. The technique Slessor uses in all three is conversational; the last two verses of 'The Nabob' can be heard re-echoing down the years in various guises, their curtly ironic realism a little watered down in later writers' reference to it:

> But in the end, one says farewell to them;
> And if he'd curse today—God damn your blood!—
> Even his curses I'd not altogether condemn,
> Not altogether scorn; and if phantoms ate—
>
> Hickey, I'd say, sit down, pull up, set to:
> Here's knife and fork, there's wine, and there's a
>   barmaid . . .

These rhythms haunt poets like Douglas Stewart (the last two lines could easily be slipped into his play *Ned Kelly* and scarcely be noticed), and through Stewart, various of the writers of the 'forties and 'fifties. But Slessor's special quality of tartness, the economical line of his wit, are altered in such later derivations to a more balladic looseness.

'The Old Play', the poem-series Slessor puts last in his second-phase poems, 1927-32, takes the anguished cry of 'Gulliver' and sets it cynically in its place. A gallery of the gods—almost forgotten Mediterranean gods like Marduk and Anubis—watches the old play that humanity still goes through; but while humanity is outworn, the gods still live, jaded with the play but still viewing its tedium, though with a yawn. The series swings between the stage, where the poet examines the unhappiness, the posturings, the real distresses and humiliations of the actors, who include himself, and the audience, where the spectators with their fantastic names yawn, doze, greet each other in the stalls, and comment on the play.

> My strings I break, my breast I beat,
> The immemorial tears repeat,
> But Beli, yawning in the pit,
> Is not at all impressed by it . . .

The series ends with a poem to the gods themselves:

> You were our statues
> Cut from space,
> Gorgon's eyes
> And dragon's face;
> Fail us not,
> You that we made,
> When the suns go out
> And the stars fade . . .

But the whole series seems a little unreal, contrived; it lacks the impact of Slessor's best later poems, where the reporting on visual and sensuous qualities is what convinces and enthrals us.

The sixteen poems that represent, in Slessor's *One Hundred Poems,* the years from 1933 to 1939, begins with the sonnet-sequence 'Out of Time', Slessor's memorable meditation or complaint on that subject that so occupied the poets of the 'thirties and 'forties. The poignant bitterness of the language of the first sonnet, sharp as the 'bony knife' of Time itself, the image of time as wave and as knife-blade, the vision of the Harbour pierced by 'quince-bright bitter slats of sun', the connection of the Harbour with death, make the poem a premonition of 'Five Bells'; but the victim of the death-by-water here is the poet, his youth, 'the moment's world'.

> Fool, would you leave this country?' cried my heart,
> But I was taken by the suck of sea.

These three sonnets taken together contain some of Slessor's most poignant images, and his most mournful; just as most of the poems of this period contain, hidden somewhere in them (like the stone thrown up by the plough, in 'Harley's field', that turns out to be a stone knife) the thought of death.

But in two extraordinary technical achievements, the poems 'Sleep' and 'Five Bells', the water imagery, of time as a wave, receives a deeper significance, that of birth and death as well. In 'Sleep' the unconsciousness of abandoned sleep is compared to the unconsciousness of the womb, 'betrayed' by 'harsh birth' as sleep is torn apart by daylight. In 'Five Bells' Time becomes 'the flood that does not flow', where midnight confuses the depth of water with the height of the sky and 'night and water/Pour to one rip of darkness'. Through this double midnight the poet tries to recall his drowned friend, detail by detail; but the picture changes to

> the night we came to Moorebank in slab-dark,
> So dark you bore no body, had no face . . .

and even the words the two had spoken were 'bitten off by the wind', so that

> . . . all I heard was words that didn't join . . .
>
> And fifty mouths, it seemed, were out that night,
> And in each tree an Ear was bending down . . .
>
> When, blank and bone-white, like a maniac's thought,
> The naphtha-flash of lightning slit the sky,
> Knifing the dark with deathly photographs.

It is easy to miss, in admiration for this passage, its deeper significance in the poem. This is not just a random recollection of a night spent with the dead man; it is itself a symbolic statement of the poem's theme, which is the fragmentariness of communication with the living, the loss of communication in death:

> Yet something's there, yet something forms its lips
> And hits and cries against the ports of space, . . .
>
> But I hear nothing, nothing . . .
>
> . . . unimportant things you might have done,
> Or once I thought you did; but you forgot
> And all have now forgotten—looks and words
> And slops of beer . . .
>
> If I could find an answer, could only find
> Your meaning, or could say why you were here
> Who now are gone, what purpose gave you breath
> Or seized it back, might I not hear your voice?
> . . . And tried to hear your voice, but all I heard
> Was a boat's whistle, and the scraping squeal
> Of seabirds' voices far away, and bells . . .

But also throughout the poem the two motifs—the 'bony knife' of Time that 'runs us through', and the water imagery, sleep or unconsciousness—are interwoven. All the imagery in fact, is taken up, altered, re-echoed; sometimes from earlier poems. The 'deathly photographs' with which the lightning 'knifes the dark' are like the vision of human life seen in lighted windows, in 'Last Trams':

> Their faces brush you as they fly,
> Fixed in the shutters of a blind;
> But whose they are, intent on what,
> Who knows? They rattle into void,
> Stars of a film without a plot,
> Snippings of idiot celluloid.

And in 'Five Bells' itself they are echoed again, in the notes in the journal, with their miscellaneous list of things the dead man owned;

> Guns, photoes of many differant things
> And differant curioes that I obtained . . .

Here, then, are Slessor's final images of human life and its failure to communicate and to endure, of the cruelty of time that allows only the briefest and most trivial contact, even between the friends, the young men who, in 'The Old Play', believe in friendship:

> —'Shang Ya! I want to be your friend'—
> That was the fashion in our termitary,
> In the gas-lit cellules of virtuous young men . . .—

but are parted by time:

> On and on, driven by flabby whips,
> To the Nine Lands, to the world's end,
> We have been scattered by the sea-captains of ships,
> Crying no more with bright and childish lips,
> Even if we wanted to pretend,
> 'Shang Ya! Let me be your friend.'

The nostalgic memory occurs again in 'Five Bells':

> In Sydney, by the spent aquarium-flare
> Of penny gaslight on pink wallpaper,
> We argued about blowing up the world . . .

The crowding imagery, the coruscating phrases of Slessor's earlier poetry, seemed to dazzle like fireworks—in fact, a poem by

Nancy Cato uses exactly this comparison for them. But behind the fireworks we are always conscious of dizzying and empty blackness, the 'cracks between the stars'. As his poetry matures, the veil of imagery thins, the darkness becomes more and more insistent. Darkness, isolated glittering lights, and emptiness—this is the background scenery of 'Five Bells'; the Harbour itself, the 'midnight water' that covers the bones of the dead men and is scarcely distinguishable from the air. And the darkness with its scattered lights seems also symbolic of the loneliness of men whose contacts are so transitory and far apart. This makes the final image of the harbour-buoys, 'tossing their fireballs wearily each to each', so obscurely moving—more moving than the bells themselves with their double reference, to time and to mortality.

This is a closely-linked and complete poem; and it is to all intents and purposes Slessor's last important communication. It closes *One Hundred Poems,* while in the later collection it is followed only by the two comparatively slight poems, 'Polarities' and 'An Inscription for Dog River', and by the deeply moving 'Beach Burial'.

This poem, written at El Alamein during the War, significantly, has the same theme as 'Five Bells'—the drowned man, the fading communication. The name scrawled on the wooden 'stake of tidewood' is itself anonymous: 'Unknown Seaman'; the indelible pencil in which it is written 'wavers and fades'; the men buried in the sand are not only anonymous but are 'joined together' by the sand, whether in life they were enemies or allies.

It is the repetition of the situation in 'Five Bells' that moves Slessor again to poetry. The poem 'Inscription for Dog River' is much slighter, but in it, too, the theme recurs: the lost identity, the anonymity of the dead soldiers, and the name of their general, which though it is cut to commemorate his victory, is cut 'next to Ashur-Bani-Pal's, Nebuchadnezzar's and the Roman host'— time scorns it as Slessor himself does.

Looking back over Slessor's poetic life, it seems as though silence was always in the background of all he has said, and has finally triumphed over his brilliant and feverish imagery. There is something about nearly all his poems that makes them seem skeletal—a construction of scintillating words, like a neon sky-advertisement against darkness. They have about them something rootless and desperate; even the increasing mastery of technique does not quite disguise their lack of content.

In the end, what Slessor tells us is that humanity is chaotic-
ally fragmented, isolated, unable to communicate with anything
other than itself; (and communication between individuals is
equally fragmentary and chaotic, subject to the whim of time and
death). Lights spring up, glitter, seem to form a pattern, but
blink out; we cannot say 'why you were here/Who now are gone'.
This is not a poetry written for the sake of communication, but
the desperate talk of a man who 'cannot escape those tunnels of
nothingness,/The cracks in the spinning Cross'. The voice has
now fallen silent.

In Slessor's work, the emotional impasse of European civilization appears as affecting Australian writing directly. Brennan had
experienced and known it; but Brennan had turned from the
impasse itself to an examination of its genesis in the psyche
of man, and he had by-passed its bitterest effects by this deeper
exploration. Even though Brennan was left desolate, there was
for him 'a peace in the heart of the winds'; and though the fight
was 'foredoom'd disastrous', the explorer of the night knew that
until man had learned to 'have care of the wastes' his battle
must go on. So, in the end, Brennan's poetry is forward-looking
and forward-urging.

But for Slessor, it seems, activity is negated before it is undertaken. His poetry is essentially static in its nature; it is not stoic,
like Brennan's, but epicurean. If human contacts are temporary
and incomplete, if the glimpse of 'the moment's world' vanishes
and 'the body dies and rots', what is left? Feeling certainly:

> . . . feeling
> Hunger and cold, feeling
> Food, feeling fire . . .
> Feeling.

But feeling too is momentary and chaotic, and may lead to
cruelty, perversion, and disgust as in 'Cannibal Street':

> 'Buy, who'll buy', the pedlar begs,
> 'Angel-wings and lady-legs,
> Tender bits and dainty parts—
> Buy—who'll buy my skewered hearts?'

> Buy, who'll buy? The cleavers fall,
> The dead men creak, the live men call
> And I (God save me) bargained there,
> Paid my pennies and ate my share.

Nothing else, in Slessor's poetry, appears to offer even a momentary satisfaction; nothing is worth seeking, except perhaps a certain elegance in living:

> Your uncle, the Great Harry, left after him
> The memory of a cravat, a taste in cheese,
> And a way of saying 'I am honoured'.
> Such things, when men and beasts have gone,
> Smell sweetly to the seraphim.
> Believe, me, fool, there are worse gifts than these.
>
> ('To Myself')

Perhaps this is the chief mark of Slessor's poetry—an elegance, a brilliance, that do not even seek to conceal the emptiness beneath, but describe their graceful figures as a skater does on ice.

In spite of his interest in technique and his twentieth-century despairs, Slessor is never an unconventional poet: that is, a poet who uses obscurity or jarring dissonance, or violence of rhythm or language, to express his personal distress. The crazy revulsion of a Kenneth Patchen at the modern scene would be entirely foreign to Slessor; even the sight of the drowned sailors at Alamein is converted into something as beautifully wrought as possible, each word and vowel and consonant meditated to produce its full effect.

Yet the despair and the lack of direction beneath the poetry are authentically twentieth-century, and they stem, not from the Australian scene, but from European civilization and the rootlessness of the city. Pound's condemnation of 'the old bitch gone in the teeth', Eliot's 'Waste Land', find their echo in Slessor, though his preference for more traditional poetic methods and his lack of depth mask the immediate likeness. Slessor's is a poetry of the surface of life; what he cannot grasp by means of sense and intuition does not exist for him.

But this very lack of thought and emotion means that despair, when he discovers it is part of himself and of the world, is all the more irredeemable. He cannot, like Brennan, widen and deepen his world-view; he can experience, but he cannot interpret. There is a sense, indeed, in which Slessor's poetry is something very like inspired reportage. He does not seek for causes or solutions; he does not try to look into history or into the human soul; and though, at the end of 'The Old Play', he calls upon the gods:

> Fail us not,
> You that we made,
> When the stars go out
> And the suns fade . . .
> Leave us not crying
> In emptiness.

the gods he has pictured as the play's audience are far too fantastic and cynical for such an appeal to touch them, or us.

At the bottom, the note of hollowness and hopelessness in Slessor's work is inescapable, and the more so because of the often quite conventional beauty of the words in which it is expressed:

> Vilely, continuously, stupidly,
> Time takes me, drills me, drives through bone and vein;
> So water bends the seaweeds in the sea,
> The tide goes over, but the weeds remain.
>
> ('Out of Time')

> Look in this harsher glass, and I will show you
> The daylight after the darkness, and the morning
> After the midnight, and after the night the day
> After the year after, terribly returning.
>
> ('To the Poetry of Hugh McCrae')

So the poet who had begun to write at a time when the Lindsays were issuing their ultimatum against the 'nihilism' of European art and writing, and proclaiming the apotheosis of the 'hero-artist, the bearer of the creative image', himself ended as the most nihilist of Australian writers—nihilist, as it were, in spite of himself and in spite of his rejection of the advance-guard of European writing, of the experimental work of Joyce, Pound and their followers. For the true nihilist is not the man who affirms the end of traditional modes of thought and feeling and the beginning of the reign of chaos; but the man for whom the meaning and significance of life are already negated by despair, no matter how elegant and technically accomplished its expression. And for Slessor, in the end, experience is rendered meaningless by its discontinuity, and communication between human beings is momentary, limited, and corrupted by time and death. Only 'the moment's world' can hold beauty and freedom and changelessness; and the moment is no more than a moment; it is not, as it is for Eliot, the guarantee of anything beyond itself.

A world of discontinuous moments, of temporary relationships, of sensuous joys promptly contradicted by their opposites, is in truth a world made up of 'snippings of idiot celluloid'. Even the Great Harry, whose dandyism Slessor once thought would 'smell sweetly to the cherubim', is in a later poem displayed in a mortuary light:

> . . . in the glass navel of his dressing-room,
> Nests of diminishing mirrors, Narcissus peers,
> Too nicely shined, parting the cracked, refracted sneers,
> And meets the Corpse in Evening Dress; Caruso's tomb.

For not all the 'accoutrements and mysteries' of the toilet of elegance can suffice to cover the abyss; and in Slessor's poetry the abyss is finally triumphant.

CHAPTER XI

R. D. FitzGerald

∽

THERE IS a strong regionalist feeling in Australia, which has always dictated that writers in Sydney and in Melbourne shall be regarded as of opposing schools. The two schools are defined by Manning Clark, in his article 'Faith' in *Australian Civilization*, wholly by their opposite qualities; the Sydneyan attitude is defined as Nietzschean, unconcerned with social responsibility, self-occupied, proclaiming the acceptance of 'life' and the cult of beauty, and scornful of the value of brotherly love and the Christian attitude to one's neighbour; the Melbourne school of thought is defined as basically social-democrat in its politics, humane in its attitude to 'the masses', believing in the value of education for all, occupied with self-improvement rather than with self-fulfil-ment, mental rather than sensational in its general outlook. The latter school of faith might be said to stem from Furphy and O'Dowd, the former from McCrae and his preceptor Norman Lindsay.

Manning Clark's definition of these two 'main schools of faith', as he calls them (possibly it would beg the question less to refer to them as 'attitudes to life'), is convincing enough so far as it goes; but it is, in its effect, somewhat separative and sim-plifying. In the chapter on Slessor, I tried to make a distinction between the alternative culs-de-sac to which a shallow Nietzsch-eanism leads: the premise that man is his own valuator and the measure of all things leads the natural pessimist (of whom Slessor is one example and Lawson, perhaps, on his different level another) to the desperate brink of a conclusion that since man is clearly not equipped to face godhood, the world he has made for himself is ultimately meaningless; but leads the natural optimist to cry Excelsior in the face of all evidence of human fallibility. One reaction, in fact, is to doubt the possibility of man's being able to pull himself up by his own bootstraps; the other is to exclaim 'No higher agency being at work in the uni-verse than man himself, it is obvious that man has always pulled himself up by his own bootstraps and must continue to do so.' Of this latter reaction, O'Dowd is probably the obvious example, as Slessor marks the logical working-out of the former.

It is clear that, from the Slessorian view of the universe, nothing further can emerge except variations on the theme of hopelessness and emptiness. Slessor's poetry is, in fact, a dead end; it does not carry thought beyond itself. Where Brennan finally accepted the fate of man as eternal wanderer in search of Eden—an Eden of reconciliation of 'doing and being', of action and dream—Slessor accepts rather the impossibility of any further movement or communication beyond a fragmentary gesture.

But, in the same Nietzschean atmosphere and from, in fact, the same involvements, another poet who had early published in *Vision* and made part of the same group of young Sydney writers as Slessor, chose the path of the optimist, though not, like O'Dowd, of the programmatic and political optimist. R. D. Fitz-Gerald, even as a young poet, took his stance on an actual measurable earth, on the realities of sense and of commonsense, and chose for his subject, not man's eternal wandering in quest of Eden, but the 'battle' Brennan had spoken of and the 'fronting of the way'.

Faced with the question of the justification of man's existence, and of his appropriation of the means for that existence, in a world without God, he replies in effect that man is his own justification; for FitzGerald, the line of progress is still upwards and onwards. The virtues he extols are those of courage, endurance, and moral stoicism, rather than the Dionysian gaiety recommended by the Lindsayans. He is the poet of progress, of conscious or unconscious tasks, of objective work and achievement; there is about him an air of masculinity and sinew, his poetry, at its worst headmasterly, is at its best noble.

Yet there is nothing programmatic about FitzGerald's faith; unlike O'Dowd (whom in some minor ways he resembles a little) he does not lay down blueprints for poetry, or call for leadership from the creative man; and though he takes a brief glance at the positivist dilemma, it is outer, not inner, circumstance that he sees as the chief menace and problem facing man. He is, in fact, the very reverse of Slessor; and it is curious to observe how differently each, contemporaries faced apparently with the same poetic situation, has dealt with the problems of poetry.

FitzGerald, unlike Slessor, has always been, when the circumstances of his life permitted it, a steadily productive writer. Though his poetry for a time tended to increase in argumentative and narrative content, and to decrease in verbal and imagic interest, over the years, he has sometimes suddenly achieved (as in the poem 'The Face of the Waters') a remarkable depth of insight and exactness of expression.

Though the force of contemporary preference has made him into a poet capable of compression and lyric shape, he has seldom been in fact a lyricist. His gift has been rather expository and narrative; and where he does (as he can) bring off a true lyric poem, it is often so compressed in thought and expression as to seem cramped into the briefer form as into a Procrustes' bed.

FitzGerald's first books, *The Greater Apollo* (1926) and *To Meet the Sun* (1929) were notable for their directness and good sense as well as for their thoughtfulness, but it was not obvious that the writer was a poet of stamina; and since his next book did not appear until 1938, and this was Slessor's most productive decade, FitzGerald suffered during this time a comparative eclipse.

In *The Greater Apollo*, too, he had specifically enough stated his position against the Lindsayan Renaissance: he would

> . . . look no more for gods among
> The lace-like ferns and twisted boughs . . .

> It is enough that trees are trees,
> That earth is earth and stone is stone . . .

He seemed, in fact, the epitome of countryman realism as against Slessor's city wit and disillusion; and he has little of Slessor's obsessive interest in technical accomplishment. He early worked out a pleasant straightforward prosody, with few fireworks but capable of expressing his often involved and qualified thought processes; and from the beginning he has elevated content to a higher place than form in his verse.

In 1938, Australia celebrated its 150th anniversary of the First Settlement, and FitzGerald won the prize then offered for a poem, with the long 'Essay on Memory'. It was a resounding success; FitzGerald overnight took his place beside Slessor as a leading poet, and the poem was praised and fêted. His third book, *Moonlight Acre,* appeared in the same year, and the poems in it, including 'Essay on Memory', confirmed his new position.

In *Moonlight Acre,* particularly in the first series, the influence of Brennan's 'Wanderer' poems is evident. There is, in fact, a certain reminiscence of Brennan's sentence-line even in the later poems; the length and involvement of clause after clause, the run-on lines and even the run-on verses, which make the argument seem even more strenuous than it is; so that at the final clause the reader feels he has been led at a long muscular striding pace through a complex climbing zig-zag of thought. A paraphrase or précis of the sentence, however, can often simplify it surprisingly—and it is characteristic of FitzGerald, though not often of Brennan, that a paraphrase of whole poems is not only possible, but sometimes even enlightening.

This is perhaps a serious criticism. Poetry, above all, is justly thought to consist in economy and exactitude of phrasing—the best words in the best order; moreover, even the attempt to paraphrase a poem of the order, say, of Yeats's 'Byzantium', or even one of Milton's lesser sonnets, ends and must end in bathos. The poem ought to subsist in an order of its own. FitzGerald's poems sometimes seem almost wilfully complicated and knotted (as for instance Slessor's never do); it is a touchstone, in his poetry, by which we may distinguish the really good from the expository poems.

If we look at the last four verses of the fourth poem in the 'Moonlight Acre' series we can see the Brennan influence at work:

> But you have not gone forth, poor fugitive
> behind stout bars—your standards, your sure trust.
> Imprisoned and safe, you are not defiled by dust;
> unquestioning, are not constrained to live—
>
> so have not known nor ever shall know at all
> that little homes in the dusk, nestling beside
> protecting hills, could halt you in your stride,
> nor how that call can be a fatal call
>
> for any whose feet are set on the stern way
> towards what truths or half-known images
> flash beyond thought; who, scourged with purposes,
> must tread defeat till nightfall, despair till day;
>
> while the hearths cry: 'Yet none would take the sword
> and go seeking, if somewhere at some end
> there were not firelight, quiet of friend with friend,
> and laughter—though death ends it, the last reward.'

The echo of 'The Wanderer' is obvious; but the message is quite other. Unlike Brennan, FitzGerald is not speaking from the bitterness of experience: Brennan saw himself as the Wanderer, the outcast who knows that 'the home of man (is) feeble and builded on the winds', who has 'come from the outer night' to call on the men who hide behind the gleaming panes that 'the winds are up and terribly will they shake the dry wood . . .'

> And when ye come forth at dawn, uncomforted by sleep,
> ye shall stand at amaze, beholding all the ways overhidden
> with worthless drift of the dead and all your broken
>   world . . .

FitzGerald's is the message, not of a prophet of disaster and rebirth, but of a less apocalyptic writer—one who can console himself with the thought that, though the search of the poet is difficult, it ends where it began, in human communication. Neither Brennan nor Slessor would have endorsed this comfortable conclusion.

So, in FitzGerald, Brennan's desperate search for an impossible Eden which alone can save man from final self-destruction becomes something much more like an exhortation to be up and doing:

> And that was the old sea, alive beyond the calm
> of those wide-reaching waters stifled in the lagoon—
> alert, masterful waves summoning beach and palm
> to be up and about and moving and ever upon quest
> of new desires of the spirit, not sunk in a soft rest . . .

Indeed, FitzGerald does not believe, as Brennan did, in any final confrontation with destiny and chaos and old Night. The end of 'Essay on Memory' is unquenchable in its optimism.

> Whatever the task, it lies in front: we must
> build upward though we guess not to what skies . . .
>   . . . We will serve out our term:
> not yet the impetus flags whose course began
> when at the blank mouth of our stinking lair
> we saw night's infinite curtain shake with grey
> and so went forth determined to be Man . . .
>   . . . So, should our best work fail us, walls we planned
> stifle in years blown over fine like sand,
> or life itself reach gulfs and lorn extremes—
> even some crag of ending . . .

> . . . then, launched above that steep,
> venture shall cant bold wings and with their sweep
> splinter such clogging silence as they met
> in older abyss where time slept stirless yet.

I think it is true to say that, though this attitude is heartening and masculine and even noble in its scope, it would hearten us more if there were any real evidence that FitzGerald had explored the boundaries of the humanist and positivist situation as deeply and completely as Brennan has done. But, up to the end of 'Essay on Memory', there is no such evidence. The 'battle' from which in 'The Wanderer', Brennan emerged disillusioned, exhausted, but serene was a battle which involved not only the very depths of personality but the very heights of thought. Brennan had not, it soon became evident, solved the problem in more than a momentary way; indeed, it still remains the basic issue which involves us all. Slessor's answer to it was a retreat; FitzGerald's is a defiance; but the defiance is often too vague, too lightly considered, to convince. For FitzGerald,

> argument is the blade-bright windowpane
> which shears off cleanly the slant sheaf of rain . . .
> Here thought may ponder in peace or work at will
> or take down book from shelf and read his fill . . .
>
> ('Essay on Memory')

The enemy to be defeated is, in fact, outside, and not within; it is the old threat of the elements, the 'encroaching dark', to be defeated by faith in life and self and sheer action. This is a pointer to his closeness to Baylebridge, rather than to Brennan, in attitude, though certainly in nothing else. Baylebridge's propagandism, and his desire to be a leader—even perhaps a Leader—are quite alien to FitzGerald's strenuous acceptance of life, and where Baylebridge keeps pointing out what ought to be done and thought, FitzGerald keeps pointing out the virtues and value of what actually has been and is being done and thought.

Yet FitzGerald, can, for instance, write with curious insouciance lines like

> Fell the tree to pluck a leaf;
> mow with swords a mangled sheaf;
> Life itself were cheaply spent
> for the frail accomplishment.

> Dreams are precious; earth is fair—
> throw them in the hollow air;
> count as dirt the race of men—
> fungus, trampled, thrives again.
>
> *(Moonlight Acre* VIII)

This is perhaps a more unchristian and inhumane statement than FitzGerald would care to stand by now; but it does point to a certain strain which has persisted in his poetry.

This blunt-mindedness—which, to do FitzGerald justice, seems to stem rather from an uncritical enthusiasm for action as such, than from lack of sympathy for slaves and underdogs—is allied to that quality in him which links him with the bush balladists and the tough-masculine strain in Australian development. He is, as it were, the poetic apotheosis of the balladists. Though he does not write in a vein that looks at all like the ballad, his longer narrative poems 'Heemskerck Shoals' (a supposed meditation by Abel Tasman) and 'Between Two Tides', a tale of the Pacific islands, seems like a philosophical translation and restatement of the attitude behind, say, 'The Man from Snowy River', with its glorification of sheer action and undaunted courage:

> . . . It is not enough
> that life should be lived justly, death met quietly,
> though that's nobility also. But man's essence
> is not nobility, it is man, unrest,
> a rushing of wind, distance . . .
>
>   Man is these things
> and life's like a wave breaking, not good or ill,
> or right or wrong, but action and pressing forward,
> a thing tested in the heart which hears and answers.
>
> ('Between Two Tides')

This is not so much an adventurous attitude, as it is the statement of an idea about adventurousness; it is the transmutation into ideal terms of the attitude to life that we sense behind the balladic tradition of the Outback.

Actually, it is very seldom that FitzGerald invokes any recognizably Australian background. His meditations range from Ireland, the country of his forebears, to Fiji, where as a young surveyor he spent some time. There is very little in his first important collection, *Moonlight Acre,* which can be closely localized (in this, too, he may have taken his line from Brennan's universality of imagery); and where he uses an actual scene or event as springboard for a poem, it is because that scene or event offers a convenient illustration for his theme. What reminds us of the bush tradition is the quality, not the subject or the method, of his work; its pleasure in the masculine qualities of strength and courage, its occasional offhandedness, its just-discernible swagger, its insistence on the realities of sense and the physical

> . . . this plain truth of hunger
> cries: Time to rouse! Put by the reading-glass
> which showed up print so clearly, a jagged mass
> of black rocks in a dangerous foam of white,
> showed more than sight could know, but not like sight,
> split into jutting patches the blunt sense
> and took more note of blots than eloquence.
> Time now to trust our eyes, which if they find
> less than the glass, less than contents the mind,
> have yet their own sure knowledge of shape and fact
> not as things purely are, but as they act . . .
>
> ('Essay on Memory')

So, in poems like 'A Weekend Miracle', he observes the sudden flowering of tea-trees in an apparently barren and ugly landscape and meditates on the significance of this regeneration of beauty and hope for 'a world which is not sick but fears it is'.

> Health is not healing . . . it is out-thrust
> of renewal from within, process of growth . . .
> and scarcity's not sickness; all between
> the road and the ridge, coarse country and starved
> green . . .
> . . . defy
> Monday's intolerable sky
> that the old urge towards living may prevail.

Contrasting this robust faith in the natural process of living with Brennan's highly wrought awareness of the logical impasse of modern consciousness, and with Shaw Neilson's very different emphasis on the eternal miracle of creation and the imminence of death, FitzGerald seems a poet for the man-of-action in need of a faith for every-day use.

Indeed, FitzGerald has also devoted thought to the moral problem of the man of action, the man who forms part of the continually interwoven chain of living and doing, which he sees as more important than the individual who is its growing-point, as it were. In 'Fifth Day', he meditates on the fact that 'what's done goes on for ever as consequence', and therefore

> it concerns all men that what they do
> remains significant unbroken thread
> of the fabric of our living . . .
> Attitude matters; bearing . . .
> . . . dignity and distinctness that attach
> to the inmost being of us each.

In the poem 'The Wind at your Door', he treats of another moral problem which lies somewhere at the back of the Australian consciousness—the conflict between the claims of heartless authority and of its victims; a conflict that was introduced to Australian soil with the First Fleet. One might have half expected the writer of those lines in 'Moonlight Acre' to take the side of authority in the age-old quarrel; it is the mark of a certain subtilizing and sensitizing over the years that in this later poem FitzGerald takes up the cause of the victim.

The poem is a meditation on FitzGerald's own ancestor, a doctor who was employed by 'the System' to supervise floggings in the early days of settlement, and on one of the men whose punishment he supervised, one Maurice FitzGerald, an Irish deportee:

> an ignorant dolt, no doubt, for all that crew
> was tenantry. The breed of clod and dunce
> makes patriots and true men: could I announce
> that Maurice as my kin I say aloud
> I'd take his irons as heraldry, and be proud.

But the doctor, not the convict, is in fact of FitzGerald's blood, and must be owned, in spite of revulsion, and forgiven with

> the forgiveness I must hope may clean
> my own shortcomings; since no man can live
> in his own sight if it will not forgive.

And contemplating the endurance of the convict under his three hundred lashes, FitzGerald writes:

> It would be well if I could find, removed
> through generations back—who knows how far?—

more than a surname's thickness as a proved
bridge with that man's foundations. I need some star
of courage from his firmament, a bar
against surrenders: faith.

'Yet,' he goes on, 'I can live with Mason . . .

. . . ill grows where ills resort:
they were bad times. None know what in his place
they might have done. I've my own faults to face.

What FitzGerald finds to admire in his namesake's resistance
and obstinacy under his three hundred lashes—the courage and
endurance, the refusal to surrender—is still what 'Essay on
Memory' celebrated more than twenty years before. The Irish
rebel and convict, refusing to disclose the secret of the rebel
armoury, is one of those

whom violence of mind,
violence of action, gave such singleness
that if they did but grow, ambitionless
except to live in the sun, they served their kind
with that straight growth of will which bears for seed
zest to create . . .

('Essay on Memory')

So FitzGerald, in his later as in the earlier poem, seems still
to affirm that

. . . all good is effort, and all truth
encounter and overcoming . . .

And though he repudiates Dr Mason's part in the proceedings,
and prefers the convict's side, it is clearly not any 'social concern'
(to use the modern jargon) that puts him there, but a more human admiration. For FitzGerald the savagery of the punishment
is, though not approved, explicable in terms of history: it is

a savagery tamed in you
only as subtler fears may serve in lieu
of thong and noose—old savagery which has built
your world and laws out of the lives it spilt.

FitzGerald has in fact been concerned with a kind of non-
Christian, conservative morality, throughout his poetic life; and
his poems, seen as a whole, are attempts to define and explain
this point of view. In *The Greater Apollo*, his first-printed book,
he explicitly rejected, not only the Greek pantheon of McCrae

and Lindsay but any concern with religions and metaphysical questions.

> What is revealed to me and known
> Beyond material things alone?
> It is enough that trees are trees,
> That earth is earth and stone is stone,

he wrote then, and time has not altered his standpoint. The basic faith underlying his optimistic stance towards history—the faith in 'effort and overcoming'—is peculiarly, perhaps, the outcome of his notion of the destiny of the European race in Australia, a simple notion enough but one which underlies the whole of the apparently intricate eleven-page argument of 'Essay on Memory' and brings it to a triumphant conclusion:

> . . . We whose scope
> clasps the tremendous leagues of summer-south,
> thunder-oppressive with curbed energies,
> least of all folk need question our day's worth
> or think its turmoil twitchings of spent earth . . .

For FitzGerald, no question of moral guilt and justification arises; there is no self-questioning, for instance, on the plight of the aborigines or the denudation of the land. Indeed, reading his poetry one might think Australia to have been uninhabited before the white man's coming: in 'Heemskerck Shoals', the supposed meditation of Abel Tasman, it is pictured as wholly empty:

> the place which lay, unleased
> beneath its empty centuries and stars turning,
> was waking under his love and would call those
> fired with the same unreasonable yearning
> who'd take it for their own . . .

And

> . . . there was one place—
> only the south was left—where spread clear floors
> for feet of the European . . .

Man is master of his own destiny, here, with a vengeance; and the Kipling notion of the universe—stripped, to be sure, of its imperial reference and put into the mouths, not of British Tommies, but of explorers and lawyers and even Tongan chiefs—is carried forward from its less subtle influence on the balladists of the 'nineties and the early years of the twentieth century, to act as a philosophical justification for a materialistic Australian culture. FitzGerald is nothing if not a materialistic poet, as a rule: he remains the poet who accepts stone as stone and tree as tree, and deeper philosophical questions of the relationship of concept and percept, of creation and destruction, it might seem, concern him very little.

But if we did think so, we would be wrong. Poets, even those that seem most predictable, are apt to be unexpected; and perhaps the most unexpected poem by any Australian poet is Fitz-Gerald's 'The Face of the Waters', written during the last war. It is in free rhythms, and it is unrhymed, where FitzGerald usually prefers more or less conventional forms, and it is a meditation on no less a subject than Creation, and on the impossibility of meditating on Creation.

It is, also unexpectedly, a very successful poem, making its point (unlike much of FitzGerald's work), more through imagery and suggestion than through statement and argument. It is indeed almost surrealist in its picture of the 'tentative migration' of 'a universe on the edge of being born':

> Once again the scurry of feet—those myriads
> crossing the black granite; and again
> laughter cruelly in pursuit; and then
> the twang like a harpstring or the spring of a trap,
> and the swerve on the polished surface: the soft little pads
> sidling and skidding and avoiding; but soon caught up
> in the hand of laughter and put back . . .
> There is no release from the rack
> of darkness for the unformed shape,
> the unexisting thought
> stretched half-and-half
> under the imminence of huge pylons—
> the deeper nought . . .
> in the shadow of beginning and that denser black

This is an attempt to go much deeper than most Australian poets have cared to trust themselves. It is an attempt, in fact, to go far beyond the region where 'stone is stone and tree is tree', into the region of 'the eternal instant', or 'nothing, which is the quick'. It is scarcely surprising that the poem's agonizing search for 'the pre-time pinpoint of impossible beginning' should be through a region of negatives. But the poem constantly refers back to the daytime world, where this impossible beginning becomes 'your hand stretched out to touch your neighbour's/and feet running through the dark, directionless like darkness'.

> Worlds that were spun adrift re-enter
> that intolerable centre;
> indeed the widest-looping comet
> never departed from it;
> it alone exists.

And the 'eternal instant' (which is also the 'pre-time pinpoint', in which are balanced the terrible forces of assertion and negation, life and anti-life), contains within itself all reality,

> the struggle to magpie-morning and all life's clamour
>   and lust
> the part breaking through the whole,
> light and the clear day and so simple a goal.

The poem, seen against the background of the rest of Fitz-Gerald's work, seems an enigma. Here is the most apparently commonsense and even at times prosaic of our writers, embarking on an excursion into the depths which seems momentarily to out-Brennan Brennan: embarking almost without warning and preparation, and returning safely (though it is an excursion he does not seem to have wished to repeat). The cruel pursuing laughter, the terrified feet on the 'black granite' (a detail that frightens like a nightmare)—how terribly authentic they seem. We wonder if the poem can rescue itself, as it were, and return to the upper levels on which alone poems can properly function; and when it does so there is a sense of relief as though some trapeze act were safely over.

Two things, however, can be observed in criticism of this remarkable poem. Firstly, though it begins with a terrible and monumental image implying a consciousness behind creation, and a mocking consciousness at that, which can laugh as it frustrates the attempt of life to break out of darkness, this image is not pursued or explained. To impute mockery to (presumably) the Creator is to introduce an alarming duality into the notion of creation. Surely, if this is a mere intuition, it needs justifying: and since it is introduced at the beginning, some reference at least should be made to it, even if only for the sake of unity, in the conclusion. It is too large and disquieting a notion to be left, as it is left, unexplained. It weights the poem profoundly at the beginning; we expect a counter-weight at the end, and instead we are presented only with a catalogue of the attributes (if such they may be called) of the 'pinpoint of impossible beginning'; the creator-notion has disappeared, and the mockery of the laughter that presides over creation is neither explained nor explained away.

Secondly, the last passage of the poem is extremely difficult to unravel; perhaps this is intentional (after all, to speak of the pre-conscious is to use words where words cannot apply at all, and to attempt to disentangle positive from negative where both may be as yet indistinguishable from each other is a thankless task). But it is worth quoting from the last lines to allow the reader to see their difficulty:

> The eggshell collapses
> in the fist of the eternal instant
> All is what it was before . . .

(that is, apparently, the potentiality of life has again been frustrated)

> Yet is that eternal instant
> the pinpoint bursting into reality,
> the possibilities and perhapses,
> the feet scurrying on the floor,
> It is the suspense also
> with which the outward thrust
> holds the inward surrender—
> the stresses in the shell before it buckles under:
> the struggle to magpie-morning and all life's clamour
>   and lust . . .

Here again, though apparently the opposite is being balanced against the frustration of the first three lines (since the 'eternal instant' is now the 'pinpoint bursting into reality', and *also* the suspense of forces)—here again the eggshell is shown as being *destroyed*, not by a thrust from within of life emerging, but by a thrust from *outside*, since it 'buckles under'. If an eggshell is broken by the emerging life, it does not buckle under, but upwards; if it is crushed inwards, the life within is injured. Yet the sentence continues: 'the struggle to magpie-morning and all life's clamour and lust'. The image is confusing; not only I think, because the 'eternal instant' is in any case inexpressible and contains all possibilities, but because the thought is unclear.

It is interesting to compare the feeling and thought of the

poem with Brennan's treatment of the same theme—the theme of the

> nought which is the hid heart of all place,

of the 'fleeting centre of the abyss' which man eternally seeks and which Brennan places, not outside man and his thought, but at the very core of both. Brennan, like FitzGerald, would tell us that

> Worlds that were spun adrift re-enter
> that intolerable centre;
> indeed the widest-looping comet
> never departed from it;
> it alone exists.

But FitzGerald does not draw from this statement the corollary that Brennan draws:

> Some throne thou thinkst to win
> or pride of thy far kin;
> this incomplete and dusty hour to achieve:
> know that the hour is one,
> eternally begun,
> eternally deferr'd, thy grasp a Danaid sieve . . .

> Rest—and a new abyss
> suddenly yawns, of this
> the moment sole, and yet the counterpart:
> and thou must house it, thou,
> within thy fleshly Now,
> thyself the abyss that shrinks, the unbounded hermit-
>   heart . . .

For Brennan the vision of the 'intolerable centre' is indeed intolerable; for it means that man is bound to the wheel of things and must suffer defeat eternally. For FitzGerald, the notion of solipsism seems to hold no terrors; it is not even mentioned. The practical and extroverted philosophy of Action as its own justification—'all truth is effort'—seems to him sufficient; if the wheel of things is a treadmill, at least, he seems to say, let man tread it with pride in the task.

But perhaps, all appearances to the contrary, it is just here that the mockery of the Creator's laughter is to be recalled, and FitzGerald is, at least in this one poem, far more subtle and disillusioned than the reader imagines. Perhaps the question had better be left open.

But one thing may profitably be said here: this poem stands alone in FitzGerald's work, both as his chief exploration of a theme which seems particularly to concern the twentieth century, that of subconscious or pre-conscious existence, and also as the only poem in which he uses a dream imagery which is almost surrealistic in its vague suggestiveness (the scurry of feet on the 'black granite', the imminence of huge pylons, the 'twang like a harpstring or the spring of a trap' which is yet 'not a string but silence plucked at the heart of silence').

The strength of his handling of these images, the sense of their dreamlike rightness, as we read, give them an impact which, it must be confessed, FitzGerald's poems do not always have. He has not, on the whole, worked through the image, but through statement; and after this poem, which was published in 1944, he returned to his former method.

During the next year he published under the title 'Said the Don' part of what was later to appear as the long poem 'Between Two Tides'. It is a discursive historical narrative to which might be profitably prefixed Jacob Burckhardt's observation that man is 'the one and only thing which lasts in history and is its only possible centre . . . this suffering, striving and active being, as he is and was and will be for ever'.

Or rather, this quotation might apply, except that, for Burckhardt, though man was the only possible subject for history, he was also a creature with moral problems and moral responsibilities, a creature subject to sin and error. For FitzGerald, error sometimes seems only of the kind implied in the phrase 'trial and error', and sin does not exist.

> Man is these things,
> And Life's like a wave breaking—not good or ill
> or right or wrong, but action and pressing forward.

The goal to which that action is directed is not a moral goal; indeed, since 'truth is effort', it is impossible that there should be a goal at all, either within history or outside it. We remember that though 'The Face of the Waters' ended in apparent triumph, with the cry

> light, and the clear day, and so simple a goal

we were given no hint of what the goal could be, or even in what its simplicity consisted. The goal, apparently, must be a constant succession of difficulties to be overcome, of steps on the treadmill of things which can never take man outside the 'intolerable centre' which alone exists.

For within history, there can be nothing but more history, and 'effort and overcoming' must be presented with more and more problems to be overcome, or they cannot be maintained. It is surely a monotonous prospect.

Does FitzGerald believe then that, in spite of the fact that the widest-looping comet cannot escape from its 'intolerable centre', there is such a thing as Progress in a straight line—progress in the nineteenth-century sense? He does not imply that man has grown morally or ethically better, over the centuries; indeed, in 'The Wind at your Door', it is clearly stated that the savagery of those 'bad times' has been tamed in man today only by fears which have taken the place of thong and noose, and that savagery has built our world and our laws.

History itself, it seems, must act as its own yardstick; we must, as he wrote in 'Essay on Memory', 'build upward though we guess not to what skies'. A historical imperative may not seem a wholly satisfactory substitute for a moral imperative (particularly if, as FitzGerald seems to imply, it stems from a mocking Creator); but it seems, in the end, to be all FitzGerald has to offer us, as a philosophy.

Philosophies, however, are not poetry; and even if FitzGerald's man-of-action viewpoint on the world does not always convince us, the poetry remains, and we would be very much the poorer without it. Though his theme is still, as it has always been, the justification of man to man, his later short poems in particular have expressed it in terms much more epigrammatic and moving than those of his middle period. Poems like 'Bog and Candle', 'Edge', 'The Wind at your Door', and 'This Between Us', are a noble and a masterly summing up of what this poet has been and done. There is about them a quality of sculpture—sculpture well and truly made, that will stand up to time and weather. They are poems that form a kind of monument to man.

CHAPTER XII

J. P. McAuley

~

MCAULEY'S FIRST book, *Under Aldebaran*, was published in 1946, when he himself was twenty-nine years old. However, it had for some time been obvious to those who had come across work of his scattered in University and other journals that he was a writer of brilliance, scope and economy. Sometimes the pressures behind his poems seemed too rigidly held under control; sometimes they seemed falsified by intellectual elaboration and too-recondite allusion. But the appearance of his poem 'The Blue Horses' in the 1943 Angus and Robertson anthology clearly indicated a talent that would mean much in the growth of Australian poetry.

It often happens that a comparatively early poem gives a kind of gnomic hint or map of the poet's later development; as Slessor's 'Stars' did, and Brennan's 'Thule'. What 'The Blue Horses' gives, however, is a kind of summary of the problems and difficulties behind the later development; the solution it finds for them is not the one which McAuley later turned to, and even the treatment is much looser and more irregular than the later versification. (In his later collection of essays *The End of Modernity*, McAuley disclaims all the 'new schemes and devices to replace traditional metre and rhyme . . . Who could bear a whole literature based on sprung rhyme, or free verse, or loosened semi-regular verse, or assonance and part-rhyme? One or two individual successes in such forms practically exhaust their usefulness', p. 169).

Similarly, in later years, McAuley was to reject all 'modernist' art movements and methods. But 'The Blue Horses' is given an epigraph 'In honour of Franz Marc' (the co-founder with Kandinsky of the *Blaue Reiter* expressionist movement in painting in pre-war Germany—a movement of which Klee was a distinguished member), and the poem is a celebration of the force of creative imagination as against a mechanic and material civilization.

> Blue Horses lift their neighing trumpets to the moon!
> They stamp among the spiritual mills
> That weave a universe from our decay . . .
>
> . . . Beneath the knocking of the magic hoof
> New spaces open and expand.
> For in the world are spaces infinite
> And each point is a mighty room
> Where flowers with strange faces bloom
> In the amazing light . . .

It is an immature poem, but its power is obvious; perhaps the most revealing verse, however, is that in which modern civilization is rejected:

> Leave to the councillors the garbage-plot,
> The refuse and the greasy tins
> Of this slum-culture—these are not
> The area where love begins . . .

And it was this side of the theme, with its implicit rejection of a good deal more than the mere overt manifestations of 'this slum-culture', that was more and more to influence McAuley's attitude. Later he was to write ('Sacred Art in the Modern World'):

> The modern movement is ambiguous. On the one hand it seems to bear witness to a dissatisfaction with the world-view of crass bourgeois humanism; . . . on the other hand, the revolt against humanism is generally of a blind, disorderly sort; the direction actually taken is not so much towards traditional order and intellectuality . . . as towards the dissolution of the last restraints and limitations of rationalism and empiricism, a descent into the abyss of subjectivity and irrationality. . . . In certain cases one might even be tempted to speak of a demoniac inspiration . . .[1]

Accordingly 'The Blue Horses' was not only his first, but his last, attempt to reconcile his own and the world's problems by an appeal to art as a healing and creative force. But McAuley has always felt the necessity for reconciliation, and moreover for a reconciliation that could be regarded, not merely as a temporary solution, but as permanent and all-embracing. His poetry's painstaking lucidity (after some early undergraduate flirtation with what he would now call 'Modernity') and his refusal to

1 *The End of Modernity*, pp. 104-5

compromise with romanticism or individualism in any way, are perhaps an indication of the urgency of his own inner difficulties and the necessity he has felt of some imposed order, external and immutable, to make his world bearable and meaningful.

Another early poem, 'Envoi', indicates both his self-identification with the Australian landscape and people, and his impatience with the new nationalism and the rising sense of Australianism which were finding expression in the war years. This upsurge of feeling for Australia, her history and her landscape had both a positive and (as always with nationalistic movements) a negative side; it was characteristic of McAuley's dry temper of mind to choose rather to prick the bubbles of enthusiasm, and to reduce the new 'love of country' theme to something closer to 'I am trapped in my country'. So his self-identification with Australia and her people has led rather to an increased sense of guilt and futility than to any inflation or self-satisfaction; rather to a cataloguing of the national vices than a celebration of the national virtues.

This uneasiness of feeling is obvious in the first version of the poem itself:

> There the blue-green gums are a fringe of remote disorder
> And the brown sheep poke at my dreams along the hillside;
> And there in the soil, in the season, in the shifting airs
> Comes the faint sterility that disheartens and derides.

> Where once was a sea is now a salty sunken desert,
> A futile heart with a fair periphery;
> The people are hard-eyed, kindly, with nothing inside them;
> The men are independent but you could not call them free.

> And I am fitted to that land as the soul is to the body . . .

So his later criticisms of Australia do often seem like a concealed self-criticism; and in view of his emphasis throughout his work on 'order and good chance', the first line of the poem (as it was first printed) takes on a significance it would not have in a writer more capable of accepting imperfection in himself and others. It seems to mark what was then, at any rate, a deep-seated sense of something wrong or out-of-place; and since to criticize the arrangements of Nature as untidy is perhaps permissible (though certainly anthropomorphic) but to call them disorderly is to make a value-judgement of a much more far-reaching kind, it is justifiable to suspect that the disorder was McAuley's own.

(It is interesting, by the way, that some years later McAuley amended the line. It now reads, at least in the Penguin edition:

'There the blue-green gums have a wild precision, a strict disorder'—

which, while it modifies, does not quite answer the criticism.)

The volume, *Under Aldebaran,* when it came out, was probably the best first book of poems to appear in Australia for many years. 'The Incarnation of Sirius', with its wild vision of man and the universe run mad together, is probably its high point; and possibly also it is the turning-point of McAuley's early poetry, away from the violent forces of the human emotions, towards the cooler, though just as precarious, uplands of intellect; away from what in his essay 'The Magian Heresy', he calls with distaste the 'night-world of the self', towards the 'daylight interpretations' of the Catholic religion.

In fact, the imposed order of the intellect, rather than of feeling, has probably always been McAuley's choice; the flux of life has no part in his poetry, which always turns away from actuality towards theory, and which is more inclined to talk about the problems of being a poet and an ethical being, than to indulge in poetry out of sheer love of being a poet and of living. Always, one feels a certain deliberation, a choice, a tension, in his earlier poems; tight-wires over the abyss, they sometimes have the air of a dialogue between a man bent on some desperate step and an authority—perhaps a very intelligent police-officer with a training in psychiatry—who is attempting to dissuade him without revealing any knowledge of his intentions. 'Celebration of Divine Love', for instance, reads more like a piece of persuasion, of special pleading, than a joyful choice of an alternative that is salvation.

I do not think that many people would quarrel with the basis of McAuley's analysis of the modern world and its dilemma: the lack of unity between man and his world, between the symbol and the thing symbolized, between the word and the thing—the withdrawal of meaningfulness from the outer to the inner, the modern assertion that man is the master of his own destiny and the accompanying assumption that the world is his to take apart as he chooses, since he is the final arbiter. For a child (as Piaget's experiments prove) even today, the word is *in* the thing; for the modern adult the word is (to use a phrase from a modern logician) 'a screen between us and reality', a dead thing, 'an end, not a beginning'. It is this separation of subject from object that marks the beginning of what McAuley has stigmatized as Modernity, his personal anathema maranatha—the exaltation of man, the denial of all else.

For McAuley, a man who has always needed, in the words of Clerk Maxwell, 'a law to guide him and a mystery to move about in', this separation, in the terrible responsibility it implies, was intolerable. Seeing the world fragmented into different meaningless objects of a madman's study, he chose to return into the only discipline that leads back into those centuries before the Middle Ages, when the world was still a spiritual reality and man a part of it; the Roman Church.

> World undistorted, world unsimplified,
> So long by me desired, so long denied!
> Open, eyes of the heart, begin to see
> The tranquil, vast, created mystery,
> In all its courts of being laid awake,
> Flooded with uncreated light for mercy's sake.

('A Letter to John Dryden')

This is obviously a legitimate analysis and a legitimate reason for conversion (indeed, no doubt all motives for conversion are legitimate). What has roused doubts is not this; it is something different, a failure in sympathy perhaps, in McAuley himself. It is possible to condemn, to be revolted by, to turn away from, the spectacle of the modern world; but in doing so the condemner forfeits all chance of understanding, and transcending through understanding, the problem that is behind that spectacle. McAuley's temper has always been a little doctrinaire; he has tended to take his own reaction to any aspect of 'modernity' as necessarily the correct reaction, and he has tended to condemn other reactions as insincere, at the very least, sinful and deliberately blind at the worst. But a condemnatory and abusive approach, such as McAuley has sometimes too easily taken up, is of no use at all to the spirit faced with terrible alternatives. If there is one thing we have learned from the past five hundred years, it is that our problem is far larger, far more inescapable, and implies far more for our whole world-view, than can be realized by anyone who refuses to grant it validity and meaning. If the movement of thought that began with (let us say) Galileo and brings us to our present situation is to be grasped and transcended, we will not do this by dismissing it as an 'illicit enterprise'.

This disquisition which I have felt it necessary to intrude on an account of McAuley's poetry is perhaps outside the legitimate task of criticism; but since much of McAuley's own poetry is based on and takes its point and meaning from his own stand-point here, I have felt it necessary to clarify my own attitude. Moreover, it is right that criticism should make its own basis clear. With much of McAuley's view of the modern situation I agree; with his resultant attitude to it and his prescriptions for its ills, particularly in poetry, I cannot agree at all; nor can I feel that they are pertinent to the situation.

I think this attitude of McAuley's may take its rise from a certain summariness, and a certain lack of real depth, in his analysis of the situation and of the alternatives it offers. Let me quote a crucial passage from his 'The Celebration of Divine Love', where he is speaking of the progress of the seeking mind through the modern world:

> Fled from his own disaster, he consults
> The learned magi casting horoscopes
> For the New Babylon. Plan by plan
> They raise the scaffold of terrestrial hopes:
> 'For thus', they say, 'when exiled man
> Disowns Jerusalem which we destroy,
> And learns to live, as the enlightened should,
> The desecrated life, he will enjoy
> The sweet fruition of all earthly good.'
> Yet, ill at ease, his steps are led apart
> To where the despised and hated remnant clings
> To the old way with undivided will:
> Out of the bowed darkness a voice sings,
> 'If I forget thee, O Jerusalem . . .'
> He listens, and his heart stands still.

This is perhaps the clearest poetic exposition McAuley has given us of the *process* of his conversion (I may add that Buckley, in his essay on McAuley, takes it also as a kind of prescription for the conversion of all, but perhaps it is better left as a personal statement). Let it be made clear that with the *fact* of conversion there cannot be any question of quarrel; it is the shallowness of the analysis behind the process that I think ought to concern us here. For there is not—alas—a simple choice between the 'modern magi' and the 'old way', as McAuley presents it, for most of us and to put it in this way is merely to beg a very great many questions. This is not to summarize; it is to over-simplify; and McAuley has set his face, in the quotation given earlier from 'A Letter to John Dryden', against over-simplification of this world. This passage is an example of the lack of depth and sympathy, the schoolmasterly attitude, which I have mentioned as rousing my own uneasiness. McAuley knows more than this—why does he not say so?

And the shallowness continues to be visible in the lines that follow. Is the 'remnant' of the faithful truly 'despised and hated?' I think this is a significant over-statement. There is obviously not much hatred or despising in the attitude of most people; certainly not among most whose opinion is worth considering. Rather, they would sigh with the dying Rochester, 'He is fortunate who can believe; it is not possible to every man.' And among the 'modern magi' of whom McAuley may be thinking, the attitude is not usually one of hatred, but of patronizing incredulity. The line is a gesture of mock-heroism, if we look at it unsympathetically; if we look again, it may seem more like a half-conscious encouragement to the potential convert. It is a call to the ranks of the religious martyrs, in a world where martyrdom is more likely, fortunately or unfortunately, to be for one's politics than for one's religion.

All this being said, it is more than time to look at the poetry itself. In the first book, *Under Aldebaran,* what perhaps is most likely to remain with the reader is a sense of tremendous tensions composed by effort; of the skill and smoothness of a skater who knows himself on the thinnest ice. The sense is conveyed, I think, by the inevitable tension between the classical precision of McAuley's versification, the careful choice of word, phrase, the controlled and directed current of the sentence, on the one hand, and the sudden unexplained and alarming images that spring up in these cultivated mindscapes. There is 'Terra Australis', with its deceptive simplicity in the second verse:

It is your land of similes; the wattle
Scatters its pollen on the doubting heart:
The flowers are wide-awake; the air gives ease;
There you come home; the magpies call you Jack
And whistle like larrikins at you from the trees . . .

through the third verse with its gradual insinuation of something stranger, in this familiar view:

> And who shall say on what errand the insolent emu
> Walks between morning and night on the edge of the plain?

to the extraordinary fourth verse:

> And northward, in valleys of the fiery Goat,
> Where the sun like a centaur vertically shoots
> His raging arrows with unerring aim,
> Stand the ecstatic solitary pyres
> Of unknown lovers, featureless with flame.

And there is 'The Incarnation of Sirius', with its vision of 'the monstrous form of God's antagonist':

> Anubis-headed, the heresiarch
> Sprang to a height, fire-sinewed in the dark . . .

Perhaps enough has been quoted to convey this sense of a quiveringly apocalyptic vision allied to a kind of forced calm of manner, of violence wedded to classicism. It is this contrast that gives much of the book its power; and when the inner tumult of the poems has been mastered and balanced by the emphasis that McAuley places on their intellectual ordering, they can rise to a sustained triumphant music as of a singer exactly striking the centre of his highest note, that is piercing in its beauty.

> O seraph in the soul, who singing climb
> The order of creation as a stair,
> And hold a silver lamp above the time
> And places of our deepening despair . . .

It is a lovely note; the very depth of the abyss below gives it resonance; but like so much of McAuley's poetry it is not so much creation, as invocation of creation: not so much poetry as a discovery of the conditions of poetry. There is, if I may put it so, something in most of these poems of deliberation, decision, imposition. It is in this sense more than any that McAuley is now a Virgilian, rather than a Homeric, kind of writer; I say 'now', because this tendency seems to have been strengthened and confirmed over the years since the appearance of *Under Aldebaran*.

His second book, *A Vision of Ceremony*, contains, however, some of the most perfect of his poems, notably the New Guinea lyrics in the section called 'Black Swans': 'To a Dead Bird of

Paradise', 'To the Holy Spirit', and 'New Guinea'. His translation of the Bird of Paradise killed for its plumage is particularly
beautiful:

> Ah, fabulous fancy,
> Now cold and forlorn,
> Go dwell with the phoenix
> And unicorn.
>
> Your opaline plumage,
> Deep-burning jewel
> Falls prey to the hand that is
> Cunning and cruel . . .
>
> But there your exemplar,
> The phoenix, survives,
> Unheeded, unheeding,
> Through myriad lives . . .

And, in 'To the Holy Spirit':

> Leaving your fragrant rest on the summit of morning calm,
> Descend, Bird of Paradise, from the high mountain;
> And, plumed with glowing iris along each curving wire,
> Visit in time our regions of eucalypt and palm . . .
> Engender upon our souls your sacred rhythm: inspire
> The trembling breath of the flute, the exultant cosmic psalm,
> The dance that breaks into flower beneath the storm-voiced
>   mountain;
> Array in your dazzling intricate plumage the swaying choir.

This deeply meaningful and effective translation of the natural
into the spiritual seems to link with a passage in 'The End of
Modernity', where he refers to 'The special valuation (Christianity) gives to the material world, finding it real and good,
and eternally involved in man's spiritual destiny, sharing the redemption . . . Has this "Christian materialism" yet been sufficiently absorbed by a Western consciousness still marked by
Platonist spiritualism? . . .'[2] And this in turn links with the
passage that concludes (and largely justifies) the otherwise too
polemical poem 'To John Dryden', from which I have quoted
earlier.

For if the external world is indeed to be respiritualized, taken
up into our inner processes and rejoined to word and symbol,
this—or something like this—is the way it can be done. The

2 ibid., p. 116

simplicity, grace and colour of these poems cannot be an accident; in them McAuley seems to show his full power.

But for some reason, this hardly happens again. His Swan symbolism, beautiful as it is, does not seem to work on the same level; the actual swan is less fused with the symbolic Swan. In 'Mating Swans', the observation is exact enough, but it seems to overweight the poem; in 'The Middle of Life', on the other hand, the swan has become no more than an idea, a piece of shorthand as it were for something the poet wants to say. And other poems of the same kind seem sometimes over-quiet, sometimes a little too laboured and sententious:

> Upon your sacral column, pure
> Presence to the inward eye,
> There rests for an entablature
> The invisible order of the sky.
>
> But mostly, stilled to trance, O palm,
> Your paradisal plumage rears
> Its fountain, and amidst the calm
> A milky flowering spathe appears;
>
> Which an ascending youth incises
> Deftly with a bamboo knife,
> Whence a fermenting fluid rises
> Like joy within the common life.
>
> ('Palm')

On the whole, these poems, and the others in the book, seem less convincing, less satisfying, than those in *Under Aldebaran*. I think this comparative drop in the tone of voice, this flattening as it were in the poetic landscape, comes from exactly what one might have expected to free McAuley to write even better, that is, the calming of his personal tensions and agonies. Where before the whole tone was of a hard-won triumph, a balance kept against appalling odds, in a land where terror was never far away from the tight-rope walker, the tone is now (what was always in fact, a danger even to the youthful McAuley) sometimes almost prosy and didactic. The words have not exactly become more polysyllabic—but their polysyllabism seems more academic; the decoration has not become obtrusive, but it seems less inevitable and more artificial:

> And thus one Sunday, with another pair,
> They found a garden; each couple sat remote;

> The sky laughed: a curling baroque air
> Ruffled the colours of the bright parterre;
> A bird sat by with soft recording note.

('A Leaf of Sage')

The series of poems, 'The Hero and the Hydra', an attempt to cast light on modern man through a re-creation of certain of the Greek mythological tales, is perhaps McAuley's most Virgilian venture. But Augustus could not help but recognize the tale of his own forebears, when read aloud, as pertinent to his own day; the Prometheus-legend, already so extensively capitalized on by other poets, is apt to recall the sweet shrill crazy voice of Shelley, so unhappy yet so much for all that a poet, and against it, rather to my own surprise, McAuley sounds curiously bathetic.

> To suffer woes which Hope thinks infinite;
> To forgive wrongs darker than death or night;
> To defy Power, which seems omnipotent;
> To love, and bear; to hope till Hope creates
> From its own wreck the thing it contemplates;
> Neither to change, nor falter, nor repent . . .

Set that against McAuley's Prometheus' last word:

>   . . . If it be true,
> Then is the phoenix also true: the mind
> Shall rise up from these ashes to repair
> Ten thousand years and build its world anew.
> The plough that turns the blackened waste will turn
> The heart to peace; again the meek will learn
> In suffering and patient thought to share
> The task of gods, and hold a world in care.

Of the four poems which make up 'The Hero and the Hydra', the lines which most linger in my own memory are those which McAuley puts into the mouth of the dying Chiron:

> I have loved the earth alone, and had no will
> To change the measures of its good and ill;
> Others give laws, and blame, and sit above,
> But there were no conditions in my love.

Can it be that the elusive doubt and dissatisfaction that McAuley's later poetry seems to create in the minds even of many of his admirers may come from the conditions that he imposes on his love? So good a poet, capable of such sustained splendour, ought to convince us more than, in fact, he does. And I think that, if he feels we are simply unwilling to be convinced, he is wrong.

CHAPTER XIII

A. D. Hope

AS A poet, McAuley, in spite of his austerity, has sometimes seemed too gracefully nostalgic to present a firm front against the disregard and mere incomprehension that this commercial age and country accords to poetry. Its much more violent adversary has always been A. D. Hope. The two have at least this in common, that both insist on the imposition of order and metrical discipline on a poetic experience that seems to each to be chaotic. But Hope has often suffered from being as much his own adversary as that of the world; so that, instead of castigating the hypocrisy and insensitiveness of others, he seems rather to be preoccupied with enormous and half-real terrors which originate as much within himself as without—terrors of sexuality, of impotence, of cruelty and of decay.

Against these, and against the world's ignorance and spite, he has armed himself with a kind of half-hysterical cocktail-party wit, a conventional gift for caricature, and a repertoire of thrusts and parries that seems sometimes designed to conceal his real feelings even from himself. This manner, which has come to stand as Hope himself to superficial readers, can however modulate into its very opposite—a moving and rhythmical speech that rises at its heights into real nobility of form and content.

Hope is, in fact, as he has come to realize, a poet of two worlds and of at least two faces. His earlier work was much more given to a particular note of angry wit which gained him his reputation—much of it was a kind of defence-by-attack. Though for years he published little and did not earnestly seek the character of brilliant young man and alarming Swiftian critic, it is possible to trace a certain not wholly admirable enjoyment of the role, in his early reviews and poems.

It was tempting at that time to doubt whether any serious and passionate preoccupation with poetry, or even with criticism, would emerge from Hope's particular kind of distaste for the world. For one thing, his targets (though they have changed with the years) were not always those that most deserved martyrdom with arrows. Polemic can be admirable; Hope's has not always been so.

But, if his criticism has been sometimes one-sided, Hope has taken his poetry more seriously and responsibly than once might have been foretold. In fact, he has increased in stature so much that, in the ascendancy of University poets since the end of the war, he has become the most important figure. From a satirist, he has turned himself into a poet, and a poet with a vision of the world that is compelling and highly organized.

Nevertheless, Hope's world remains painfully dualistic. He is, more than any of our poets, torn between a loathed reality and a vision of eternal meaning. To his first world, he presents a frenetic puritan violence; of his second, until recently, he has not been able to speak with any certainty.

The difference between the two is perhaps best demonstrated in such poems as 'Observation Car'. This appears in his first book, *The Wandering Islands*, but is not reprinted in his collection *Poems*. It is a very characteristic poem, however, with its bitter knock-about farce, its vulgar-postcard figures, its self-disgust projected on to the outer world, and its revealing self-pity. It is, in fact, a thoroughly self-conscious poem; and from the beginning Hope has been a poet of self-consciousness, and of the torture of the self exposed in a merciless limelight both to itself and to the outer world.

The central metaphor is itself revealing. It is of Hope as a small boy, put into the observation car of the train for his first journey alone—a journey which lengthens like a nightmare into the whole journey of life. The rhythm and construction of the poem lend themselves to a particular tone of hysterical wit:

> . . . I am bored and a little perplexed
> And weak with the effort of endless evacuation
> of the long monotonous Now, the repetitive tidy
> Officialdom of each siding, of each little station
> Labelled Monday, Tuesday—and goodness, what happened
>   to Friday?

The lonely bewildered child in the observation car has already begun to talk with one eye on the audience.

> . . . And the maddening way the other passengers alter:

The schoolgirl who goes to the Ladies' comes back to her seat
A lollipop blonde who leads you on to assault her,
And you've just got her skirts round her waist and her
    pants round her feet
When you find yourself fumbling about the nightmare knees
of a pink hippopotamus with a permanent wave
Who sends you for sandwiches and a couple of teas,
But by then she has whiskers, no teeth and one foot in
    the grave . . .

By this time the kind of audience the writer is talking to seems
to be established; and it is hardly likely to be an audience which
wants to hear about the private agonies of a sensitive poet. So
when Hope's switch from the cocktail-party to the confessional
comes, it cannot help making us uneasy. Somehow it seems like
trickery, to be suddenly buttonholed by the rueful poet, ex-
plaining how he 'planned to break the journey

                              . . . to see
My urgent Now explode continually into flower,
To be the Eater of Time, a poet and not that sly
Anus of mind the historian . . .

In the end, neither aspect of the poem is convincing; there is
even a certain vulgarity about it, the vulgarity of the man who
has misjudged his listener. Either we want to be amused, or we
are interested in the private self-analysis of the poet; we cannot
attend to both in the space of the one poem. One way or the
other, the poem is a confidence-trick; our sympathy is demanded
on false pretences.

Yet it is the note of the second personality, the despondent and
ever-so-faintly maudlin self-analyst, that has deepened, changed
and matured over the years since the poem was written, sub-
merging the easy glitter and sword-play of the earlier Hope and
finally turning him into someone far more important: into, in
fact, one of the Eaters of Time.

In a society whose puritanism takes the form of making a
more-or-less neat division between the less and the more respectable occupations of the normal man—a kind of vision-proof com-
partment as it were—Hope's unsuitable habit of confronting the
flesh and the spirit has caused him to be regarded as outrageously
taken up with sex, and, moreover, ambiguous in his attitude
towards it. It is perfectly true that Hope's most obsessive image
of his first world, the world we call 'real', is in terms of sexual

cruelty and sexual possession; just as his vision of the second world, the eternal verity, takes its rise from the image of sexual fulfilment. But in his best poems the imagery becomes, as Eliot said in another context, 'only a way of putting it'. In the worse poems, however, such as 'Massacre of the Innocents', 'Pygmalion', 'Three Romances', a certain kind of distaste is aroused in most readers which I think has a valid basis.

In these and other poems, what is really, and rightly, objectionable is not the nature of the imagery (though this of course adds to our dislike of the poems); it is rather that the imagery seriously overweighs what is actually being said—what the poem is about. This is an architectural fault, as much as a fault in taste. Poems as rococo as, for instance, 'Lot and his Daughters', simply cannot support their weight of emphasis on sexual detail; it becomes apparent that the poem is written for the sake of the detail, rather than the detail put in for the sake of the poem. Moreover, this particular fault in construction, which is excusable where a poem is over-decorated through sheer enjoyment of decoration, in that it enhances life, is inexcusable where it is mere Grand Guignol or where the object is just to 'make our flesh creep'. It is even more inexcusable where, as in 'Ascent into Hell', the poet's object is to emphasize his own anguish and self-pity, to blackmail the reader, as it were, into sympathy. This is the worst weakness in Hope's poetry; and from such poems we are right to draw back in distaste.

For we can seldom feel, in such poems, that Hope's immediate audience of admirers is dispensable. Rather, like his own Byron:

> through the Infernal Fields he makes his way,
> playing again, but on a giant stage,
> his own Don Juan . . .

—and playing to an audience that, in his best moments, he must at times have felt to be no less suffocating. Yet he cannot help assuming the tone, acting the part; and this is why in his worst poems he appears to be talking at, rather than speaking to us. Hope has his own self-occupied rhetoric:

> That breed is in my bones; in me again
> The spirit elect works out its mighty plan—
> Yes, but that birth is hard. In the grown man
> Habit corrupts the will with terror or pain . . .

> ('Invocation')

It is the more admirable in Hope to have passed, in so many good poems (particularly in the later collection), beyond the temptations of his particular Slough of Despond. Cleverness and self-consciousness have spoiled more good writers than most other qualities, and simplicity and humility are difficult virtues for poets accustomed to use wit as a weapon.

Hope's present strength and maturity as a poet seem to have been reached, moreover, through a cultivation and exacerbation of his perception of his own loneliness and despair, a meditation on the moments that have seemed to offer a way out (such as the moments of love), and an enlightened submission to the necessities of poetry. Through these three aspects, he has found a basis for faith in some kind of universal process in which man is an instrument, not an end. This instrumentality is to be, curiously enough, through art and not through an increase in knowledge. If Hope cannot believe in Brennan's apotheosis of consciousness, he has at least had a glimpse of some kind of apotheosis of the creative side of man.

It is interesting that, whereas McAuley abandoned the notion of art as a saving and redeeming force, after writing his early poem 'The Blue Horses', Hope seems to have been led to it, and through it to a new vision of the possibilities of mankind, in his later years. In 'Pyramis or the House of Ascent', what is celebrated is the 'great work', the pyramid that remains when the race is gone.

> Neglect and greed
> Have left it void and ruin; sun and frost
> Fret it away; yet, all foretold, I see
> The builder answering: 'Let the work proceed!'

This turns into a meditation on the builders,

> men who put aside
> Consideration, dared, and stood alone,
> Strengthening those powers that fence the failing heart:
> Intemperate will and incorruptible pride.

This comparatively early poem shows Hope in a Nietzschean mood; for him, 'the builders', it would seem, worked for themselves alone and in defiance of the gods who must be 'overcome'. Yet his exemplars, Blake, 'Milton twice blind groping about his soul/For exit, and Swift raving mad in his', would not have spoken so of their art or of its motives: Blake who insisted that he had written his Prophetic Books 'from immediate dictation, and even against my will'; Milton who lamented his blindness because it made useless 'that one talent which is death to hide', not for himself but 'to serve therewith my Maker'; Swift, who also understood that the world's sin and his own were not to be mended by strengthening 'intemperate will and incorruptible pride'.

The poem is in fact an emblem of Hope's failure in understanding; his emphasis on the achievement of the defiant ego, in the face of all else, is sheer modern *hubris,* the self-dramatization of the hollow self-occupied mind.

Yet the poem which, in his later volume, Hope chooses to put next to this, 'The Death of the Bird', is an indication that he is capable of wider and deeper insights into the nature of the world. Where Hope is overtly or covertly self-occupied (and this happens in almost all his early work) his poetry is apt to be somewhat artificial in tone; his use of language can be flashily academic. In poems such as 'The Death of the Bird', where he finds a metaphor that allows him to escape from himself and objectify his problems, the miracle is worked and simplicity comes easily:

Season after season, sure and safely guided,
Going away she is also coming home.

And being home, memory becomes a passion
With which she feeds her brood and straws her nest . . .

The theme—of division, of the two homes of the migrant bird —is one that Hope makes especially his own. No poet is more conscious of dualism, no poet more vehemently rejects the temptation of an artificial unification of the two sides of his and the world's nature; and perhaps no poet has gone farther in exploring his own oppositions. The challenge of black to white, of female to male, of evil to good, of flesh to spirit, and of life to legend, occupies him in all his work, and the problems of reconciliation are the more terrible for him in that he knows himself to contain all these opposites and to be at home nowhere and everywhere.

For a poet so deeply divided and so despairingly aware of division, the question of reconciliation must seem impossible, and the comparative peace of death must seem the only final answer. So, in 'The Death of the Bird', there is a certain note of

triumph as well as compassion in the very current of the last
verses, with their piling up, first of despairs,

> Try as she will, the trackless world delivers
> No way, the wilderness of light no sign,
> The immense and complex map of hills and rivers
> Mocks her small wisdom with its vast design.

and then of elemental forces that by their strength justify her
relinquishment of the struggle:

> And darkness rises from the eastern valleys,
> And the winds buffet her with their hungry breath,
> And the great earth, with neither grief nor malice,
> Receives the tiny burden of her death.

The death itself comes as relief, not as sorrow; the divided heart,
Hope seems to be saying, can only find peace and unity here,
where the earth from which the opposites spring reunites them in
indifference.

This is the final message of *The Wandering Islands;* it is re-
iterated in the impressive poem 'The Return of Persephone'.
This re-creation of a legend of rebirth has a characteristically
twentieth-century turn. Persephone has been the rebel bride of
Dis; it is only when she leaves him to return to the world and the
spring that, seeing him in despair and resignation,

> Foreknowing all bounds of passion, of power, of art,
> for the first time she loved him from her heart.

This deep recognition of the hopelessness of 'passion, of power,
of art', this disillusion and search for the peace of death, is Hope's
contradiction of his own assertion of the powers of the conscious
self, the 'builder', the artist. It has always been in an ultimate
refusal to believe in his own statements, a creative spark springing from the clash of one side of his personality on another,
that Hope has found the strength and impulse to move on out
of his insoluble dilemmas and pose fresh contradictions at a
new level of insight. It is a painful method of progress and a
bruising one, but for Hope it has been fruitful.

So in the more important new poems in his second volume,
this deathward-turning denial, this vision of Persephone herself
in love with resignation, finds its own answer in a new kind of
statement of the 'bounds of passion, of power, of art', in a vision
which for the first time allows of the entrance of eternity into
mortality, of essence into existence, of the world of legend into

the world of corruption. The new note of triumph sounds in the first poem of the book, *Soledades of the Sun and Moon*—a poem about the relationship, less of poets with each other than of poets to poetry, and of poetry to the 'immortal images', the archetypes and symbols of legend, typified in the constellations.

> The mortal hearts of poets first engender
> The parleying of those immortal creatures;
> Then from their interchange create unending
> Orbits of song and colloquies of light . . .
>
> . . . In the star rising or the lost leaf falling
> The life of poetry, this enchanted motion,
> Perpetually recurs.

The theme is taken up again in 'An Epistle'—where again a man addresses a woman; the meditation this time is on the theme, not of poetry, but of love, denied yet triumphant:

> The soul sitting apart sees what I do,
>   Who win powers more than Orpheus knew,
> Though he tamed tigers and enchanted trees
>   And broached the chthonic mysteries.
> The gate beyond the gate that I found fast
>   Has opened to your touch at last.
> Nothing is lost for those who pass this door:
>   They contemplate their world before
> And in the carcase of the lion come
>   Upon the unguessed honeycomb . . .

This honeycomb is symbolic of a vision and knowledge beyond that of the flesh and time—a knowledge of the eternal images and their reality, which is far greater than that of individual man and individual love:

> As on the rough back of some stream in flood
>   Whose current is by rocks withstood,
> We see in all that ruin and rush endure
>   A form miraculously pure;
> A standing wave through which the waters race
>   Yet keeps its crystal shape and place,
> So shapes and creatures of eternity
>   We form or bear. Though more than we,
> Their substance and their being we sustain
>   Awhile, though they, not we, remain.
> And still, while we have part in them, we can
>   Surpass the single reach of man,

> Put on strange visions and powers we knew not of—
> And thus it has been with my love . . .

This magnificent metaphor is perhaps the high point of Hope's thought so far. It makes most clear the new trend of his thought, both about the legend and about humanity's part in it; for humanity, like the rough chaotic stream, is that which, though bound by time, is now seen to sustain, even to make the fleshly incarnation of, that which is eternal and beyond time's limitations. Humanity, then, however its immediate manifestations may disgust and dismay him, has for Hope been redeemed and justified by its part in the creation and sustention of eternity. The breadth and splendour of this vision, even if Hope should carry it no farther, are in turn enough to redeem and direct his poetry and our own.

In the poem which concludes the first section of this volume, 'An Epistle from Holofernes', the relation of the poet to this world of the eternal images, and the second world—that of the coarsely human temporality of event and action, where Love manifests itself as Lust and where compromise, habit and custom 'mask us from ourselves'—is set out and examined. The poet's function is to act as mediator between legend and actuality:

> It is the meaning of the poet's trade
> To recreate the fables and revive
> In men the energies by which they live . . .

But in doing so he must not lose sight of that world, in which after all our salvation or damnation is worked out, and by ourselves: the fables must be truly re-created, not simply repeated.

> If in heroic couplets then I seem
> To cut the ground from an heroic theme,
> It is not that I mock at love, or you,
> But, living two lives, know both of them are true.
> There's a hard thing, and yet it must be done,
> Which is: to see and live them both as one.

This is, of course, also the task of all poets; but in Australia only Hope has seen and stated it so clearly. This may be because of all our poets Hope has thought most about the task of poetry. There is something in this concentration of consideration that reminds us of a French rather than an English habit of mind; like Mallarmé, like Valéry, his greatest gift to poetry has been as much his elucidation of the poetic task as his actual examples of poetry. With McAuley and Harold Stewart, he early theorized about the forms and subjects of verse; and like McAuley's, a good deal of his poetry since then has been about poetry. The visible sensuous world is not his starting-point—it enters his poems with sometimes startling impact, but it is more often used as an illustration and concretion of an intellectual or emotional insight, than as itself a provocation to poetry, or even as what Baudelaire called it, a 'forest of symbols'. For Hope, the poetry is the thing; it is the mediator between doomed time and saving eternity; its function must be clarified and defined, the poet must understand what it is that he is doing.

This new readjustment of our hitherto most contradictory poet to his task is, or ought to be, an important happening for poetry. Hope is what is called an 'intellectual' poet; he is neither a poet of humanity nor a poet of the senses and their objects. For 'intellectual' poets, there is seldom any escape from a basic confrontation with the problems of intellectual man—the solipsism, the second-hand mulling over of opinion, the abstraction of thought that, hypertrophied and self-generating, can lead only towards despair. The intellect is only of real use in poetry when it begins from a starting-point of faith—not necessarily religious faith, but simply belief in a meaning in the human world, a direction that governs the flow and eddy of event, an underlying and overriding destiny that is not confined to man's own conscious purpose and knowledge.

This faith seems to have come to Hope, rather as an intuitive perception than an intellectual conclusion. His long poem 'Conversation with Calliope', a discussion of the situation of epic poetry in our present world, and incidentally of the situation of the poet as well, elaborates the idea behind it into a sketch of Hope's new world-view (though he is careful to emphasize that any such sketch must be regarded as a 'fable', not as an exposition).

> In the beginning was the Word . . .
> but though it *was*, it was not heard.
>
> . . . And then the Word began to move,
> Itself unmoved . . .
>
> The endless edifice of love
> Felt life's first step upon its sill,
> And in that primal globule furled
> Lay all the orders of the world.

These orders are then explained; the first is Life, the second consciousness. The third order, however, is beyond our grasp; it is a new creation through us as its instruments, the order of Art, and this, though we can see its products, we cannot fully understand:

> The arts themselves propose the free
> And unknown ends which they fulfil . . .
> New modes of being, till their laws
> Prevail, cannot be understood
> Beyond the process and the cause . . .

But the modern flood of increasing population, increasing synthesization and mass-production, of 'Man disposing', is leading to Art's disappearance.

> The Great Society produces
> Only the arts it can afford,
> Stamped, sterilized and tinned and tested
> And standardized and predigested.

Even to this, however, the Muse can reply, though her answer may not provide much consolation for man as he now is; 'The Word withdraws', she says, 'but never fails'. Even in the coming barbarism, 'Small clans we choose, and hold apart./Some few in whom the heavenly rage/Still blazes and keeps pure the heart,' and from these pilgrims the 'new forms of being' will still arise, though the poets of the present day (including Hope) may have to accept their own impotence.

The interest and importance of the new status Hope is postulating for art seems to me to lie less in the terms of his postulation than in the fact that, after years of self-disgust and disgust for the worse manifestations of humanity, he has, as it were, found a use for mortality that stretches all the way into eternity. Whether his readers can comprehend and credit the notion of the eternal images as a 'third order of being', higher than and incomprehensible by consciousness, is possibly beside the point. Indeed, he has himself carefully told us that we cannot grasp the notion of this 'third order', since we ourselves do not enter into it except as 'forming or bearing' the images that move above and beyond us. This means, in effect, that we act because of forces that move us beyond the comprehension of our own will and consciousness; that what we do has meaning in the state of eternity which it cannot have in the state of time, and which we therefore cannot believe in or even see in its full dimensions.

He himself gives the example of colour-vision, which may have arisen among a few while the mass of their fellows were still unable to perceive colour as such—no attempt at communication could make those who were unequipped for colour-perception understand or believe in the reality of colour for their fellows. (An even better illustration might be found in the fantasy 'Flat-land', where a sphere tries to bring to a one-dimensional world of flat circles the notion of extension in three dimensions. The circles dismiss him, however, as merely a circle which can make itself smaller or larger at will—since as he tries to demonstrate his own sphericity, he merely passes through their one-dimensional world.)

There is, decidedly, nothing new in the notion of forces that manifest themselves through us, though they themselves move on a different plane, and are incomprehensible to our senses and intelligence. But, as ever, what does have perennial interest and importance is that every now and then someone—like Hope— declares the discovery that they exist; and not merely as attenuated notions or universals, but as living and acting entities, 'orders of being'.

And there is a good deal in Hope's proclamation of them which recalls Rilke's even more painfully arrived-at perceptions: for Hope, as for Rilke, mankind exists for the sake of art, of transformation. For Rilke, this transformation is that of the material of everyday life, the simple images of the world around us:

> Are we, perhaps, *here* just for saying: House,
> Bridge, Fountain, Gate, Jug, Fruit-tree, Window,—
> possibly: Pillar, Tower? . . . but for *saying,* remember,
> Oh, for such saying as never the things themselves
> hoped so intensely to be . . .
>
> ('Ninth Elegy')

For Hope, it is rather the archetypal images of human life—the images that already hang before our eyes in the constellations, and the legends and the myths from which the stars are named— that themselves take their life through and from us, requiring of the poet a continual reinterpretation and re-creation that they may in turn give life to man.

But, archetypal force or Angel, both require that man should be able to serve, perhaps even, unknown to himself, to harbour powers greater than he knows; and this is the conception which frees poetry at last from the limitations of conscience and consciousness into which the rational and intellectual life of the eighteenth century first betrayed it, into the service of faith and praise of what is.

CHAPTER XIV

Poets of the 'Forties and 'Fifties

∽

NO DOUBT it was in part the stimulation of danger and of the war years that set off the burst of poetic activity of the early 'forties—which carried on until the end of the war, and beyond. A number of poets of those years are still writing: some of them are (like Hope and McAuley) influences on the younger generation of poets; some, like Blight, Hart-Smith, Roland Robinson, have pursued poetry single-mindedly but without wide recognition and acclaim; some like Francis Webb, have sent up brilliant bursts of poetry at irregular intervals. But it is still remarkable how many of Australia's present poets—and how many poets—first began to publish their work in the years between 1940 and 1950.

Perhaps that war was the last in which there will be time for poetry to seem important. The universal uprooting, the deprivation, and the sharpened sense of what this country had come to mean to its new, and hitherto spiritually divided, inhabitants, all combined to force out of us poetry that for the first time began to accept Australia not as a political ideal, nor as a makeshift home, but as the ground of our seeing and feeling.

This is perhaps what is meant when it is sometimes said that during the war years and after, Australian writing 'came of age'. Of course, it had been adult enough long before, in Brennan and Neilson at least. But only now was Australia—its presentation to sight and hearing and feeling—taken as an absolute, not a relative, condition of our lives.

The feeling, which seemed so novel at first in the poems, for instance, of David Campbell:

> The Murray's source is in the mind,
> And at a word it flows . . .

has to some extent been lost in the post-war years, or has receded into the background. It became confused with the exploitation, by shallow writers and critics, of the 'Australian outlook', the Legend made commercial; it was further overlaid by the other cynical exploitations of the country that came with the boom years and with high migration rates. It no longer seems important because of these confusions and because of the natural and honest reaction against the revival of the old attitudes and notions of 'Australianism' which accompanied the post-war commercialism.

Nevertheless, it was both real and solid, the basis of much good work done since; a kind of earnest, to those who remember it, of the possibility of a real bond between the European and the Australian who mingle in our blood, and sometimes contradict each other still.

There was, of course, much more to the poetic revival of the 'forties and early 'fifties than simple patriotism. The Jindyworobak movement, even, had more behind it than appeared on the surface; its supporters were not as simple as they were made out to be, and its justification lies in the poetry it produced, best represented by the work of Roland Robinson, and by much of the early William Hart-Smith verse.

The issues that brought it into being were real enough, and though they have sunk into the background, will sooner or later and on some new level, recur in our poetry until we have transcended them. They are not a mere matter of Sydney versus The Bush, as some critics have wanted to believe; they stem from one of our built-in emotional problems, not to be exorcized by the cultivation of a poetic suburban garden.

Then, too, the 'forties were a time made famous by the 'Angry Penguins' attempt at an acclimatization of Freud, André Breton and Apocalypse, and by the exorcism of these spectres of Europeanism by the more solid spectre of Ern Malley. After this débacle, it is quite true to say that the atmosphere of Australian writing changed, on the whole for the worse. A certain distrust and suspicion, a certain chip-on-shoulder attitude and irreconcilability, have haunted the local cliques ever since, even though their origin may have been long forgotten.

The Angry Penguins' passing would probably not have been long delayed in any case, since few writers of importance came out of the movement and its congeners were young and not particularly wise. But the manner of its death left Australian poetry often too conservative and timid, often uninteresting in content and ambition. Poetic theory has never flourished here, Brennan excepted, but Ern Malley gave its first timid appearance a rap over the head that discouraged it more than ever. The outcome

of the battle did not much affect the broad roads of development
that had already been laid down (the simpler lyrical poetry that
followed Neilson and Gilmore, the *Bulletin* balladry and
political poetry such as that of Manifold); but from then on
poets tended to keep more strictly to their track and to eschew
the glance beyond.

The question of the actual merit of the Ern Malley 'hoax
poems' has been argued to and fro a good deal; but a conviction
seems to be settling on us that they were indeed a good deal
better than true hoax poems need be. In fact, of course, it is
necessary to point out that poems written by poets, in a state (as
they have admitted) of hilarious excitement, are at least apt to
contain flashes of really exciting prosody, and to have a degree
of internal organization and (conscious or unconscious) allusion
much higher than can be achieved by non-poetic minds applying
themselves to verse.

The hoax, in the end, proved little except that the 'Angry Penguins were young and naive and that their enthusiasm blinded
them to certain obvious hints and certain esoteric traps. A poem
cannot be made out of isolated brilliant images; but the whole
cadence and management of these verses was obviously expert,
even without the images:

> I had read in books that art is not easy
> But no-one warned that the mind repeats
> In its ignorance the vision of others. I am still
> The black swan of trespass on alien waters—

Such a verse contains, to hindsight, a warning and even an
audacious 'dare' to the reader, but it is not, in fact, a 'repetition
of the vision of others', it is something both individual and deft.

The only conclusive experiment on the critical faculties of the
Angry Penguins would have been whether they in fact accepted
verse clumsily turned and unpoetic in essentials, if it complied
with their other desiderata. The Ern Malley poems were really a
trap only for cross-word puzzle addicts.

The results of the whole Malley situation, with the publicity
that raged round it, were not good for poetry in Australia; not
because the Angry Penguins' bubble did not need pricking, but
because (as the perpetrators themselves have practically admitted) the chronic middle-suburban suspicion of everything that
cannot readily be understood, the anti-intellectual and anti-art

bias of Australian society, were reinforced into an attitude of positive righteousness by the supposed exposure of hypocritical ineptitude in the 'Bohemian' cliques of artists and writers. The celebrated and hysterically funny prosecution of *Angry Penguins* for obscenity was only one symptom of this attitude.

But the real damage done to the public attitude to poetry was less immediately definable, and more persistent. The Press exploitation of the hoax, and a certain misunderstanding of the attitudes behind it, certainly tended to reinforce a confusion between poetry and sensationalism and later between poetry and polemic, which has always been a danger in Australia. The lack of a rooted poetic practice and tradition; the fact that Gordon was the first poet to win really wide recognition and that he led a rather crudely adventurous life; the polemic verse of Lawson and his scapegoat poverty and personal unhappiness; the popular appeal of the bush ballad and its later pandering to public taste; the audacious Lindsay-McCrae sallies against prudery and bourgeois values—all these factors and many more, in the brief history of Australian literature, have tended to make audiences here less disposed to value poetry as an art or a discipline, and more inclined to demand of it an immediate impact one way or another, an obvious and public 'message' or self-exposure.

Above all, the Australian audience has felt the Malley situation as justifying it in a refusal to attempt to transcend its own experience or give credence to the unfamiliar. What cannot be immediately understood is too often dismissed as unimportant or over-subtle, or even as a shallow attempt at self-aggrandization. So the critical atmosphere that greets the new poet in Australia is thoroughly unfavourable to experiment or to adventurousness —a fact which perhaps has something to do with the number of poems written in the 'fifties and 'sixties in either an academic and classical, or a rumbustiously masculine, vein, both these manners being recognizably 'safe'.

One cannot help wondering, too, whether this demand for the sensational has not perhaps been a more or less unconscious influence on the poetry of A. D. Hope. I am not suggesting that his emphasis on sexuality, his rages of disgust or fascinated horror or (more rarely) tender delight, his charnel-house or abattoir similes, do not come from something inherent in his own personality as a poet; I am suggesting, however, that it is with a certain theatrical malice, a chuckle behind the horrific mask, that he has often presented his audience with something to feed their curious notion of what poetry is and does.

For Hope's deepest and most basic themes are not at all what they are often thought to be; they are deeper, bitterer, and based more solidly on universal human experience and on the poet's continuing task, than his surface sensationalism would admit. For myself, I prefer to go beyond the 'masks and images' to the poet who hides behind them; and I am not at all convinced that Hope has not harmed his own work here and there by a somewhat adolescent proneness to attempt to shock (and therefore titillate) a public whose notion of poetry is often a long way from the poets' true mark and impulsion. If this is so, the fault probably lies on both sides of the footlights.

In any case, it is possibly truer in Australia than anywhere else that the quiet persistent poet who refuses to be side-tracked from working out his own poetic method and subjects, or to court public favour or disfavour, is apt to be overlooked and even somewhat despised. The work of several of the poets who began writing in the nineteen-forties comes to mind here; that, for instance of David Campbell, which has seldom been examined as a whole or considered for its inner direction and significance; more particularly, that of John Blight, who works far from other literary influences in fierce and self-involved independence, and (though his poetry is represented in practically all anthologies of Australian poetry published since 1943, and several overseas collections as well) has been able to have published (until 1963) only two small and not very representative books of verse.

Blight makes no concessions to popular taste, to the demands of readers for intelligibility or grace; if he is lyrical it is almost in spite of himself, and the chief characteristic of his poetry is its knotted awkward struggle with meanings and with the intractable shapes and events of the outer world. Because he is an example of the kind of poetic integrity that is almost submerged and overlooked in today's literary cliquism and the cross-currents of poetry-reviewing-poetry, and because he is one of those poets who has made an almost unnoticed journey between the years of 1942 and 1962, commenting, as he went, with increasing perspicacity and unfailing honesty, his almost inaccessible poetic production is worth considering against the better-known work of his contemporary Francis Webb.

Both began to write at roughly the same time; neither is an immediate part of the literary scene, since both have chosen to go their own way; but the work of each has something significant to tell us about what has happened to poetic perception and human values over the twenty years and more since they began to write. Perhaps the very fact that both have chosen a solitary struggle—one with the world of objects and meanings, the other with an inner world of menaces, terrors and illuminations— makes their poetry, however opposed in tendency, shed a light on man's present preoccupations and bewilderments as such, rather than on the special scene presented by Australian writing.

Blight's use of his own immediate environment as a reflector of thought may make his verse appear on the surface like 'Austra- liana'; but on deeper examination it achieves universality—a universality of the kind that, I think, Australian poetry should now find easy, but which it is in fact scarcely daring to aim at. The poet who is most unashamedly himself is also likely to be most human; and perhaps of all our poets Webb and Blight have least chosen to study or reproduce the manner of other writers. This is why I have chosen to end this book with a superficial account of the poetry of each, as it has grown and changed, from the early nineteen-forties to the nineteen-sixties.

Blight's first collection of verse, *The Old Pianist* (1945), though the verse it contained was sometimes immature, already showed his talent for suddenly twisting apart the seen to reveal the inner relationship or the unseen reality; as in, for example, 'To a Farmer, Fencing':

> Where hides the spider, mortal or machine,
> Whose web is stranded from each telephone;
> Light bulb to light bulb strung like beads of dew?
>
> Indeed, I noticed you ensnared inside
> The web that's spun about the countryside;
> And though the lure of lissom gossamer
> Will trap the best of flies, a wily spider
>
> Lurks out of sight of web upon a thread
> That links a telephone beside his bed;
> He sets a net and seldom after toils,
> Bul sleeps and smiles and feasts upon the spoils . . .

The second book, though severely edited and far too exclu- sive to be thoroughly representative of Blight, contained such remarkable evocations of the coastal bush-country as 'Friar-bird':

Bracken, sand and bush. Barely a dozen thoughts
Creation scattered here. Oh, who thinks like this?
How wizened is his mind! Thicker than these nuts'
Rind is his skull . . .
But who can speak to lonely bush, who can speak with trees?
Only the friar-bird may call, speak like this.
Blady-grass would cut the throats, put dead men at ease
When their tongues from talking grew black like his . . .

And the fantastic imagination that the first book showed seemed
to be growing even more gnomic in its wit, and more economical
in its expression:

Behind the black lace of the printed page
Did you see everlasting life or age
Dressed in its leper's skin of crinkled paper?
Look! Who walks through the sheet with lighted taper? . . .
The veil was never lifted, but the lace
Showed well enough the presence of a face;
Or, hanging on a peg, an empty skull,
It looked like cobweb spiderless and dull.

('Black Lace')

This gnarled, compressed language, sometimes awkward and
obscure but always meaningful, seemed to need for its comple-
ment an equally compressed form; and in this second book
Blight was feeling his way toward the form he wanted—a four-
teen-line 'sonnet', with a variable rhyme-scheme—sometimes
ABABCDCDEFEFGG; sometimes ABBACDDCEFFEGG, sometimes simple couplets throughout, or even ABCABCDDEFGEFG.
It is full of irregularities however, both of rhyme (which can
become assonance, or dissonance, or even repetition of the
rhyme-word) and of metre, which is in fact not metre at all but
a conversational counterpoint of beat and cross-beat that defies
conventional scansion:

The island is lost ground; an acre or two
In the realms of the sea. Is country
Once loved of mother earth. Now, a whale's back
Of wet mud, black, sliding back out of view
Into the lost regions of a trackless sea; . . .

('The Island')

Over this flat-pan sea, this mud haven,
This shelf of the sea floor, sea-birds paddle
And the red mud raddles the sea.

You are on creation's level. Proven
Your lowly origin, where, in one puddle,
Sea-snails and your toes agree—
The same spasms and rhythms. Stub
On a rock, or a sharp stab of a beak,
They draw in . . .

('Sea Level')

There is something curiously authentic about Blight's later work; the voice of a man meditating, seeing, experiencing, all at once, it is unmistakably active and factual, a kind of shorthand of poetry. The very fact that this poetry sometimes seems to owe little or nothing to contemporary influences and to have inherited as little from the past, gives the best of it a kind of primitive immediacy, such as it might not have if the writer were more in touch with the 'literary movements' and cliques.

Blight seems to recognize this; his later work has tended to exploit the very oddness of his particular vision and mode of expression; and perhaps the somewhat earlier poem 'Totems' points to this recognition.

This page be cursed. It is the worst page
I have ever used as a stage
For my evocations. My poems
Like totems,
Are tortured wild dreams here.
They have nothing of the clear
Lyric mask of the lark:
Only the dark,
Sinuous casts of a mind
Sealed by eyes that are blind
To natural graces;

Only the impossible carved faces
Of wooden gods, stolid
As they are solid,
And wooden, and brooding,
All life eluding.

Yet, totems,
Are they not the wild poems
Of dark minds?
Though talent blinds,
Still in the murk
The carvers work.

This kind of poetry is extremely unfashionable in the Australia of the 'sixties, in which Hope's polish and McAuley's plaintive grace are at present the strongest influence. But there is perhaps something in common between the elder Blight and the younger Randolph Stow, who both turn away from current developments and beckon the reader into different paths. Blight, however, believes in the power of the intuitive mind to find its true correspondences in natural forces; Stow's thought is less downright, more self-conscious and conscious of others, yet more ethereal. Where Blight's thought is in constant reference to the things seen and felt, Stow moves more easily through time and abstraction.

Blight's pursuit of concreteness, fact and image, and the brevity of his recent poems, have not meant that his later work has been scrappy; for all his 'sonnets' over the past few years have centred on one subject, the sea. The single sonnets have taken their grip on single aspects—flotsam, sea-creatures, boats, seamen, rock-pools—but each sonnet, like a shell or a stone picked up and deeply pondered, contains in the end its hidden reference to the whole or throws an oblique light on some other meditation. And the whole series of something over ninety brief poems refers in the end, not to the ocean only, but to the emergence of man and of thought from those inexhaustible depths.

> For the blue-print sea charts shapes, a launching
> Of ideas that, now, settle on land . . .
> I think there
> Came all art from the sea, when the land was square.
>
> ('From the Sea')

Blight chooses his language with deliberation and precision; what he has to convey is, however, no more precise than life itself. The art lies in the very awkwardness, sometimes, of his verse, that carries with it a sense of the immediacy of experience, the seizing on it before it vanishes, the hurried salting of its tail.

> Ghost-crabs, their fleetness, have made me
> Desperate to delineate the norm
> Of the effacing creatures. I must
> Describe nothing less ephemeral than dust;
> And you who read, must barely hope to see
> A creature, an image, but a mere scrabble of foam . . .
>
> ('Ghost-crabs')

And if he takes a permanent stand anywhere, it is just on this flux and rush of experience:

> If I am to tell you what I believe,
> I am to go ashore, to stand on sand,
> And tell you my margins are here, and here.
> Yes! I can point to the limits of the sea; retrieve
> A reef, submarinely joined, to expand
> My continent of importance. But, dear,
> Really, I am better to speak to you in a way
> That is not based on a continent of rock,
> But has the wish-wash of water—is, is
> The Sea . . .

Yet certain notions do present themselves, do recur time and again like a pattern of tides; and one of them is the correspondence between sea and land—between, to put it fantastically, the physical in man and his thought-processes, between what is 'below' and what is 'above'. The movement from one realm to another is unpredictable, but it is always to be reckoned with.

> And, next, this
> Thought on the lines of the Lord's creating—these green tallow
> Leaves like harrow tines that rake the dunes
> Have their flowers at their tips, like stars
> Impaled: may have impaled starfish, moons
> Ago, and got the idea of beautiful flowers . . .
>
> ('Beach Flower')

> These are the first shapes: stonefish and starfish.
> Imagine the stone falling, tumbling down the scree
> Through the upper atmosphere . . .
> Starfish, I know you, now, staring as I have,
> Where a star would long gaze for its image to move . . .
> These are the first shapes, life in its first steps.
> See, now, man gazes into the outer deeps.
>
> ('Stonefish and Starfish')

And, even more deeply, the shapes of the sea become the shapes of thought, the patterns from which the logic of destruction begins:

> Isn't it ominous that Nature has not yet cleared
> Away the carpenter models of her evolution?
> So the sawfish still threshes in the shoals, and should be feared

As the first pattern of a saw. When chaos
Rules, after the last bomb, the solution
Of the bomb's rebuilding will be there. It would pay us
To catch all sawfish, first . . .

('The Sawfish')

The sea-horse, of course, can't canter; the sea-hare
Never runs anywhere . . .
All this topsy-turvydom of the sea proves
Through such nomenclature, man moves
In a looking-glass world . . . All that he sees,
Dreamed from the lees of some experience he suffers,
Toping the heady bottle of the world's globe . . .

('Sea-Beasts')

Wry, ironic, often thoroughly frightened by his double world
of sea and thought, Blight keeps his sense of the comic intact. It
is a rare sense today, and ought to be prized the more for that.
There is his 'Fisherman and Jetty':

Old jetty, wade with me out into the sea
And, there, let us watch ship and shag pass;
Knee-deep I, thigh-deep you. We
With our reasons to be there: standing in the glass
Sea, rod in hand, crane on deck . . .

or 'Dinghies',

. . . those disreputable carts of the sea,
Driverless, and horseless, idle on the mud;
Out-of-date, yet still suffered; tied up
—As if they'd bolt—with chains to the jetty.
Touch one, and watch the red furious blood
Rising in some Lilliput admiral . . .

or his trim spinster lighthouse, with

. . . the kind
Spectacles of benignancy beaming truth,
Honesty, and pride in all who ride
The sea the right way . . .

But though this wry humorous comment is characteristic of
Blight, much more characteristic is the slow, almost laborious
clarification, the parallel between sea-world and world of
thought, that like his 'comber from the unknown',

Comes at me with a crash of columns and light . . .

So his iceberg:

> strange range of crystal stillness; living glass
> Gliding, glistening past us, blistering white.
> Taut piano-string of sound; ear-vibrant wall . . .

becomes also a

> Woman, so beautiful, whom none may trust,

and a 'phantom island lost and found again'.

And the sight of the surf sets him meditating on knowledge:

> All about movements of surf, some thought-device knows;
> Its curvatures, stresses, its tension . . .
> I can't tell you. Such knowledge cannot be bought,
> But thought out, somehow. Somehow it is thought out,
> Or the surf couldn't be there, only vacuum of doubt.

> ('Surf')

So the poems are, in the end, neither about nature and the sea, nor about man, but about the primal puzzle, the relationship of the two—of thought to world, of man to earth. Blight's struggle with the problem is a lonely wrestling-match; he rejects all ready-made solutions and glib suggestions, preferring the raw touch of experience on eye and mind, a self-discovery that proceeds at the same time as a Columbus-discovery of experience itself. It is this authentic solitary process that gives the best of his work the salt taste he wants it to have:

> —for who doesn't know
> That a poem couldn't capture the sea
> Save as a cup holds it? Then the sea tastes
> Warm and not unlike blood; and though
> It has water's colourless anonymity,
> Like blood it is all too savage to drink, and wastes
> And is thrown away, once you taste its fierce flavour,
> Which is all I will you to taste, my few words to savour.

> ('A Cup of Seawater')[1]

The second of the two poets I am choosing to illustrate the work of those who were young writers in the 'forties, Francis Webb, has taken a very different path from Blight's, though no less solitary. Always a writer of dazzling verbal and technical

---

[1] Quotations from the 'sea-sonnets' are taken from *A Beachcomber's Diary*, Angus & Robertson, 1963.

efficiency, he has sometimes seemed even to trust too much to
words, so that the reader stumbles in his search for meanings
among these towering and sliding metaphors and sentences.

So in a comparatively early poem, 'Images in Winter', he
writes:

> This is why
> (In an era of free-verse, poor company)
> I pin my faith on slipping images
> Twisting like smoke or a fish caught in the hand.
> These are some company for the crumbling galleries,
> The brain of this, our black synthetic dusk.
>
> A broken harp smouldering from the brush of wings
> A ship's brown wooden wheel that brings the spar,
> The gull in a green storm clear as the maker's name;
> Such huge conceits as these, while the dodging flame
> Of the candle writes cunning shadows on the air.

And the images that cast their 'cunning shadows' on his poetry
were from the first vague yet alarming, as in 'Bush Fire':

> For what moves on the horizon, hoodwinks the blinded sky
> Is one far threat gathering flame. Remote, now, lovely,
> That spring-toothed vision bearing towards the dream:
> Only a blade of hatred, working and swaying,
> Bursts through the lying saffron and shows itself.

His longer early poems were influenced by, and in turn influenced, the narrative poetry movement of the 'forties and early
'fifties, which used the explorers' and navigators' stories as land-
marks and signposts to our modern times. But about Webb's
'Ben Boyd' and 'Leichhardt Pantomime' there was from the first
something that related less to the man who was the ostensible
subject, than to the poet's own problems and, by extension, the
problems of the human soul.

His 'Leichhardt' is scarcely more than the centre for certain
great questions, set against a backdrop carefully arranged:

> There may be agony in furnished rooms;
> Rather, they are its perfect setting. Walls
> Clamp down on motive, and the flesh of motive
> Puffs up whiter in prominence. The rage
> Contracted in the mirror; the sea-passion
> Trembling in the painted shell . . .
>
> . . . A question stares
> Relentless, from the dust; the answer traces

> Legends of fright upon his brain; he turns
> Swiftly back to the mirror, and as one
> Aloof for a moment, watches fear at work.

And of 'Ben Boyd' nothing remains but a story, seen differently by different minds, and a skull, which may itself have nothing to do with the story, but which triumphs over the seekers by its very ambiguity:

> Dead men have the power
> To mock us even while we juggle their very bones.
> They have slipped clean out of illusion and they grow—
> Six feet when he died—this fellow would top a cloud!
> The thing's too full of ghosts. I hate the feel of it:
> Holding it is like splintering a mirror
> And finding a thousand faces round your boots.

So says the sea-captain, holding the supposed skull of Boyd. And the Author's Prologue to the poem has already put the possibility of an end to the search out of bounds:

> I follow charts of guesswork, shape a cloud
> Formless, unplotted, rotten with endless change
> And the sky's blue mockery plummeting through its heart.
> Yet truth itself is a mass of stops and gaps.

('A Drum for Ben Boyd')

Webb has, in fact, always been searching for the same thing—the truth about man and his relationships. to himself. to other men, and in the end, to God. So his symbols have always been 'huge symbols figuring strangeness'; his early poetry is full of shadows, mirrors, clouds; his Leichhardt is a figure in pantomime and his Ben Boyd is a legend vanishing in memory, changing according to the view of the beholder, a mirror splintered into a thousand faces.

But as time goes on Webb's poetry, too, alters; searching in man for the truth about man he discovers there the Christ who is henceforth that truth for him:

> . . . Lamp in the spectrum's tent,
> Homing shades to the one mirror
> And white of embodiment.
> Given, the kiss of peace,
> Given, a white way,
> Love aloft in those hands.

('The Canticle')

Nevertheless, his celebration of Christ (Webb is a Catholic) has not altered the peculiar qualities of his poems. Webb's images have always been obscure, forceful, painful. Where his poems struggle through to triumph, it is always a hard-won triumph, a temporary peace found through an insight that seldom seems more than a fragmentary solution. So, in 'A Drum for Ben Boyd', the author's prologue is written as if out of despair even of writing:

> In jags of stone
> My thoughts hang perilously, in silver cliffs:
> Huge symbols figuring strangeness—the sky's edges,
> Ships toppling, and rigid, green, dead seas;
> Striking out so blindly, so often, I clasp some shape
> Tortured into beauty, with wet frozen lips,
> Only that I, too, stiffen, that the will freeze;
> Only that snippets of lightning, cords of the wind
> May drive my dreams onto Time and break their backs.

And Webb's very vocabulary is hurtful, with its dazzling lights, its cliff-faces, its hospitals and their electric terrors and boredoms, the crazy haste and frustration of its inhabitants. His one bush-ranger poem, characteristically on the subject of Morgan, Australia's most dangerous and hated member of the fraternity, is as agonized as it is psycho-analytic:

> The grey wolf at his breakfast. He cannot think
> Why he must make haste, unless because their eyes
> Are poison at every well where he might drink . . .
>
> But the Cave, his mother, is close beside his chair;
> Her sunless face scribbled with cobwebs, bones
> Rattling in her throat as she speaks. And there
>
> The stone Look-out, his towering father, leans
> Like a splinter in the seamed palm of the plain . . .

This is an interior kind of drama, as is almost all of Webb's narration or description: Ben Boyd is less a person than a figure in some obscurely meaningful legend or dream, Leichhardt is set to act the pantomime-part of a man mazed in guilt and memory; Eyre (in 'Eyre All Alone') is a man returning from a nightmare to common day:

> The final days, with grey straight lines of rain,
> A geometry ruling without angle or curve
> The scoured eyeball. But these outlines of mountains,

Shapes of the breast, of the ranges back of the Sound:
These would pick expedient pockets of the eyeball and
    soul . . .
We struggle through the last ditch of the King's River . . .

But their faces will be golden when the doors open,
Their dress shining. My torn stinking shirt, my boots,
And hair a tangle of scrub; the long knotted absurd
    beard
That is my conscience grown in the desert country.
How shall I face their golden faces, pure voices? . . .

And in 'The Sea', the Greek expedition, struggling through
sharp-edged images of destruction ('See, the sun's withers, letting
blood, inform us/Of haunted villages past this giant hill') and
harried by fear:

Little dangerous men attack without warning,
We loot and kill, singing hopelessly in the foreign morning,

finds the sea, 'A carved golden gymnasium . . . Genesis of lights',
'our mother, our revels'; much as Eyre himself conquers peril
and loneliness and reaches the end of his journey. In 'The
Gunner', even sleep itself is perilous and must be guarded
against: so the air-gunner talking in his sleep is another symbol
of struggle:

Listening, you crouched in the turret, watchful and taut
  Bogey two thousand, skipper, corkscrew to port—
Marvellous, the voice, driving electric fires
Through the panel of sleep, the black plugs, trailing wires.
                      . . . Yet you might find
Forgotten genius, control, alive in the deep
Instinctive resistance to the perils of sleep.

In the later poems, which sometimes seem to turn into 'slipping images, Twisting like smoke', and in which it is sometimes
hard to sense the interior guiding thread or argument, all nevertheless seems meaningful, however shadowy. It is as though
Webb's personal ordeal, issuing in poems as violent and difficult
as the struggle itself, does when it reaches its moments of peace
and exaltation discover a truth that, though it is perhaps no
more than a ledge on a cliff that is not yet scaled, affords us, too, a
foothold and a triumph.

The setting of the poems in *Socrates and Other Poems*, and
the later work, is desolate, grey, hygienic, sharp-edged, full of

electric terrors; yet the moments of pity and revelation, when they come, are tenderer and more deeply acceptant of life than Webb's vision has ever been before. The poems of mental and physical agony ('The Brainwashers', 'Hospital Night' and others) can issue in a revelatory peace ('A Death at Winson Green'); poems like 'The Bells of St. Peter Mancroft' escape altogether from terror into pleasure:

> Gay golden volleys of banter
> Bombard the clockwork grief;
> A frisson of gold at the centre
> Of prayer, bright core of life . . .

And 'Five Days Old', that gently marvelling celebration of a newborn child, ends

> If this is man, then the danger
> And fear are as lights of the inn,
> Faint and remote as sin
> Out here by the manger.
> In the sleeping, weeping weather
> We shall all lie down together.

But the poem which perhaps shows most clearly how deeply Webb has felt his way into man, his miseries and glories, is 'Harry': where a moron in an institution writes his letter:

> Was it then at this altar-stone the mind was begun?
> The image besieges our Troy. Consider the sick
> Convulsions of movement, and the featureless baldy sun
> Insensible—sparing that compulsive nervous tic.
> Before life, the fantastic succession,
> An imbecile makes his confession,
> Is filled with the Word unwritten, has almost genuflected.
>
> Because the wise world has for ever and ever rejected
> Him and because your children would scream at the sight
> Of his mongol mouth stained with food, he has resurrected
> The spontaneous though retarded and infantile light.
> Transfigured with him we stand
> Among walls of the no-man's-land
> While he licks the soiled envelope with a lover's caress,
> Directing it to the House of no known address.

In the work of Webb, as in that of the younger poet Stow, perhaps Australian poetry sets off on a new level. At the beginning its main preoccupations were with various aspects of the question, 'What is the relationship of man to his world,' For Australians this was posed in two main ways: 'What is the relationship of a transplanted European to this wholly unfamiliar and unawakened country, with which his past and therefore his heart has yet formed no ties?' and, 'How can this transplanted European alter his new world so as to make it more tolerable than the old?'

These are the half-acknowledged questions behind the work of Harpur; I have tried to indicate their recurrence in later poetry and their complication by the much greater issue which arose out of the breakdown of the basic unity of faith that had kept Western consciousness active and self-confident. Brennan's work has concerned itself wholly with this problem and with its roots in the history of conscious thought and feeling; his answer, the answer of the wanderer, dispossessed of the Eden of unconscious joy in which he had once been king, and of the unquestioning faith that had led him, was that no answer was final—'no ending of the way, no home, no goal'.

As Australian poetry began to mature, the problems remained but grew wider in their scope and more general in their implications. Australians ceased to believe that this country might hold the key to any Utopia, political or spiritual; what has now begun to occupy them is less the means of altering the world or of assimilating and interpreting this particular part of it, than the means of regaining faith in man through a new kind of exploration of human meanings, human language and metaphor.

So Blight, staring at his sea-shapes and noting resemblances to human thought and feeling, searches for the ancestry of meaning itself; and so Webb, gazing at the newborn child or the idiot in the institution, searches for beginnings, innocence, 'the Word unwritten', the 'gradual dawn/At an eyelid, maker of days'. Though one poet is a Catholic, the other not, the parallel may still have its significance. Both poets, in the end, are concerned less with creation than with Creation.

Index